IMAGES
of America

PALMDALE

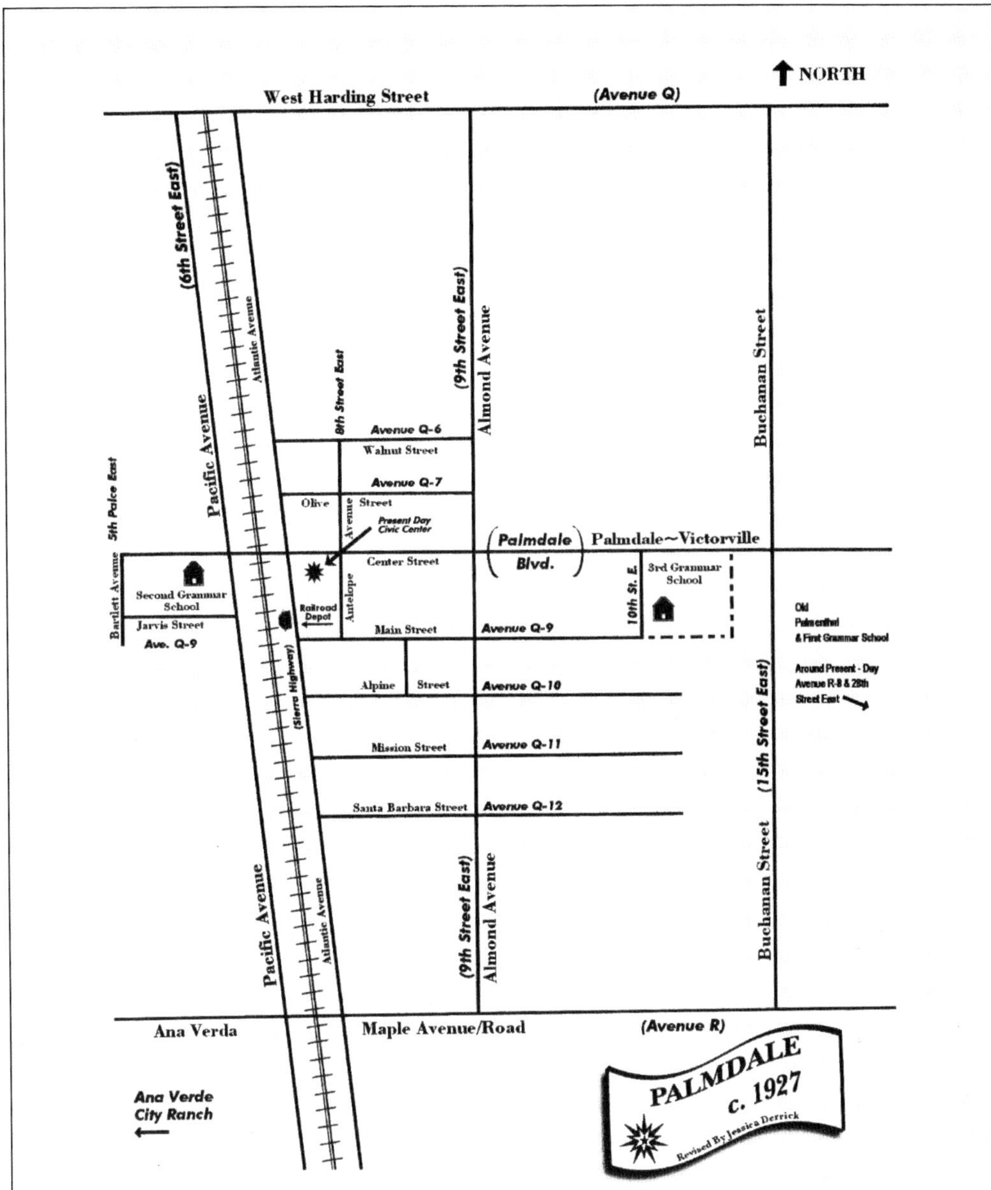

Notice something odd on this 1927 real estate promotion map of downtown Palmdale? The listed streets are completely different from today's streets. How these streets were named is not known although some obviously refer to the importance of local agriculture. The oldest Palmdale map dates to January 1886. Labeled "Palmdale Colony Lands," it was created for Moses Wicks and John Jones by surveyor B. Bassell. (Courtesy of LMAG.)

On the Cover: The Palmdale Hotel was one of the first buildings in New or West Palmdale (c. 1892); it stood at 38428 Eighth Street East at the corner of Avenue Q-7. Rudolph Primmer's family ran the hotel for several months. This photograph (1903) was taken immediately after Russell Primmer [Primer] had painted the words "Palmdale Hotel." The boy in the tree is Clyde Primmer. (Courtesy of Walt and Mickey Primmer.)

IMAGES
of America

PALMDALE

Norma H. Gurba
with Nicholas J. West

ARCADIA
PUBLISHING

ISBN 978-0-7385-8122-4

Published by Arcadia Publishing
Charleston, South Carolina

Printed in the United States of America

Library of Congress Control Number: 2010924356

For all general information contact Arcadia Publishing at:
Telephone 843-853-2070
Fax 843-853-0044
E-mail sales@arcadiapublishing.com
For customer service and orders:
Toll-Free 1-888-313-2665

Visit us on the Internet at www.arcadiapublishing.com

This book pays homage to all the wonderful people and pioneers of Palmdale and Southeast Antelope Valley who shared their lives and stories with us.

Contents

ACKNOWLEDGMENTS

No historian can ever do justice to the adventures of the first settlers. However, the authors and the City of Lancaster Museum/Art Gallery Associates, the fund-raising and volunteer organization for the facility, are dedicated to recognizing and preserving the rich history of the greater Antelope Valley for present and future generations. We sincerely thank the late Dorene and Glen Settle, who donated their extensive regional archival photographic collection to the museum/art gallery, which helped to make this book possible.

We are indebted to many colleagues who supported us, especially David Earle and Dayle DeBry of the West Antelope Valley Historical Society (WAVHS). We also owe our deepest gratitude to Arcadia Publishing for working with communities to save regional history.

Lastly, the publication of this book could not have been possible without all the wonderful additional contributors who supported our efforts of keeping local history alive by sharing their historic photographs, facts, and oral histories. They include: Antelope Valley Old Timers Association, Chuck Bostwick (*Antelope Valley Press*), Larry Chimbole, Jessica Derrick, Yoshio Ekimoto, Phillip Elkins, Cheryl Fletcher (*Antelope Valley Press*), Kern Antelope Historical Society, Ron and Maddi Kleit, Littlerock Library, Cora Sweet McCrumb family, Lil Stradal McDonald, John Munz family, Jessica Neighbors, Pacific Southwest District of Lutheran Church–Missouri Synod, Palmdale City Library, Palmdale High School, Denece Bones Parsons, Walt and Mickey Primmer, Anthony Ray, John Ritter family, Phil Serpico, J. Gordon Shelton, Tom Shiokari, Charles Snodgrass family, St. Mary's Catholic Church, Milt Stark, Irma "Babe" Story, Fred Strasburg, Ann and Tony Tyson, University of Southern California—on behalf of the USC Special Collections, U.S. Geological Survey, Josephine Williams, Kevin Wolff family, and the *Herald-Examiner* collection/Los Angeles Public Library.

Unless otherwise noted, all images appearing in this book were provided by the City of Lancaster Museum/Art Gallery (LMAG). All proceeds from the sales of this book will go to the LMAG Associates so the group can continue to preserve local history. Designed as a companion book to *Lancaster*, which provides additional information on historical Antelope Valley, this book concludes historically during the period of the mid-1950s.

INTRODUCTION

The settlement of the bulk of the Antelope Valley proper dates from the mid-1880s, the era of the famous Southern California "land boom." Two early small communities, Harold and Palmenthal, established in the late 1880s, are considered to be foundations of what would become Palmdale.

In 1886, a group of 60 to 70 German-Swiss Lutheran families—including a couple of gold miners—migrated from Nebraska and Illinois to California. Land promoters had told them that palm trees grew near the Pacific Ocean. When these pioneers entered the Antelope Valley and saw the Joshua trees, which they mistook for palm trees, they decided to settle in the area. It was also a period of very heavy rainfall, and the surrounding lush green hills reminded some settlers of their homeland. They called their new town, Palmenthal, German for "valley of palms." The little hamlet was also called Palmdale. Palmdale was one of 18 land-development colonies in the Antelope Valley at this time.

The newly created burg of small, unpretentious homes built on well-kept 20-acre homesites, with irrigated orchards and gardens, continued to prosper during the wet years of the late 1880s and early 1890s. The thriving town also had a church, school, and various business establishments. Residents applied for a Palmdale Post Office, but a post office with the same name was already being used by another Palmdale near present-day Palm Springs. The settlement was officially named Palmenthal on June 17, 1888, when a post office was opened in John Munz's general store. However, in May 1890 the other Palmdale post office closed and the Palmenthal Post Office was granted a name change. The Palmdale Post Office was established on August 13, 1890. The town, with around 40 buildings and 150 residents, was located about 3 miles southeast of the present-day Palmdale Civic Center, near Avenue R-8 and Twenty-seventh Street East.

Despite its promising start, the situation radically changed for Palmdale's pioneers due to dwindling local water supplies, drought, land title problems, and agricultural failures in the late 1890s. People lost their homes and had to move; many relocated to "New" or "West" Palmdale, which was created when the Southern Pacific Railroad put in helper engine facilities to push freight trains up the grade to Soledad Pass between Palmdale and Acton (c. 1891). Most of the new town was located around Eighth Street East between Avenue Q-7 and Palmdale Boulevard. Harold (also known as Alpine Springs, Alpine Station, and Trego Post Office) was located 2 miles south of modern Palmdale, established at the crossroads of the Southern Pacific Railroad on present-day Sierra Highway and Fort Tejon Road (now Barrel Springs Road). Inhabited primarily by railroad employees, as New Palmdale grew, Harold lost its importance.

At first, New Palmdale was a busy little town with a growing population. But the drought continued, and by 1905, there were fewer people living in the Palmdale area than in the late 1880s. Climate conditions began to improve after that date, and the resettlement of some abandoned areas began to take place. With the completion of the Los Angeles Aqueduct and the development of well irrigation on the basis of gasoline and, later, electrical pumps, a tremendous expansion of alfalfa cultivation took place in the valley. By the late 1920s, Palmdale was a prosperous little farming and ranching community. Although alfalfa, pears, and apples became staple crops in the area, Palmdale, nevertheless, was not excluded from tough times during the Great Depression. Agriculture remained the primary industry of the Antelope Valley until World War II.

The first major population explosion occurred during the early 1950s with the development of the aircraft industry and USAF Plant 42. In 1951, Palmdale had fewer than 3,000 inhabitants, but by 1954 it doubled to more than 6,000. Although another downturn in growth followed, the opening of the Antelope Valley 14 Freeway, the construction of the California Aqueduct, and developers producing inexpensive housing caused Palmdale's population to boom once again.

In addition to Palmdale, other early colonies and communities appeared or were reborn as new towns in Southeast Antelope Valley. The old settlement of Myrtle was founded in 1888. It was resurrected a few years later as the Almondale Colony, which was located 4 miles east of present-day Littlerock. Established in 1895, the Almondale Colony was settled mainly by Midwesterners who were promised agricultural riches by real estate promoters. At one time, it had 200 residents but a combination of the drought at the end of the 1890s, tax problems, and the concern about clear titles to individual properties contributed to the colony's demise. The area was later revived as Pearblossom.

As with old Palmdale, water was very necessary for the development and survival of old Littlerock, which acquired its name from the Little Rock Creek (spelled differently from the community). Littlerock and surrounding areas became known as the "Fruit Basket of the Antelope Valley." According to some pioneers, Littlerock was first started as a racehorse farm by Nathan Cole and his brothers. However, upon discovering that fruit trees did so well in this area, the brothers decided to forget the horses and turned to agricultural ventures. Cherries, apples, peaches, almonds, olives, prunes, cantaloupe, and figs were all grown, but pears, first planted in 1893, made the area a "pearadise."

After the end of the drought, during the first decade of the 20th century, settlement revived in the old Almondale Colony region and the new name of Pearblossom reflected the importance of the pear industry on the south side of the Antelope Valley in the 1910s and 1920s.

Now regarded as one of the most beautiful residential sites in the Antelope Valley, Juniper Hills, also known as Cima Mesa, is located between Littlerock and Pearblossom. Dr. James Booth, a local surveyor, gave the foothill area the name Juniper Hills because so many large juniper trees grew on the hillsides. It was during the late 1950s that X-15 pilot and the first man to walk on the moon, astronaut Neil Armstrong, lived in this small community.

Before the famous industrial cooperative colony of Llano del Rio was started by Job Harriman, there was the thriving 1890s Quaker Llano Colony located nearby. However, there is very little information about this settlement. Today only crumbling stone walls and foundations mark the location of the Llano del Rio Cooperative Colony, which has been called the most important nonreligious utopian colony in Western American history. During the colony's period of growth and after its demise, other residents in the Llano region continued to make the area their home.

The Valyermo and Big Rock Creek areas have also played vital agricultural and water roles in the development of Southeast Antelope Valley. Dr. Levi Noble, part owner of the famed Valyermo Ranch, was the nation's leading geological expert on the San Andreas Fault and was also considered the "father of Death Valley geology."

All of these communities were composed of settlers who represented every segment of society. They were people rich in strength and resourcefulness, and everyday people partake of the fruits of their labor. They are responsible for making Palmdale and the greater Southeast Antelope Valley what they are today.

One

The Saga Begins

PALMDALE COLONY LANDS

LOCATED TWO MILES NORTHEAST OF ALPINE

CHEAP LANDS WITH WATER RIGHTS FROM LITTLE ROCK CREEK

The colony has so much Orchard and Vineyards planted as the whole of the Antelope Valley put together. Come and see the fine orchards and Vineyards of the Colony.

Lands in Small Tracts at $25 per Acre with Water Rights for each acre of land. A Discount in Large Tracts. No First Payment to Actual Settlers - Only one Year's Interest in Advance.

❖ ❖ **TERMS EASY** ❖ ❖

Will take Los Angeles City Property In Part Payment

---CALL ON OR ADDRESS---

JOHN J. JONES

West First Street, Los Angeles, Cal., P.O. Box 509
OR PETER JONES, Palmdale, Los Angeles County, Cal.

August 1, 1889
Antelope Valley Times

As soon as Palmenthal was established, the real estate boom began and prices went up. Prosperous Palmdale was growing. In 1890, the *Antelope Valley Times* wrote: "We have great faith in the future of Palmdale. It would not surprise us to see a town of 500 people there before 1891." By March 1892, there was talk of a possible new "Antelope Valley County" with Palmdale as the new county seat.

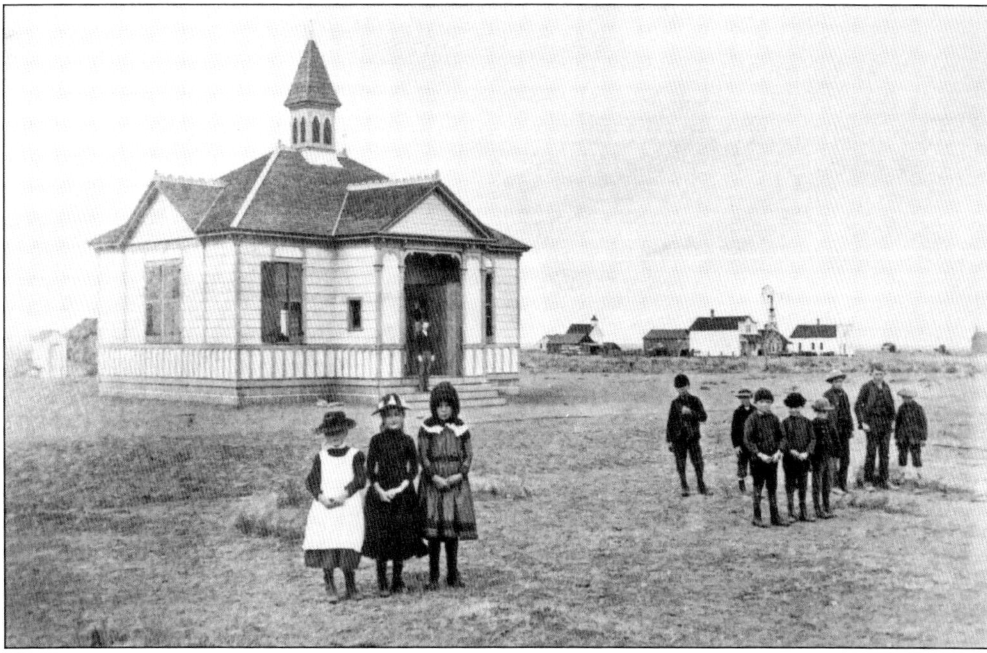

Some of the buildings of old Palmenthal (c. 1888) are, from left to right, the school outhouse, the schoolhouse, Rev. Christian Meyer's house, the Zion Evangelistic Church, a barn, John Munz's general store, the Munz house and windmill, the Palmdale House Hotel, and a saloon. The school children are, from left to right, Martha Munz, Ingeborg Munz, Maude Dowler, Fred Schmidt, and David Schmidt with an unidentified group of boys.

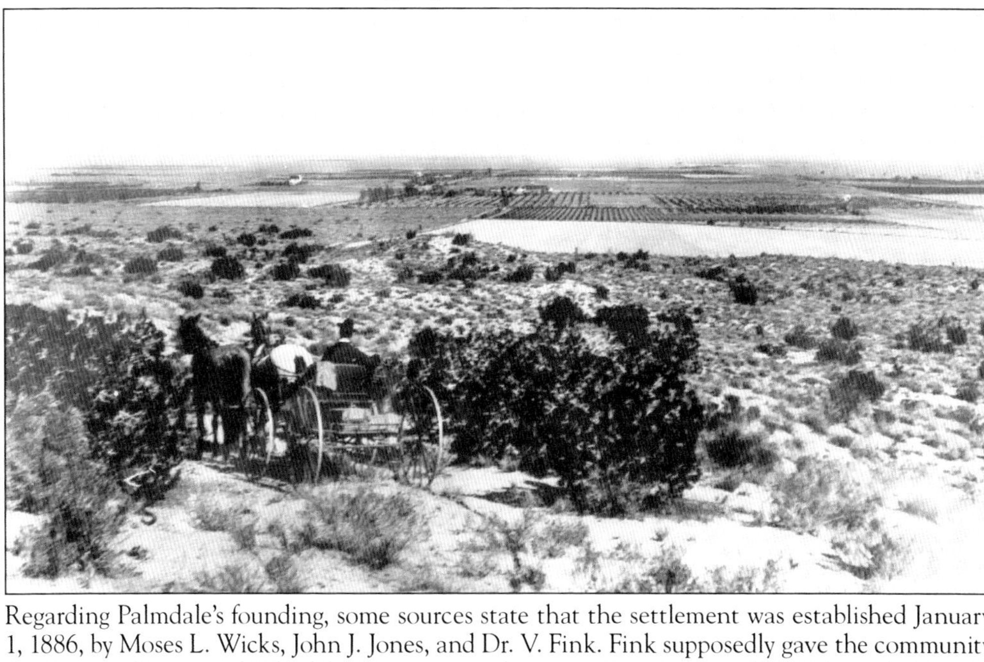

Regarding Palmdale's founding, some sources state that the settlement was established January 1, 1886, by Moses L. Wicks, John J. Jones, and Dr. V. Fink. Fink supposedly gave the community the "poetical" name of Palmdale. However, at the same time, it was called Palmenthal by the German settlers. This view of Palmenthal (c. 1895) is looking northward from Joshua Hills. The town's three streets were Magnolia, Yucca, and Palm.

Swiss-born John Munz (1848–1925) and his wife, Amalia (1860–1898), ran the Palmenthal General Store. Water for the settlement came from the Little Rock Creek, and the irrigation ditch ran in front of the store. Munz was also the postmaster and received the mail at Alpine. One time during the walk to Alpine to pick up the mail, he was attacked by coyotes. Munz's descendants still reside in the Antelope Valley.

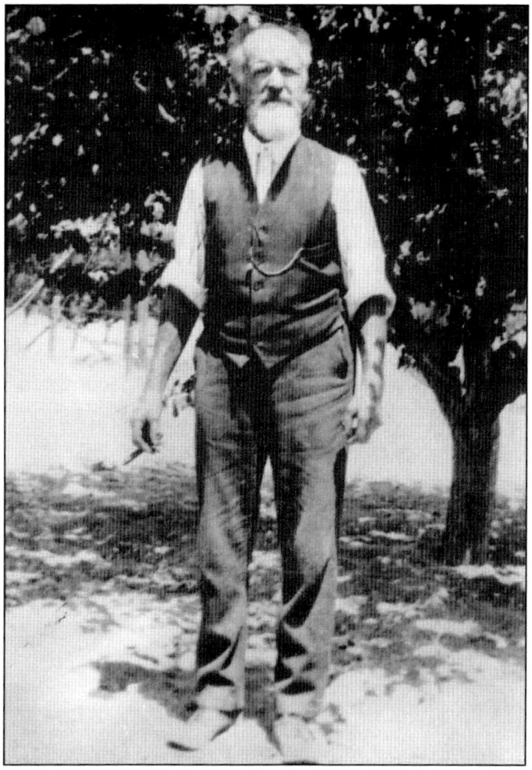

Other early Palmenthal families were the Ritters, Rathkes, Nagles, Joneses, Tetzlaffs, and the Fintels, among others. Since 1933, people with pride in the Antelope Valley gather each year for the very popular Old Timers Barbecue. This photograph dates to approximately 1947. Anyone who has lived in the valley for at least 25 years is considered an old-timer. The traditional gathering still continues today.

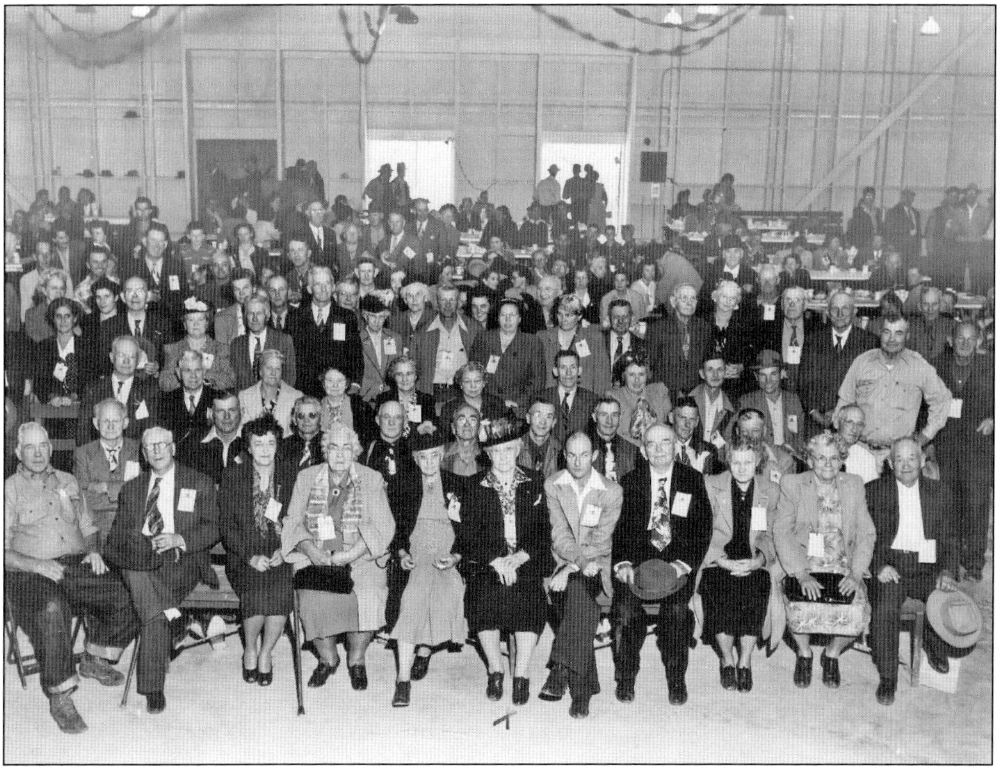

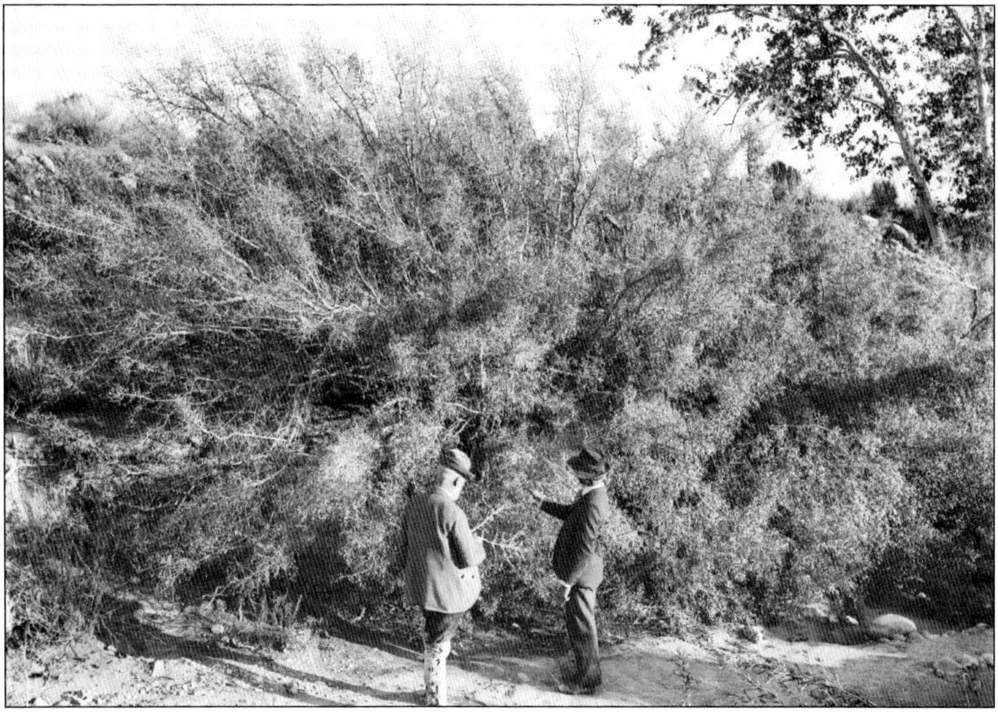

Palmdale pioneers grew a variety of crops, including pears, almonds, grapes, figs, and apples, among others. During the 1910s, schoolchildren encouraged new classmates to try the wild, nonnative, tasty olives that grew south of the town. They had a good laugh when they ate the bitter olives and spat them out in disgust. (Courtesy of University of Southern California, on behalf of the USC Special Collections.)

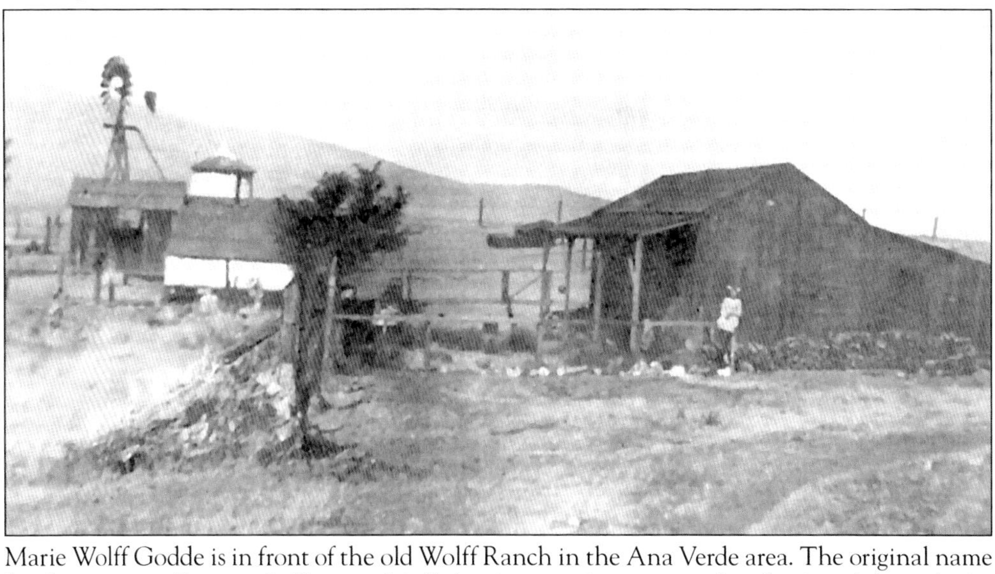

Marie Wolff Godde is in front of the old Wolff Ranch in the Ana Verde area. The original name for the area was *llano verde* ("green plain"), but it was mispronounced and misread through the years and eventually became Ana Verde. The earliest pioneer here was probably a Fernandeño Indian named Septimo who worked as a sheepherder for rancher Chico Lopez during the 1850s and 1860s. (Courtesy of the Wolff family.)

John Wolff, pictured here with Katherine Meehl Wolff and baby Marie (Mae) Wolff, became a Palmdale saloonkeeper in the 1890s. The Wolff family was related to Mom Evert of Lancaster, an early midwife who delivered many Antelope Valley pioneer babies. During the early 1900s, Palmdale was experiencing water problems so John and his family moved 4 miles west to Ana Verde. (Courtesy of the Wolff family.)

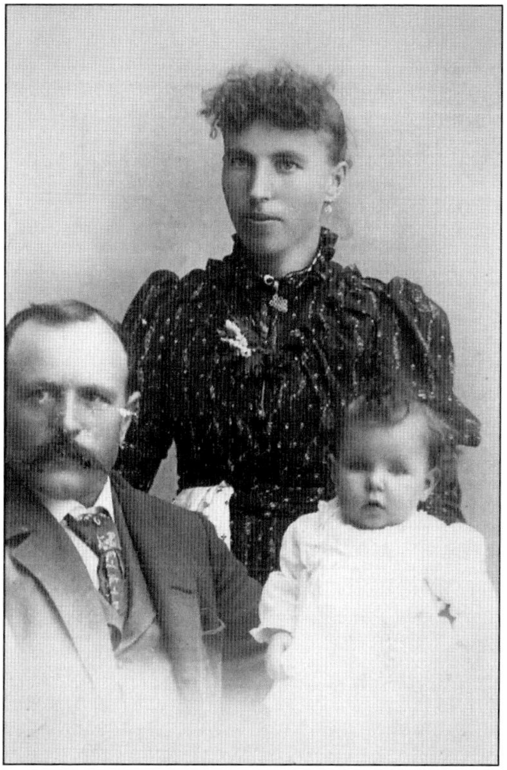

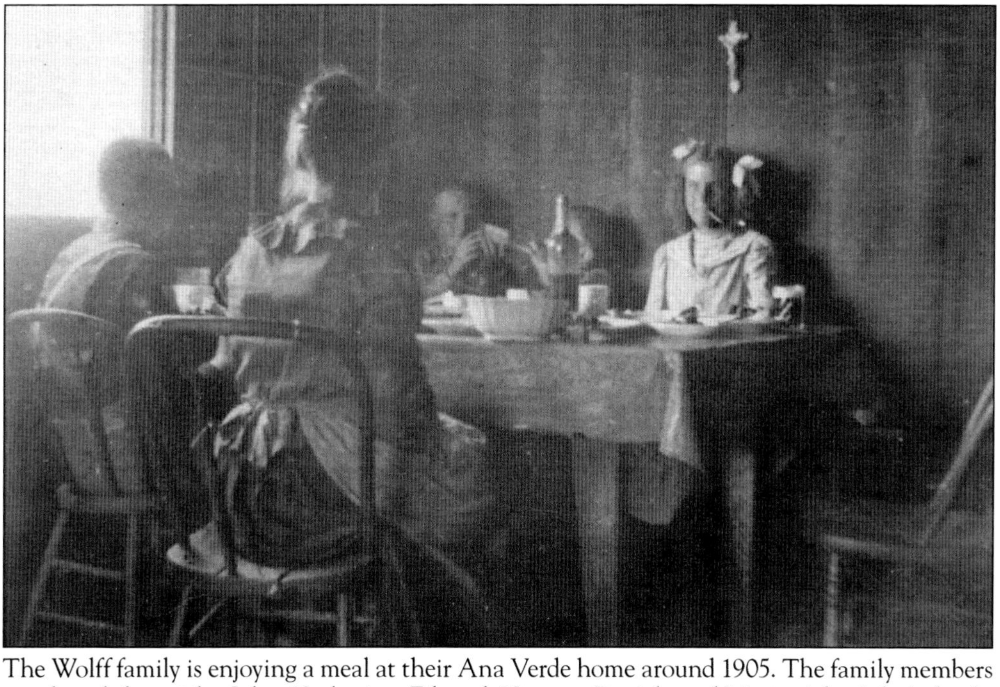

The Wolff family is enjoying a meal at their Ana Verde home around 1905. The family members are, from left to right, John, Katherine, Edward, Herman Patrick, and Marie. After John's death, Katherine was forced to sell the ranch to the City of Los Angeles at a very low price to make way for the construction of the aqueduct. (Courtesy of the Wolff family.)

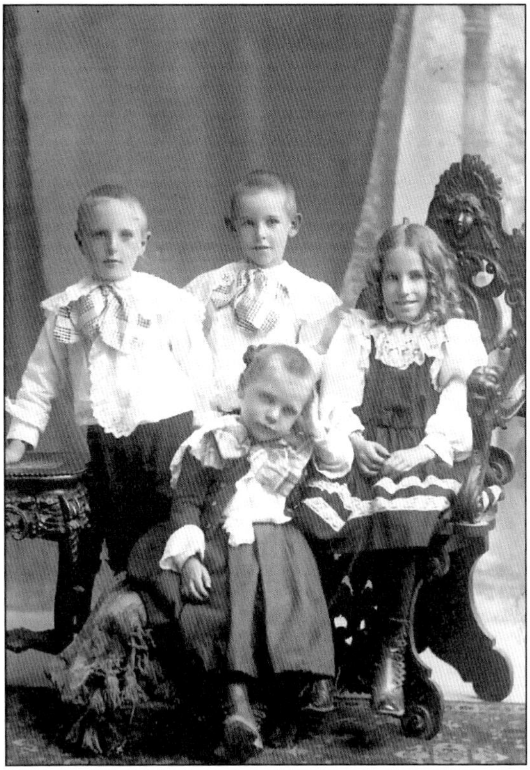

Herman Patrick (seated center) and, from left to right, Edward, John, and Marie Wolff were all born in Palmdale. The Wolff family lived in the saloon's second story. When they moved to Ana Verde, Herman Patrick recalled that for fun, he and his siblings would hide in the ranch's tall grass, jumping on and riding the surprised pigs when they came along on the trails. (Courtesy of the Wolff family.)

Unlike other Antelope Valley communities, Palmdale was not a "dry town" in the 1880s and 1890s. This old Palmenthal saloon was moved to Eighth Street East and Avenue Q-7 in New Palmdale; it stood here for 65 years. It was said that two men were killed in the saloon's gambling room. Afterwards, it was the home of Rev. Jessie Wilson of the First Presbyterian Church for many years.

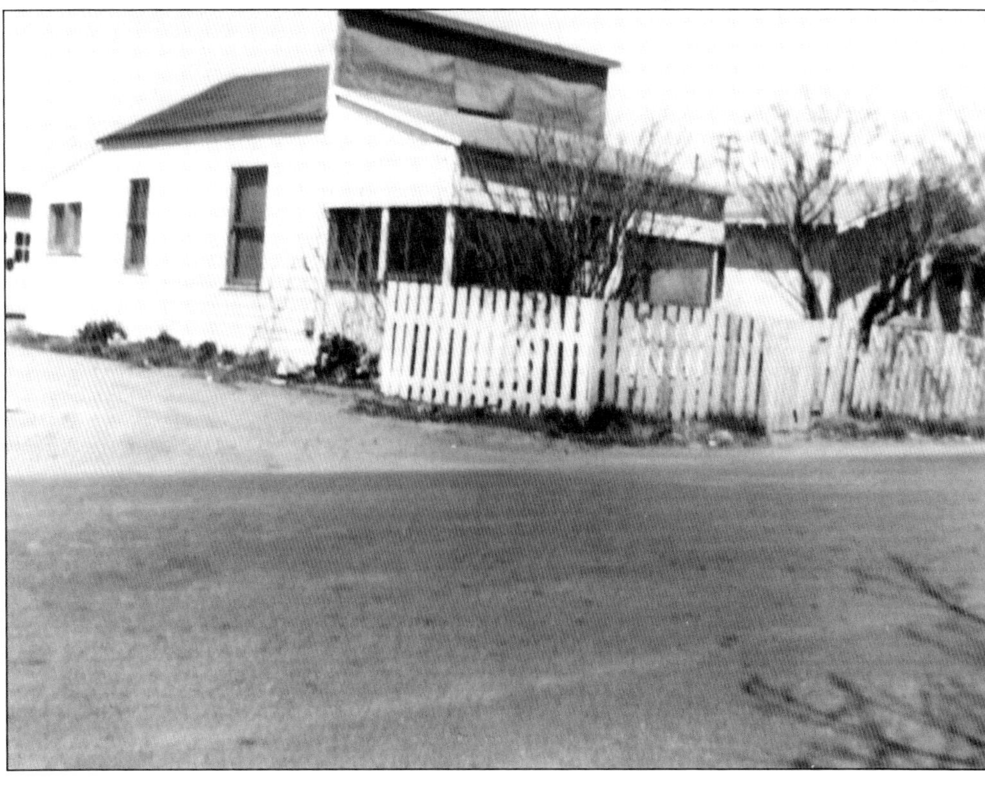

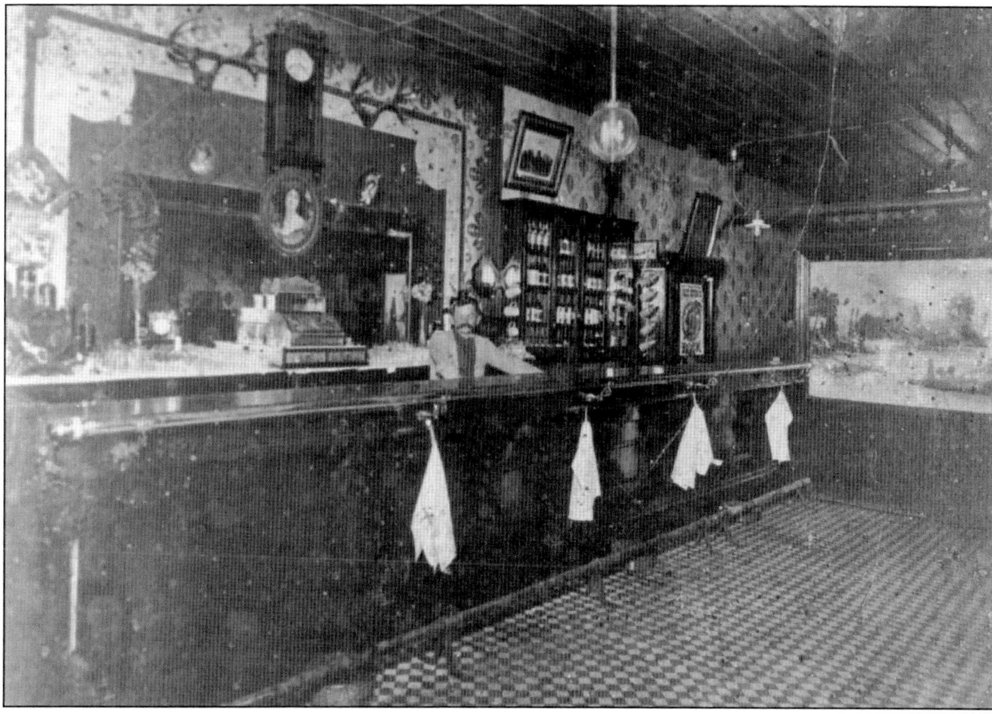

Although this bar was located in neighboring Mojave, it illustrates a saloon's interior. Other early Palmdale saloonkeepers included G. B. Poggi, T. Billings (1892), and Joseph Kirby (1893). During the early 1900s, several Palmdale businessmen, including "the czar of Palmdale," Joseph Kinchline (a constable, hotel keeper, and school trustee), were accused of running a "blind pig," an establishment that sold alcoholic beverages illegally. (Courtesy of Lil Stradal McDonald.)

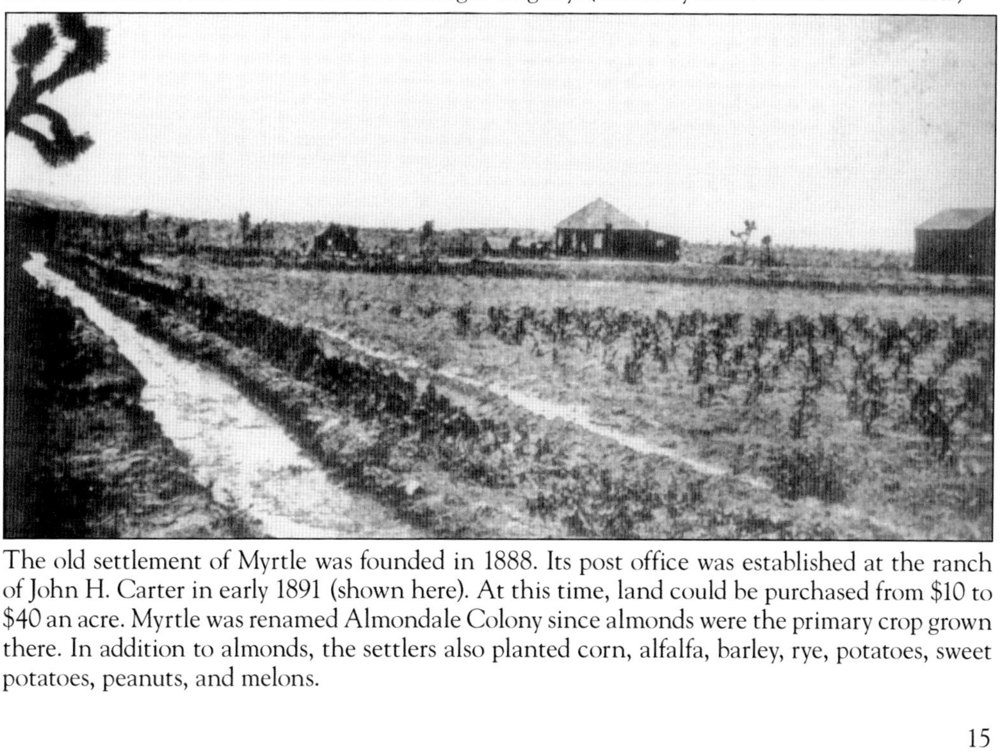

The old settlement of Myrtle was founded in 1888. Its post office was established at the ranch of John H. Carter in early 1891 (shown here). At this time, land could be purchased from $10 to $40 an acre. Myrtle was renamed Almondale Colony since almonds were the primary crop grown there. In addition to almonds, the settlers also planted corn, alfalfa, barley, rye, potatoes, sweet potatoes, peanuts, and melons.

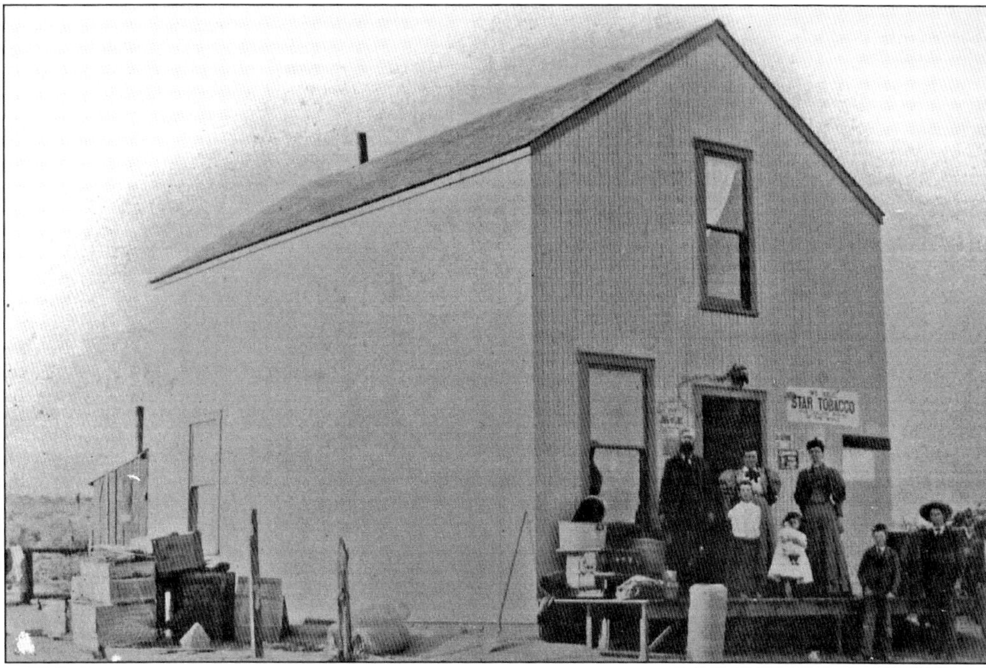

The Almondale Colony was located 4 miles east of Littlerock. It was settled mainly by Midwesterners who were promised agricultural riches by real estate promoters. Old real estate maps show Almondale Colony potentially being a very large town with a circular system of streets. By 1895, its estimated 200 residents were served by three stores, the Almondale House, a post office, a newspaper, a blacksmith, and other businesses.

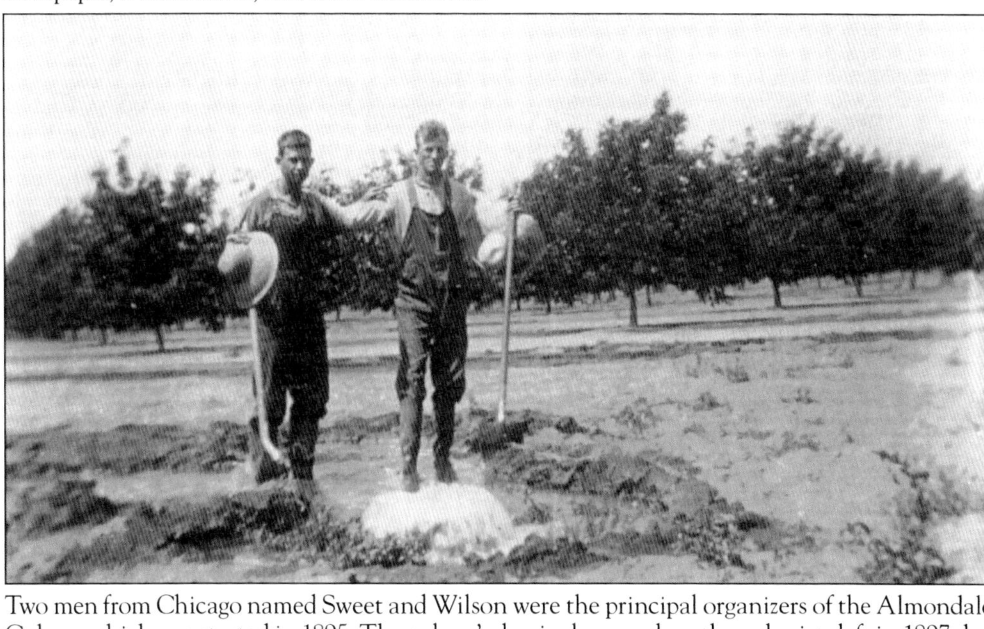

Two men from Chicago named Sweet and Wilson were the principal organizers of the Almondale Colony, which was started in 1895. The colony's demise began when the colonists left in 1897 due to a drought and tax and property title problems. The area was later revived as Pearblossom. In neighboring Littlerock, Frank Stanton (left) and George Bones Sr. are shown irrigating orchards in 1915. (Courtesy of Denece Bones Parsons.)

Two

The Railroad and Harold

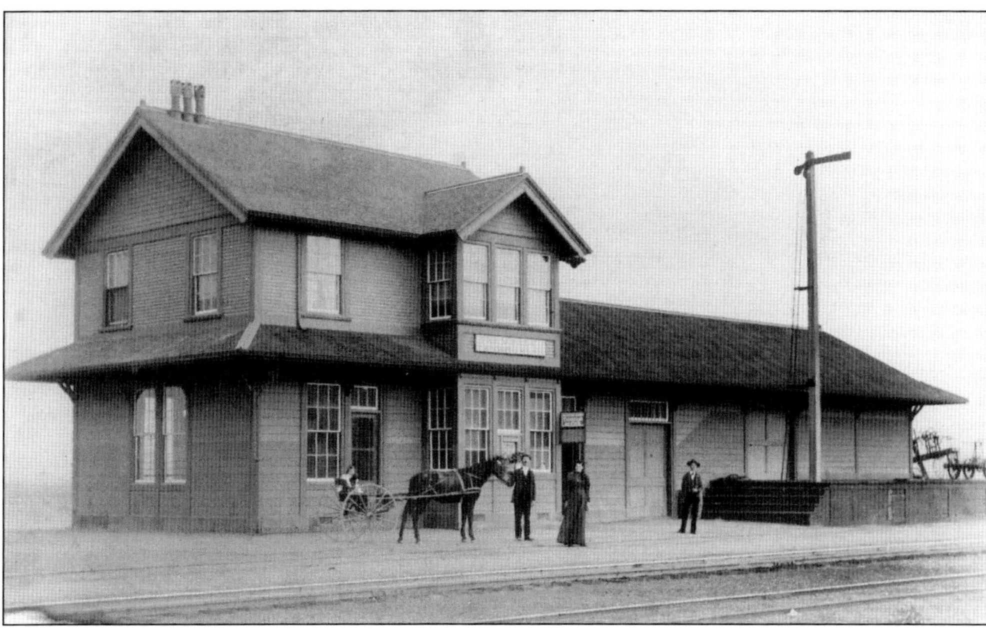

When the Southern Pacific Railroad passed through the Antelope Valley in the summer of 1876, it established small station stops at Lancaster and Mojave, but not the Palmdale area. Prior to the 1892 establishment of a little depot (moved from Harold) in New Palmdale, locals had to travel to Harold/Alpine for service. This is the Palmdale depot sometime after its completion in 1895. (Courtesy of Phil Serpico.)

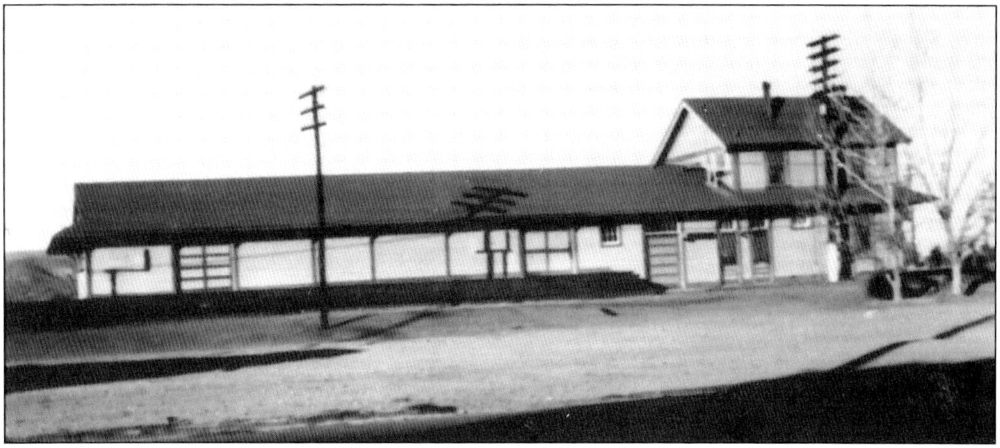

In 1892, Palmdale became a helper station; two or three large engines were kept there to help all the southbound freights up the hill to Vincent, where the helpers would uncouple and go back down to Palmdale. No agent was assigned here until around March 1892. Pioneers claimed one could also stop the train by setting a fire on the tracks! This scene dates to the 1940s. (Courtesy of WAVHS.)

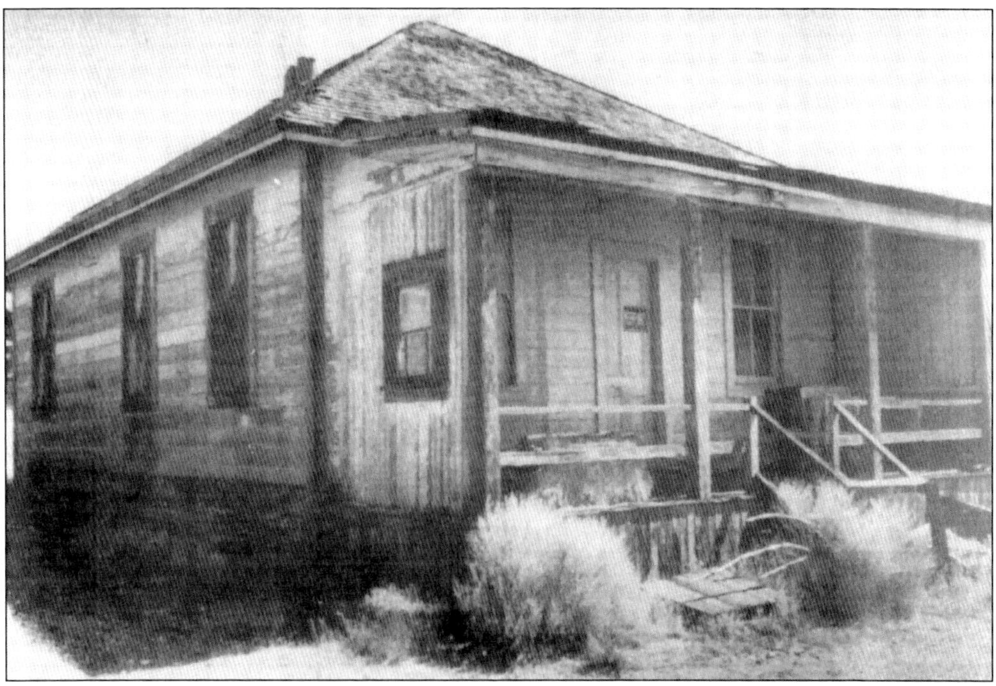

The late Antelope Valley historian, Glen Settle, was born in 1911 in the Palmdale railroad section foreman's house. It had a kitchen, a living room, and two bedrooms. It was very crowded with eight children running about. Currently located at the Tropico Gold Mine, Dayle DeBry (Lancaster cemetery manager) and the board of directors are in the process of having this structure moved to the cemetery to become a museum.

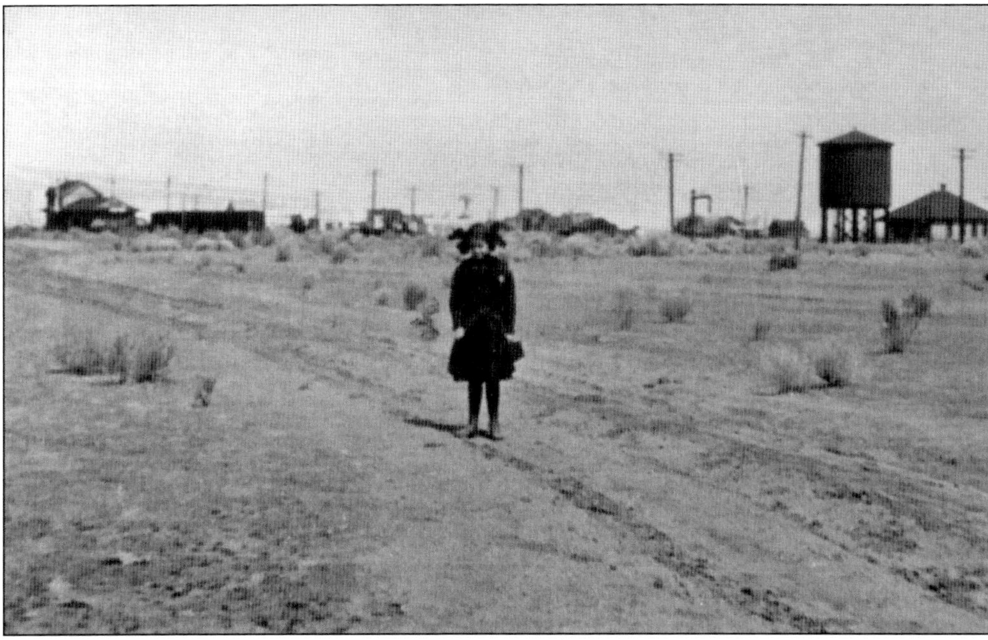

A solitary, young Myrtle Tinkham stands near the Palmdale Southern Pacific Railroad depot around 1913. The station is on the left side while the water tower and the section foreman's house are on the right. The railroad depot stood south of the southeast corner of Sierra Highway and Palmdale Boulevard, across the street from the present-day Larry Chimbole Cultural Center.

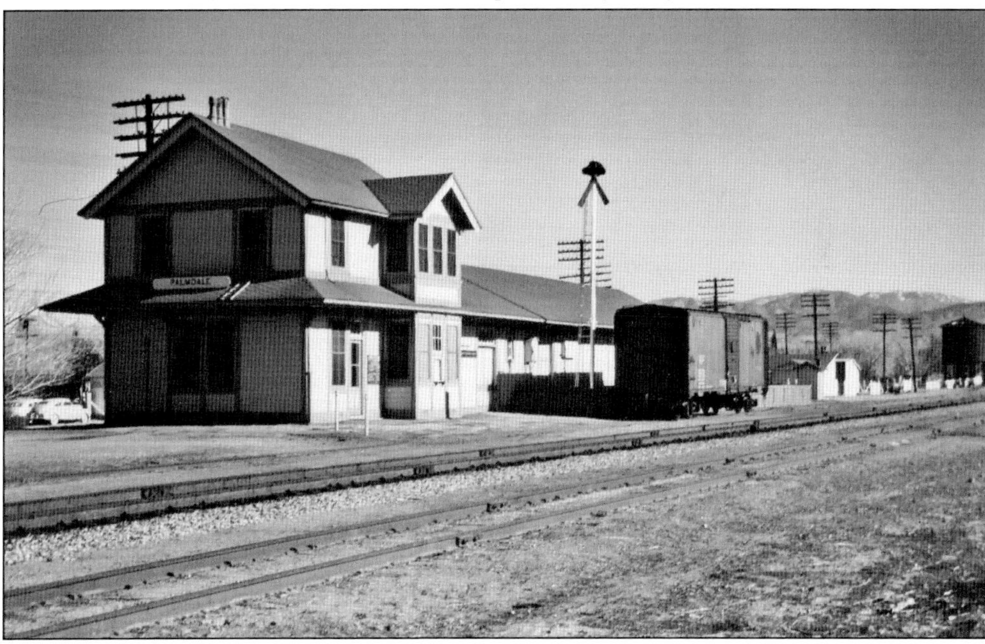

The fortunes of the railroad often waxed and waned. In 1903, it comprised the largest part of town and was the community's biggest employer. The Depression was a difficult period, but things improved for a while afterwards. However, when Southern Pacific (SP) opened a new office in spring of 1969, the old depot was dismantled in October 1969. This is the depot in the 1940s. (Courtesy of Ron and Maddi Kleit.)

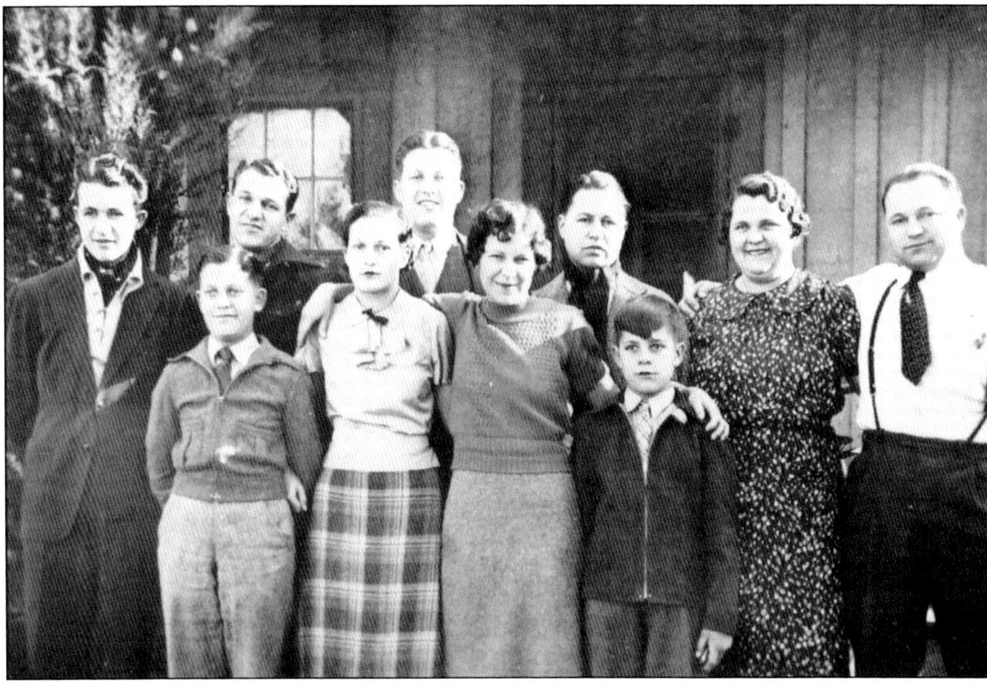

William and Marion Settle came to the Antelope Valley in 1909 when William became a section foreman for the SP Railroad in Palmdale. Marion's father came to California during the Gold Rush and was stationed at neighboring Fort Tejon during the Civil War. The family lived in a railroad-provided house in Palmdale. The Settle children included Bill, Glen, Earle, Irving, Mark, Robert, Jack, Ruth, Maude, Mildred, and Aileen.

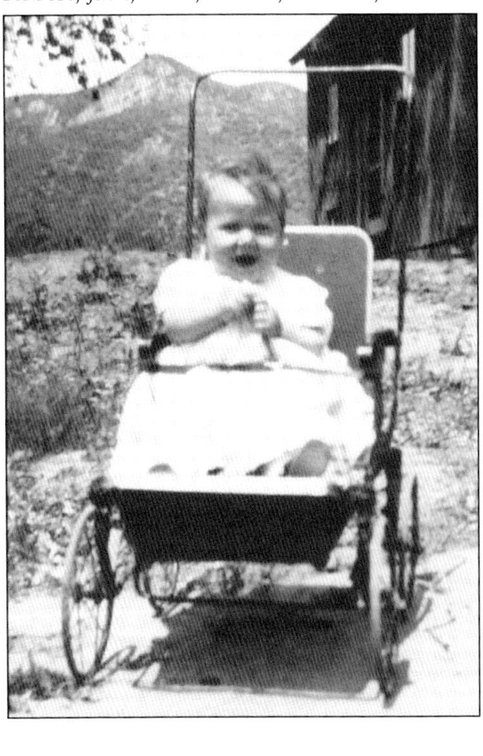

This book would not have been possible without the contributions of Glen Settle, who died during its writing. Born in Palmdale, his family moved to Lancaster when he was in the third grade. He lived almost his entire life in the Antelope Valley. Settle married Dorene Burton (1923–2000), whose relatives were some of the first non-Hispanic settlers in the valley (1869). "Baby" Glen is enjoying himself on a family vacation.

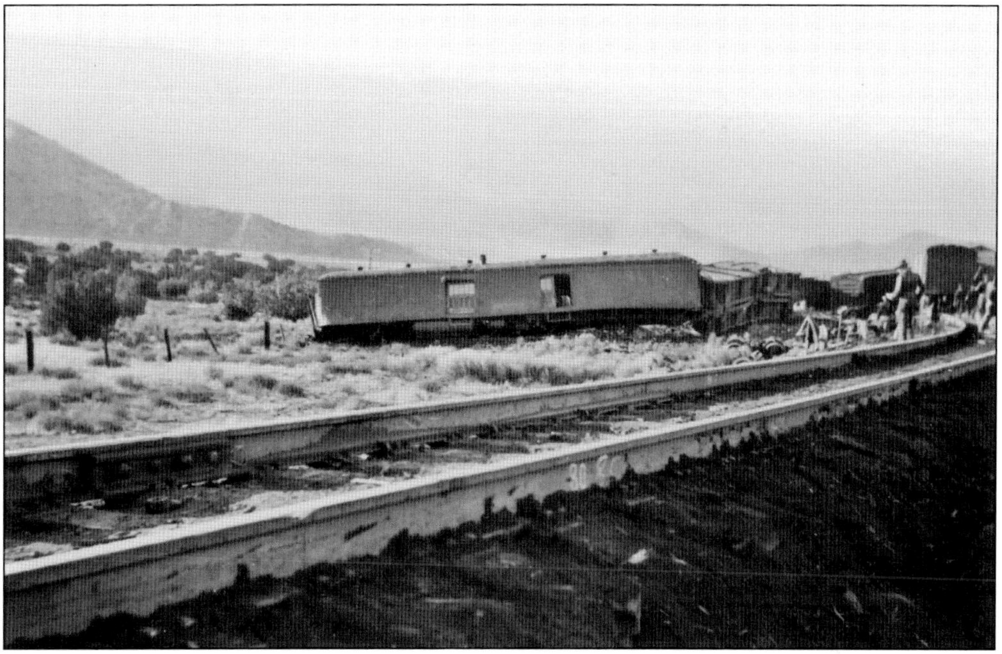

Accidents and even death were common occurrences for travelers and railroad workers. Some workers lost their hands or died after being trapped between cars. In May 1903, a large SP Railroad oil storage tank at Palmdale collapsed and killed the night watchman and Schneckenberger's four-year-old son, who had been playing near the tank when it fell upon him. The train wreck shown here took place south of Palmdale near Acton.

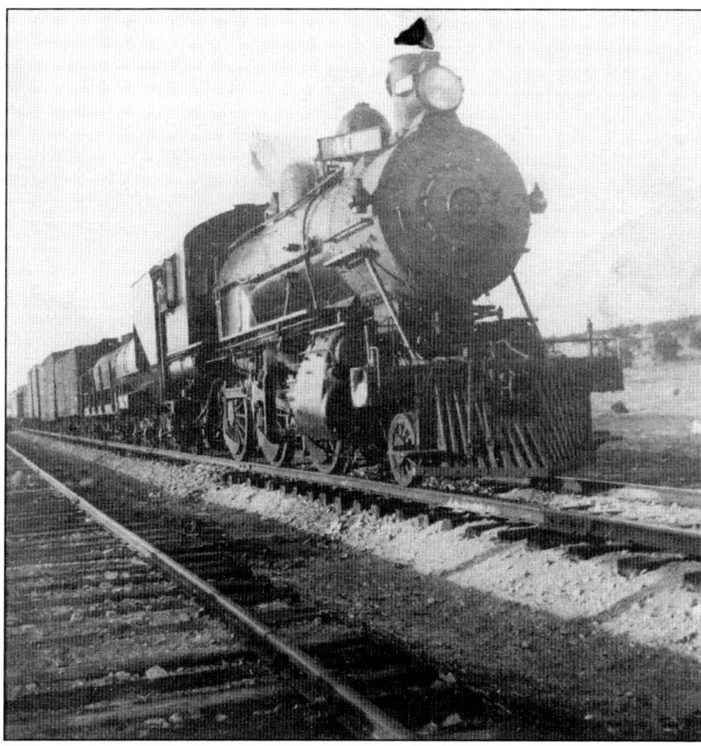

This train may be in the vicinity of old Harold, which was also known as Alpine Station and Trego Post Office. Located about 2 miles south of Palmdale, Harold was at one time a very important community, as it was at the crossroads of two major routes on the valley floor: the SP Railroad tracks and Fort Tejon Road. Railroad employees and Chinese laborers mostly inhabited it.

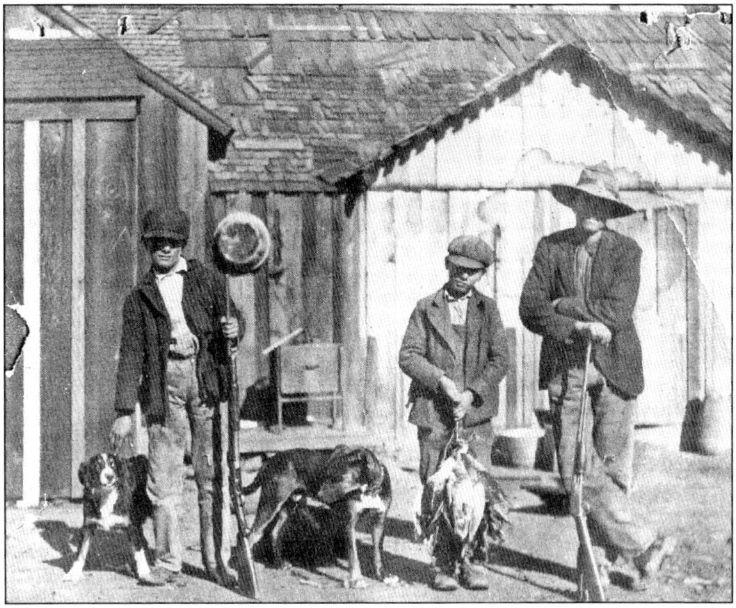

By the early 1890s, Harold consisted of a combination hotel/saloon and a few houses. As New Palmdale grew, the town gradually lost its importance, and by 1926 it had dwindled to only the Harold Square Deal Garage and a few little shacks. A mobile home park now stands in the vicinity of old Harold. Three Harold hunters and their dogs enjoyed a good bird hunting day in 1905.

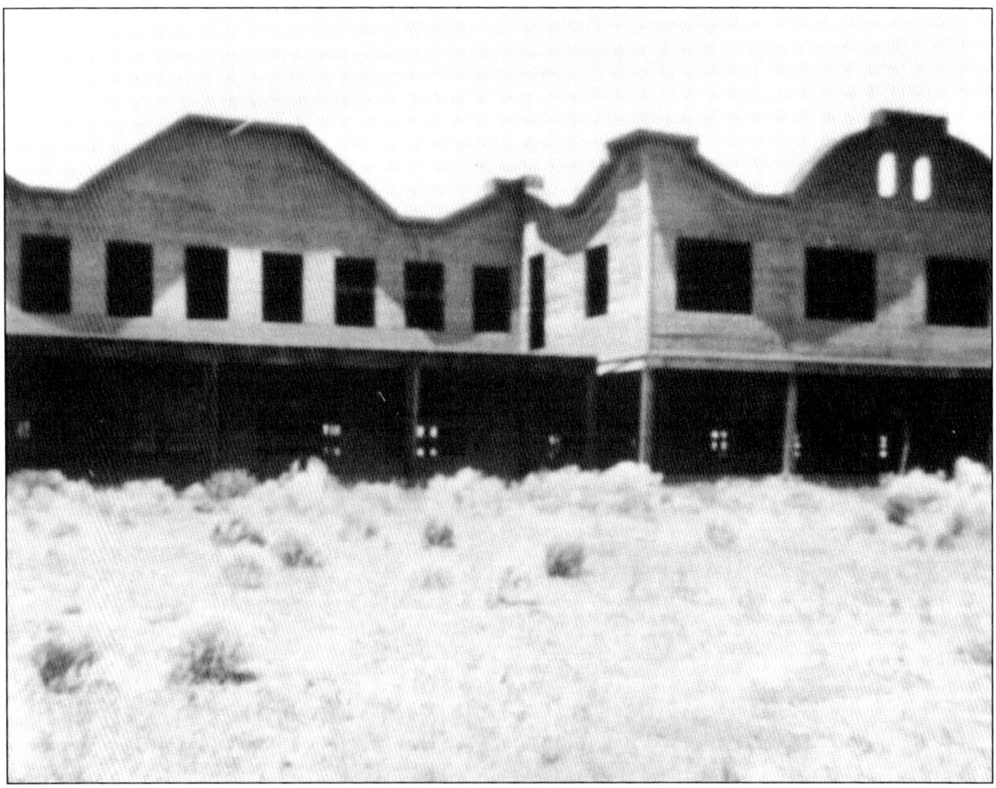

There are some present-day reminders of old Harold; local streets are named Harold Second, Harold Third, Harold Beech, and Harold Ash. Unfortunately, this building, the unfinished Alpine Springs Hotel and Sanitarium built on the west side of Sierra Highway, no longer exists. In 1908, investors had hoped to make the area into a health and rest resort. Constructed in the mission style, this structure's building cost was $40,000.

Three

Littlerock, Juniper Hills, and Pearblossom

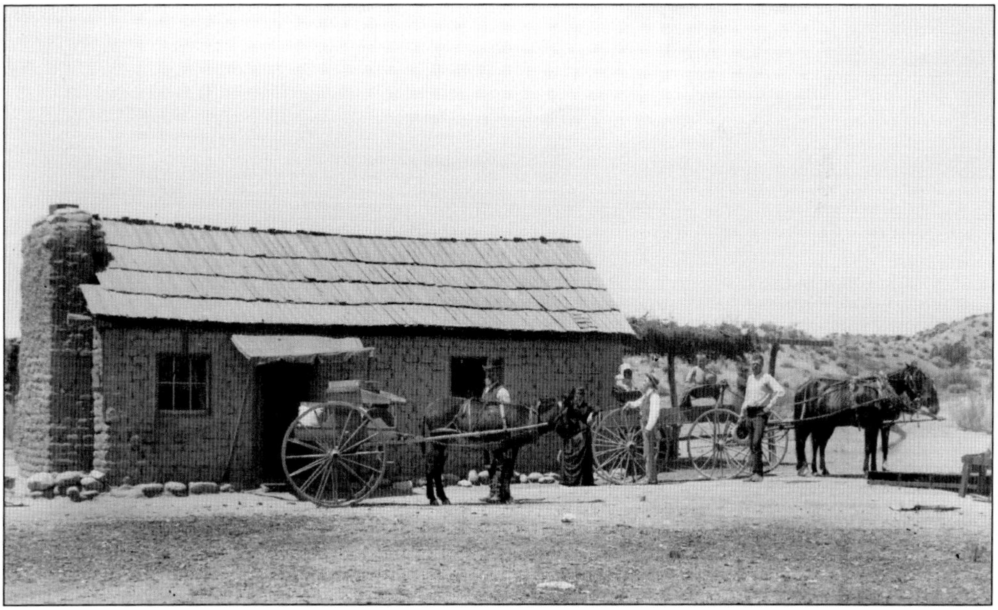

The first nonnative settlement on Little Rock Creek is believed to be that of the Santiago Garcia family. The adobe's exact date is not known, but it probably coincides with the mining boom of the late 1860s. It was later used as a stage stop. According to local oral tradition, Garcia was killed in 1873 by a grizzly bear in what was later named Santiago Canyon. (Courtesy of Fred Strasburg.)

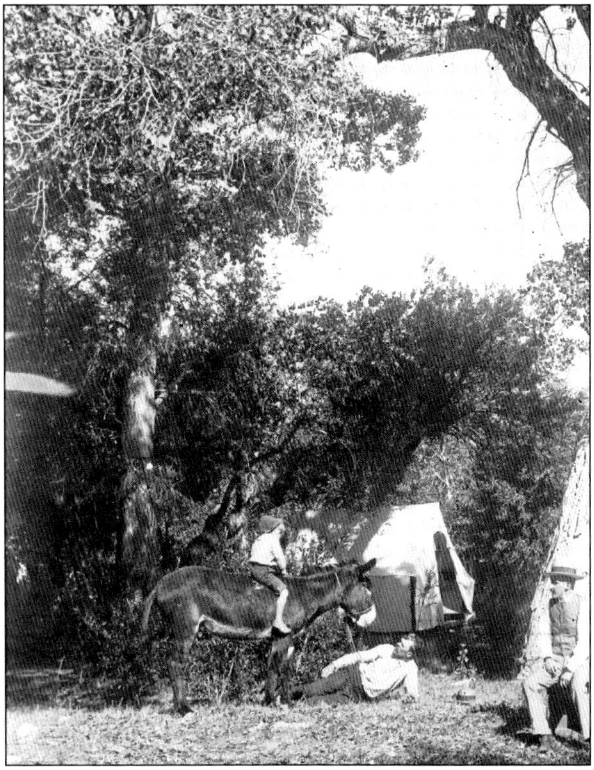

In the late 1880s, the Alpine Springs Land and Water Company was formed by the Cole brothers, Charles, Zack, and Nathan (reclining), and Charles's son, Burt. They planned to establish a colony at the mouth of Little Rock Canyon. They originally set up a horse ranch here but became intrigued by the potential for establishing orchards there. (Courtesy of University of Southern California, on behalf of the USC Special Collections.)

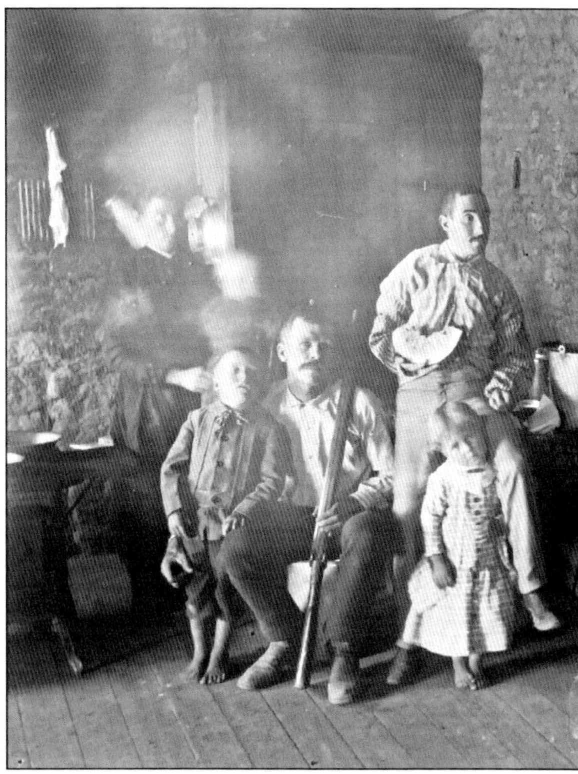

Nathan Cole and his family are posing in their cabin. Around 1893, the Coles involved the firm of Palmer and Chapin of Chicago in promoting the early Tierra Bonita Colony on the east bank of Little Rock Creek. This agricultural colony was laid out in the vicinity of the northern "suburbs" of modern Littlerock. (Courtesy of University of Southern California, on behalf of the USC Special Collections.)

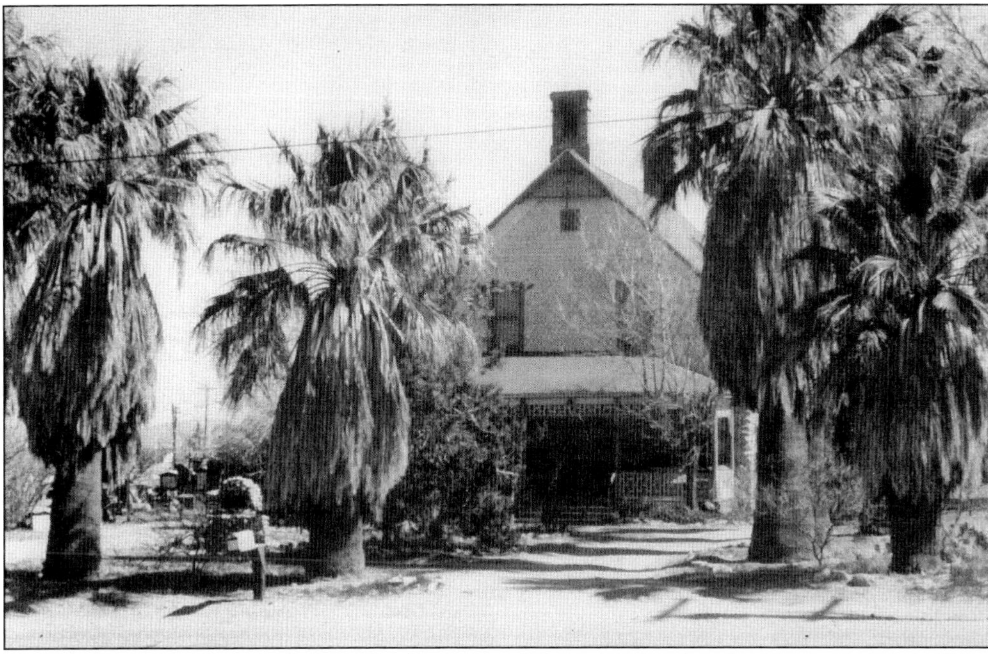

Originally known as the Palmer and Chapin Guest House of Littlerock, this is one of the oldest houses in the Antelope Valley. Built from local river rocks, its purpose was to accommodate the Midwestern land buyers who came to see their land in the 1890s. An early promotional brochure described it as measuring 41-feet-by-50-feet with nice large rooms and redwood throughout. Mrs. S. Brubaker was an early proprietor.

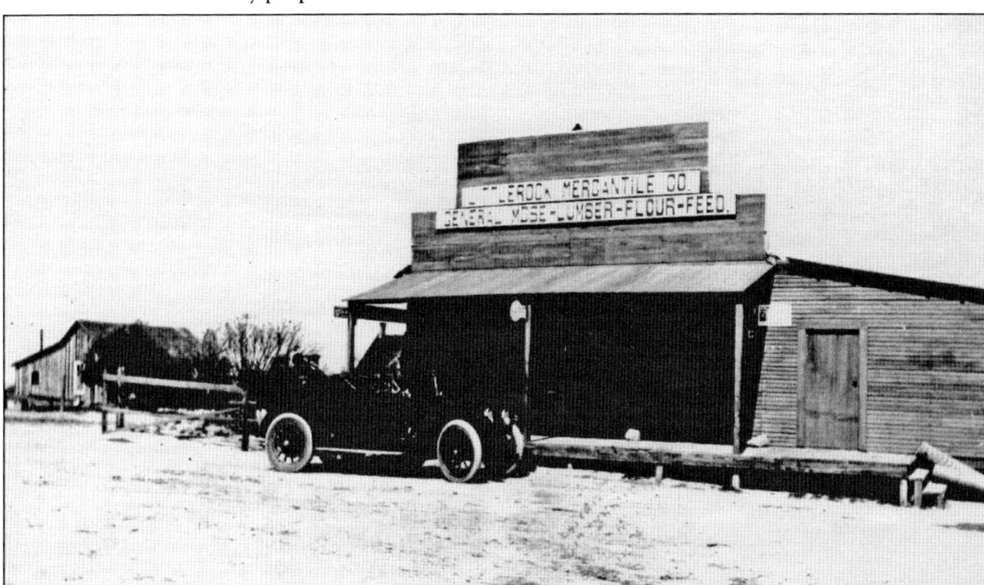

The first Littlerock Post Office was established on September 6, 1893, by a Mr. Billings at Seventy-seventh Street East and Pearblossom Highway; Frances Bonham was the postmistress. The first general store opened in 1894, but failed after about a year. Mr. and Mrs. Olaf Lewis owned the new store around 1911. A. O. Miller also ran the general store and post office at one time. (Courtesy of Fred Strasburg.)

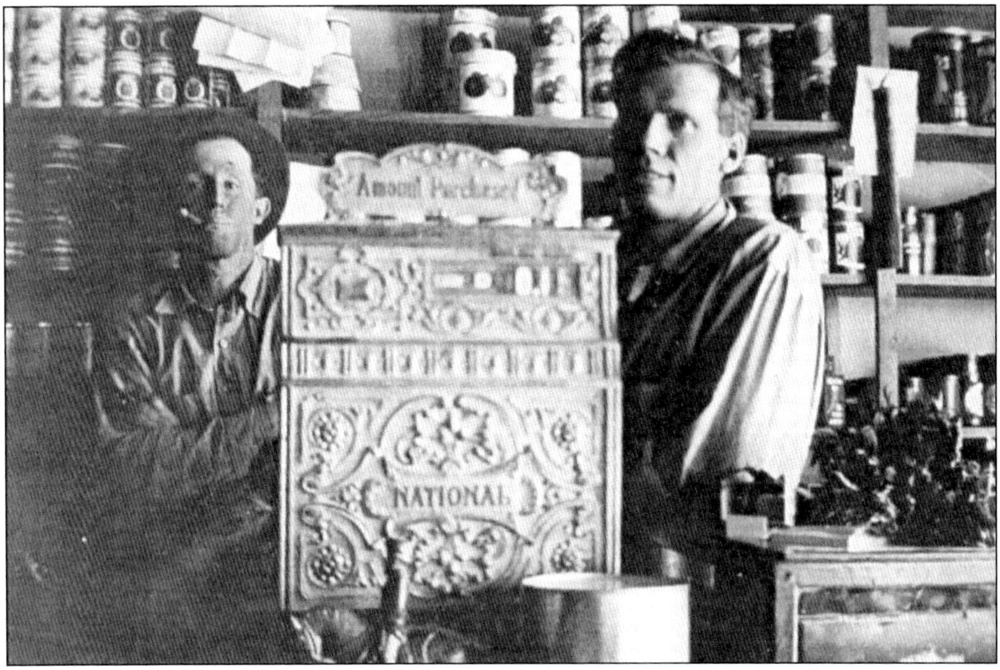

The downtown area of Littlerock has always centered near Seventy-seventh Street East and Pearblossom Highway. On the north side of Highway 138, there was a two-story building with a grocery, one gas pump, and a post office downstairs and apartments upstairs. Its different proprietors were William Morse, Olaf Lewis, and Jay Stockton. Lew Bones (left) and Frank Stanton are shown inside the Lewis store (1915). (Courtesy of Denece Bones Parsons.)

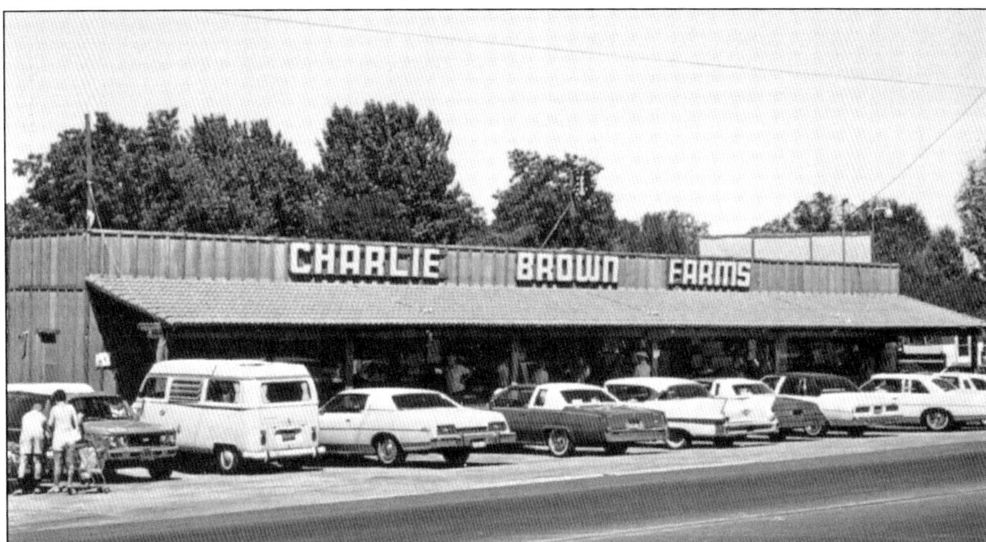

Littlerock's landmark Charlie Brown Farms is located on Pearblossom Highway. Today it is owned by Jackie Hallgren. Before it was constructed, however, there was an earlier little fruit stand and store on the same site, owned by Alfred and Marian Sweet and later by Frank and Mary Sweet. One of Frank's sons, Tom, gained fame as the Ajax "White Knight" in "stronger than dirt!" television commercials. (Courtesy of Jackie Hallgren.)

Early female Littlerock pioneers like Mrs. Rosa worked a variety of occupations, including farmers, teachers, boardinghouse cooks, stage drivers, postmistresses, sales people, and bus drivers. August was pear-picking time, and women from all over the Antelope Valley obtained temporary work in the packing sheds. During the mid-1910s, a group of Littlerock women established the Get Together Society at the local school for community support.

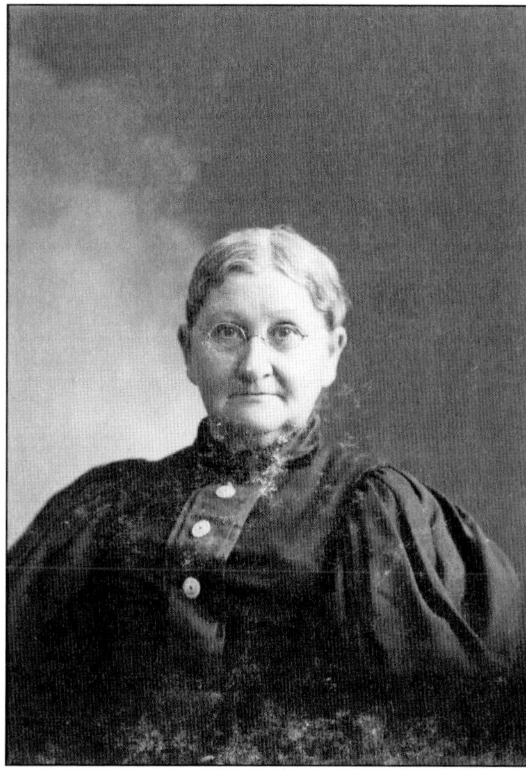

In 1890, Everett Martin came to the valley with his family and settled on a homestead in the Llano area. Because of water problems, they moved to the Littlerock region. In 1907, Amasa, Everett's father, purchased 40 acres at what is now Pearblossom Highway and Seventy-seventh Street East, which included the old rock guesthouse. This is the old Martin packing facility on Seventy-seventh Street. (Courtesy of Denece Bones Parsons.)

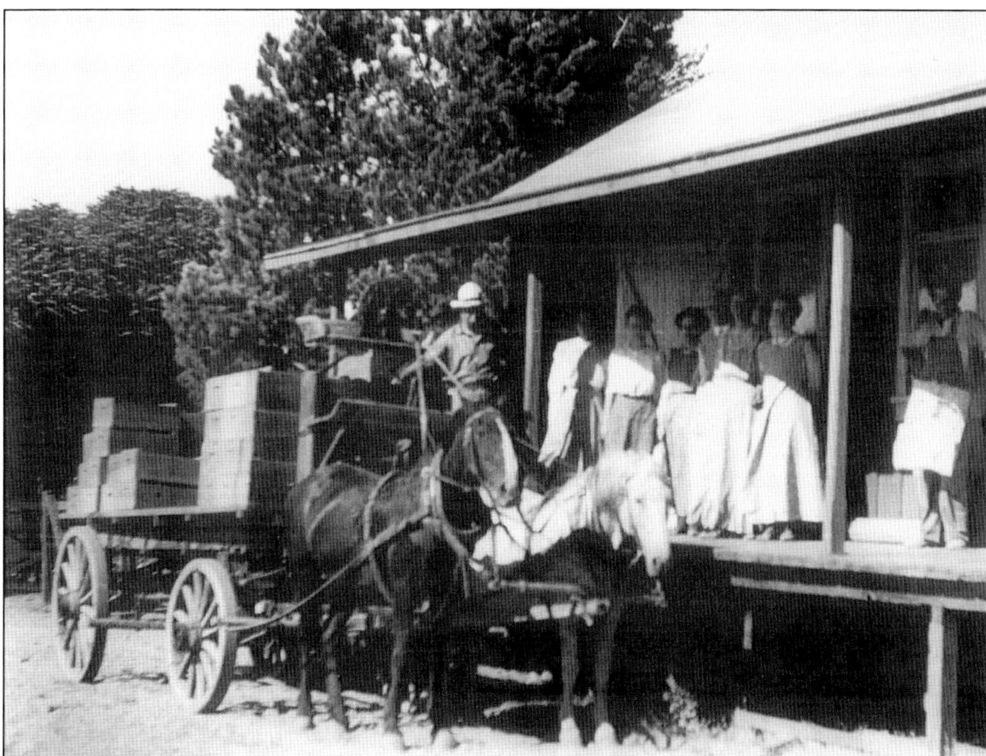

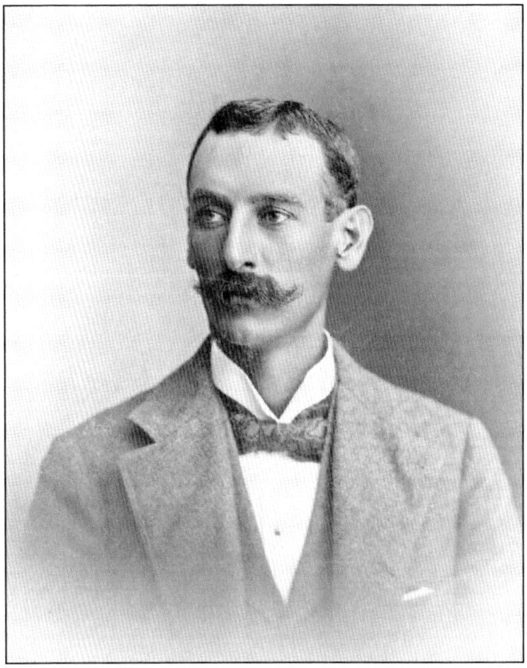

Born into a prominent Los Angeles family, George Weinshank, a nurseryman, florist, and experimental planter, temporarily moved to Antelope Valley when he became sick. He was also related to James Ward of Lancaster. Weinshank was very impressed with the local orchards and studied them. In 1907, he planted an experimental walnut tree near downtown Whittier, California, which is now California State Historical Landmark No. 681.

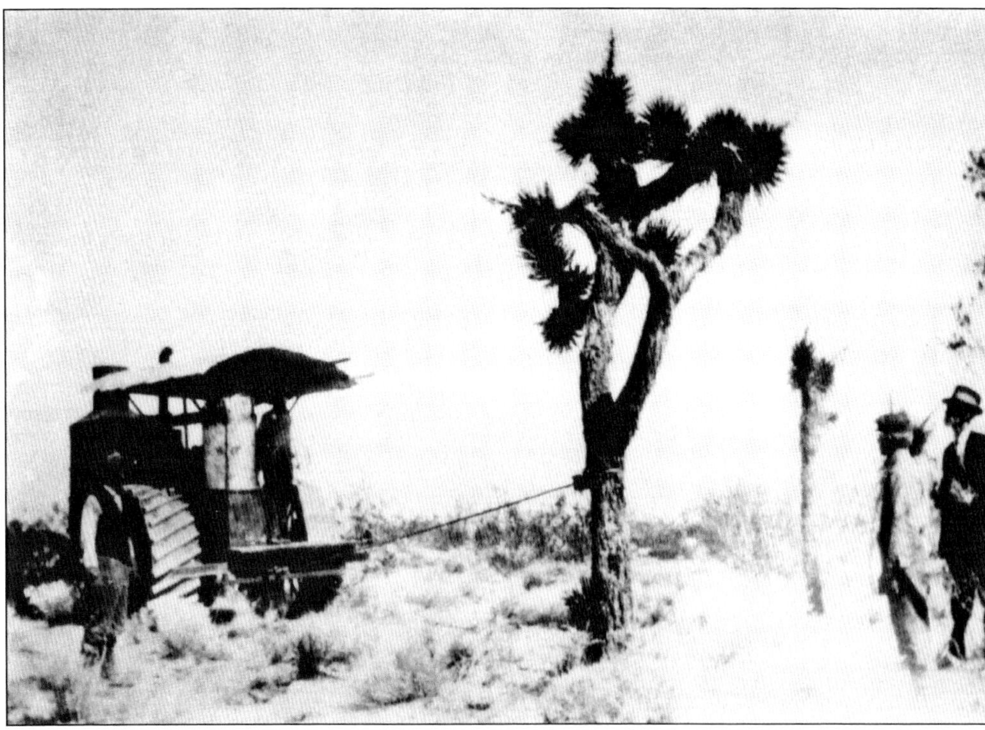

Early farmers thought winter rainfall would be sufficient for their crops, but after disastrous droughts they recognized the need for irrigation. During the 1910s, the introduction of gasoline pumps and, later, electric pumps, helped to revive fruit and nut cultivation. Native vegetation, including Joshua trees, had to be removed for orchardists to plant their fruit trees. This scene is from Llano del Rio Colony in 1915.

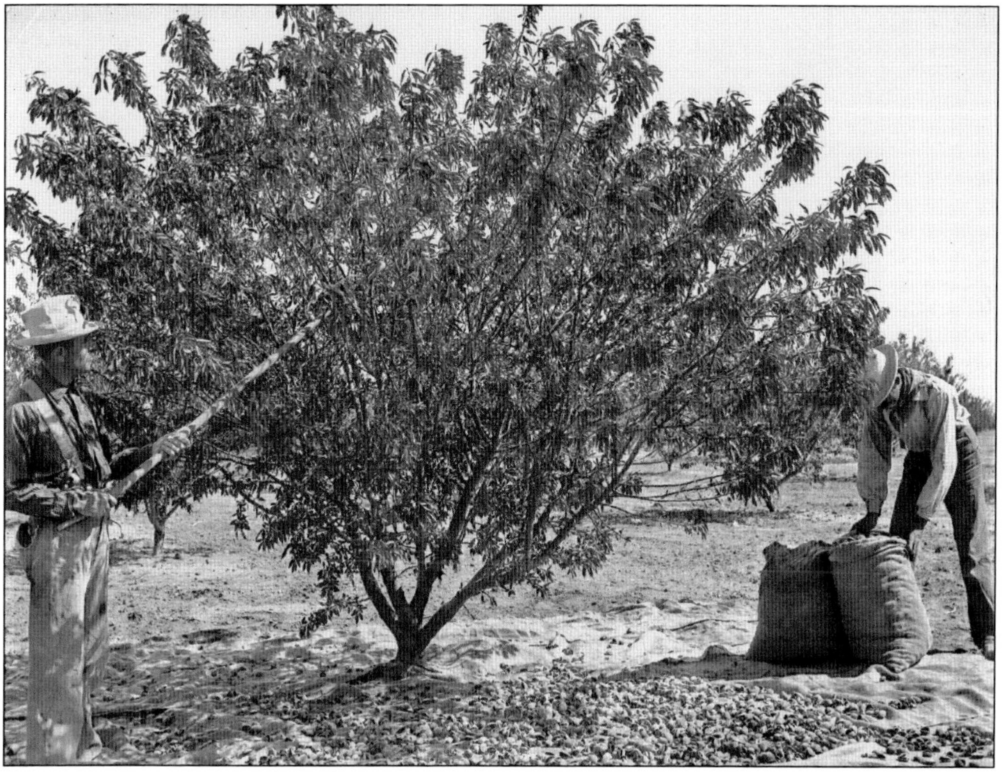

Between 1910 and 1915, almonds were removed and replaced with Bartlett pears in the Littlerock area. Two men are picking almonds by shaking the branches with a stick, causing the almonds to fall to the cloth spread below the tree. The man on the right is very busy loading the sacks with the loose almonds. (Courtesy of University of Southern California, on behalf of the USC Special Collections.)

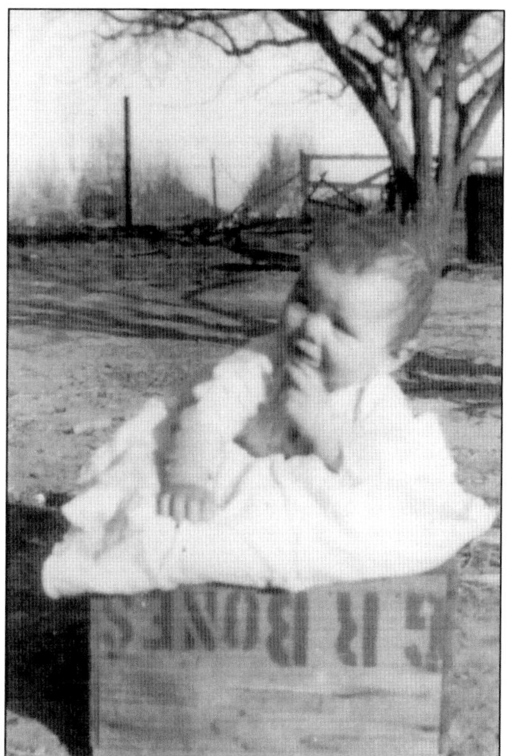

The community-minded Bones family has owned pear and peach orchards in Littlerock for almost a century. Lew Bones came here in 1903 to work as a pear ranch laborer. In 1915, his brother, George, came here to pull and cut almond trees for firewood as they were being phased out in favor of pear trees. George Bones Jr. is resting in a fruit box in 1925. (Courtesy of Denece Bones Parsons.)

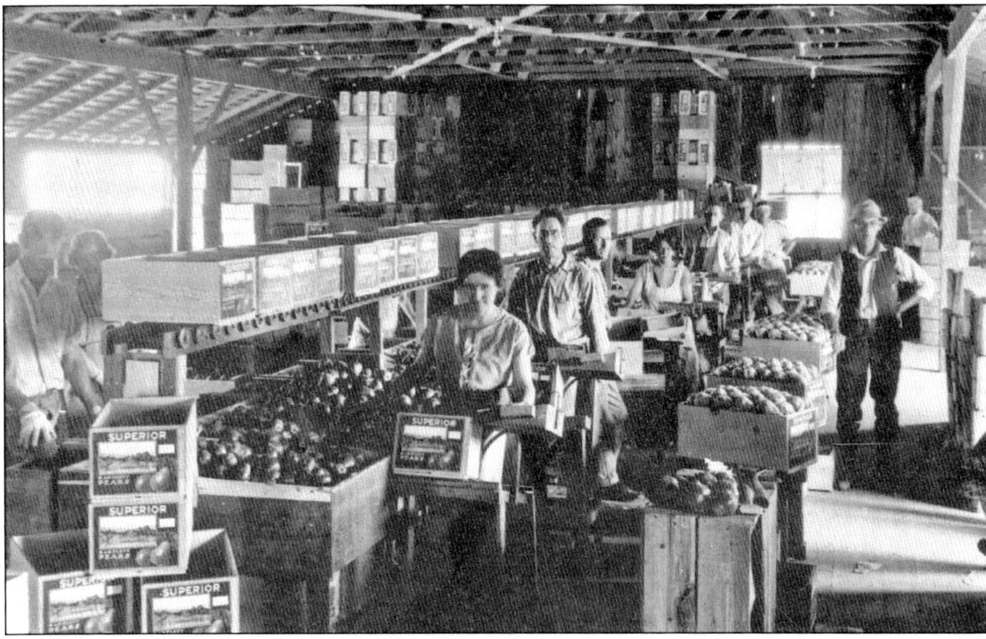

The pear harvest provided employment for many residents. The Farm Bureau had packing schools in Littlerock and Palmdale with a University of California, Davis professor for those who desired to learn how to pack pears. After all the hard work, it was common to have a dance at the Brubaker and Barton packinghouses. Locals would gather and play their instruments so others could dance until early morning.

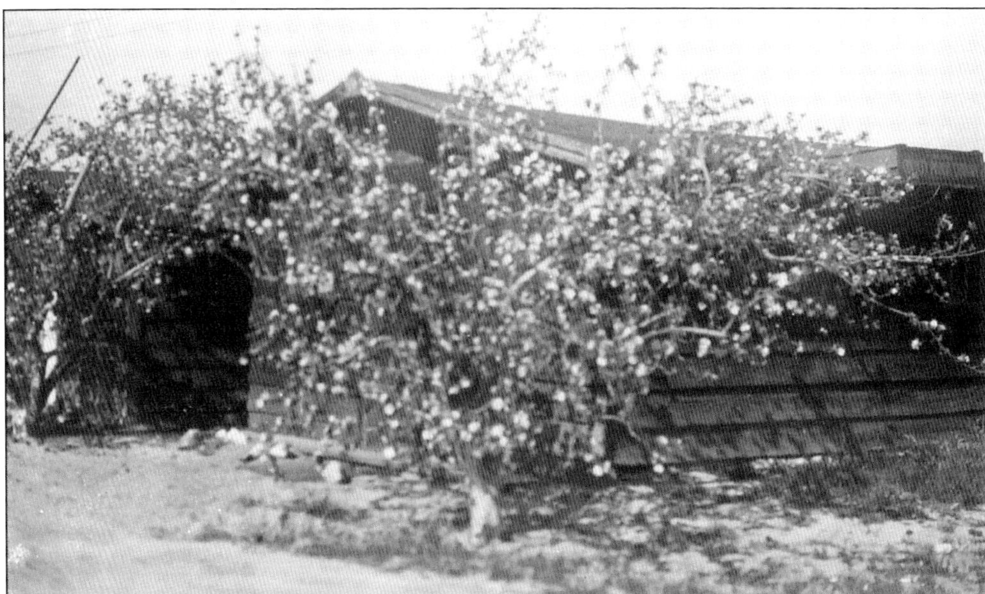

In 1918, Amasa Martin inaugurated a Pear Day Festival. Ben Brainard was the first chairman of the Littlerock Chamber of Commerce, which was formed in 1928. He and later presidents worked hard to promote Littlerock's agricultural ventures. A popular advertisement was "good pears without worms." Apple trees like these at the Littlerock Library (1937) were also planted. (Courtesy of Littlerock Library, County of Los Angeles Public Library.)

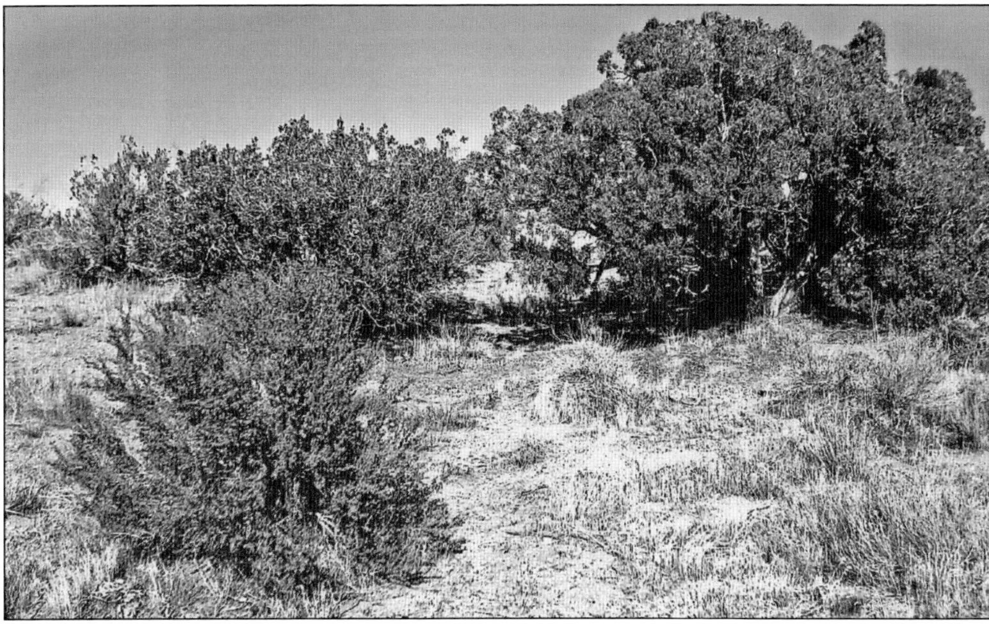

Juniper Hills, also known as Cima Mesa, is located between Littlerock and Pearblossom. Dr. James Booth, a local surveyor, gave the foothill area its name because so many large juniper trees grew here. In 1921, Bert Colbeck ("Mr. Juniper Hills") filed on a homestead. At this time, all water and supplies had to be hauled in by horse and wagon through the gulches as there were no roads here.

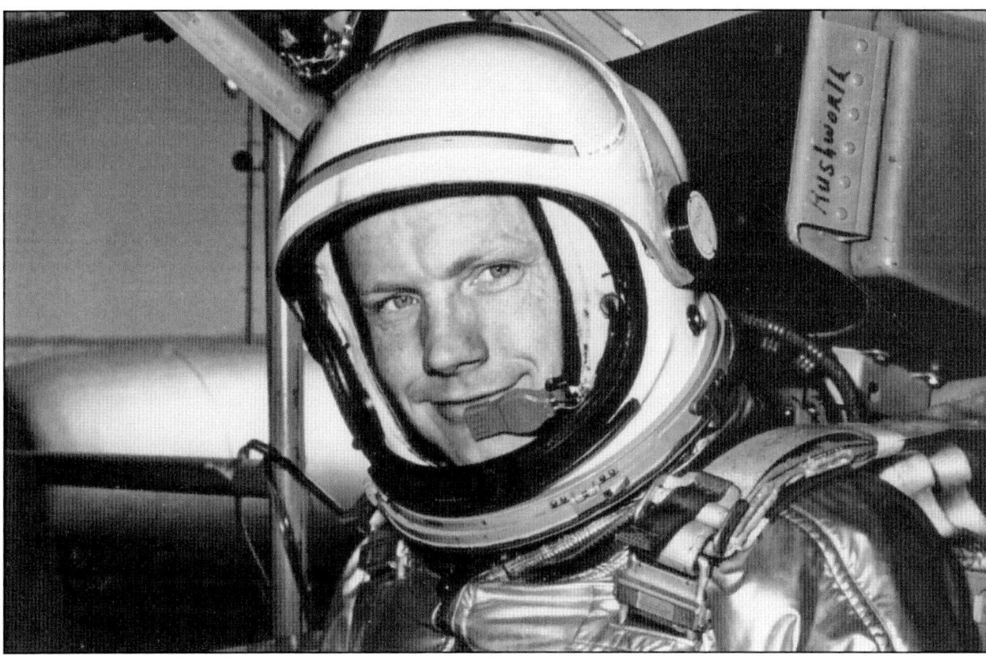

Before he became the first person to walk on the moon on July 20, 1969, Neil Armstrong and his family lived in a rustic cabin in Juniper Hills. At this time, he was employed at Edwards AFB, where he was a project pilot on many pioneering high-speed aircraft, including the 4,000-mile-per-hour X-15. His wife, Janet, taught Red Cross swimming classes at a local community pool.

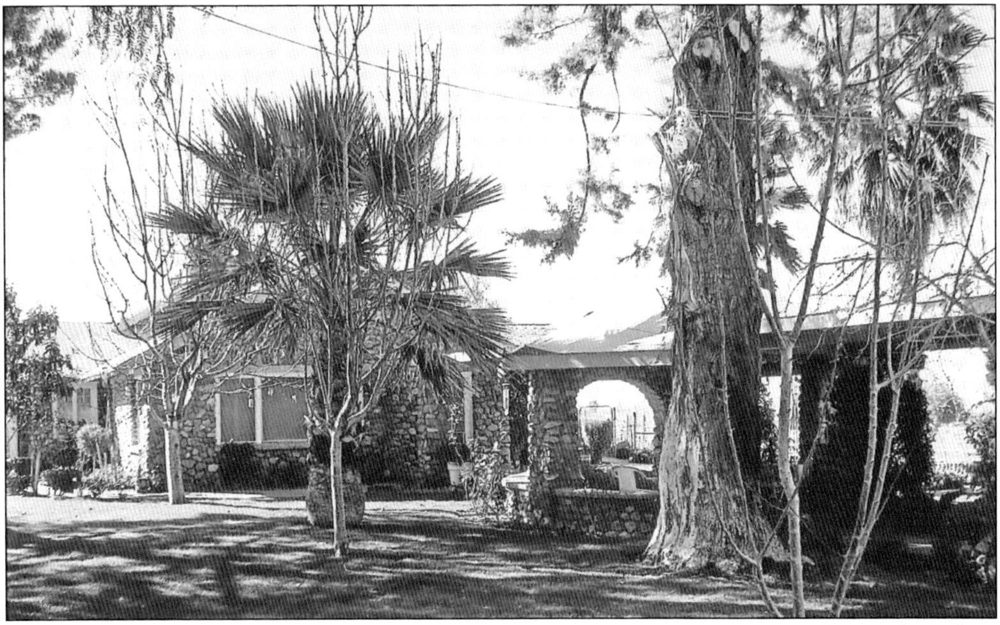

During the mid-1920s, Mr. and Mrs. L. F. Hughes owned one of the finest ranches in the valley. Formerly the Rush Ranch, it was located on Longview Road. It was often described as a palatial cobblestone and was worth $10,000. The main house was constructed from stone by Italian craftsmen. The Pearblossom property even had its own electric light plant. Robert St. Clair's family resided here for a while.

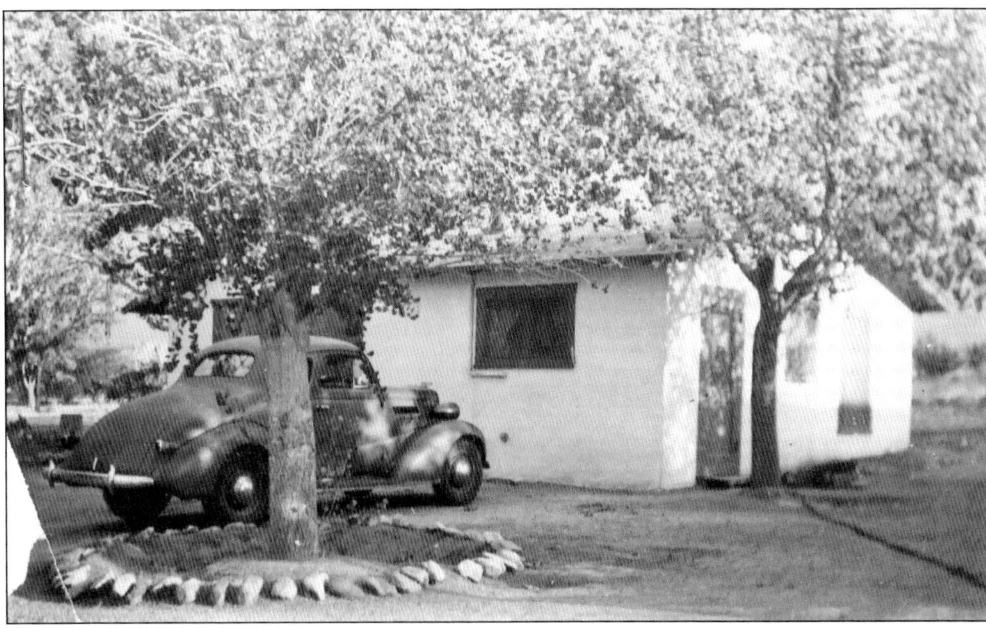

The credit for naming the community of Pearblossom is usually given to Guy Chase. A former Santa Monica resident, he named it for the area's once abundant pear orchards. By 1928, there was a "Pearblossom" gas station here. Chase also built several business structures on Highway 138. The area also became a favorite Hollywood locale for early Western movies. This is the Lee house in Pearblossom (1946).

Four

LLANO, VALYERMO, AND BIG ROCK CREEK

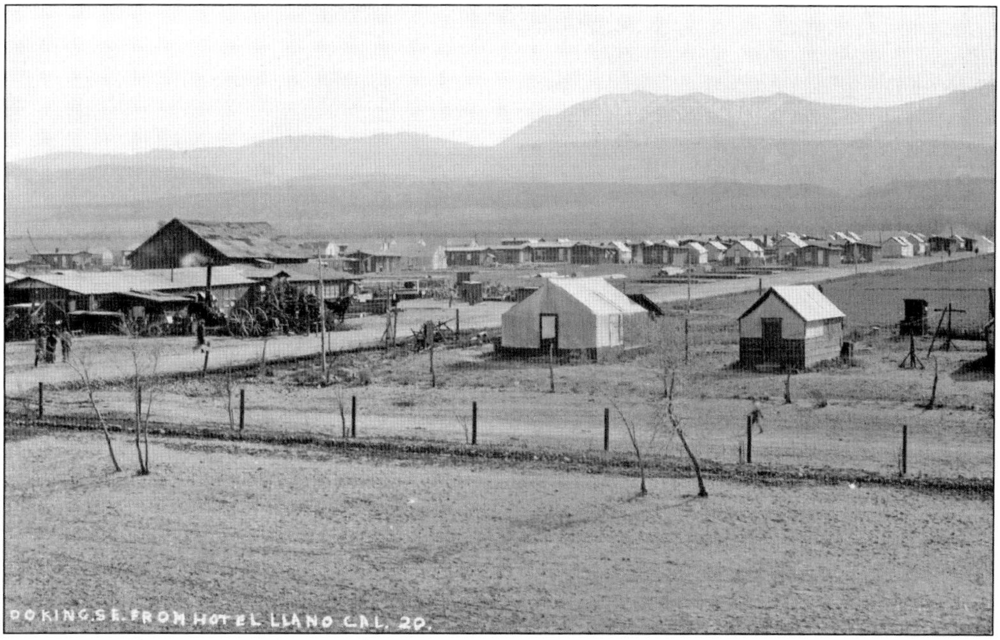

A few crumbling stone walls are all that remain of the Llano del Rio Colony, which was one of the most notable industrial cooperative experiments in California history. Located along Highway 138 near 165th Street East, the historic colony was founded on May 1, 1914, by Job Harriman and 50 settlers. By mid-1917, the colony's population reached a peak of 900, making it the largest town in Antelope Valley.

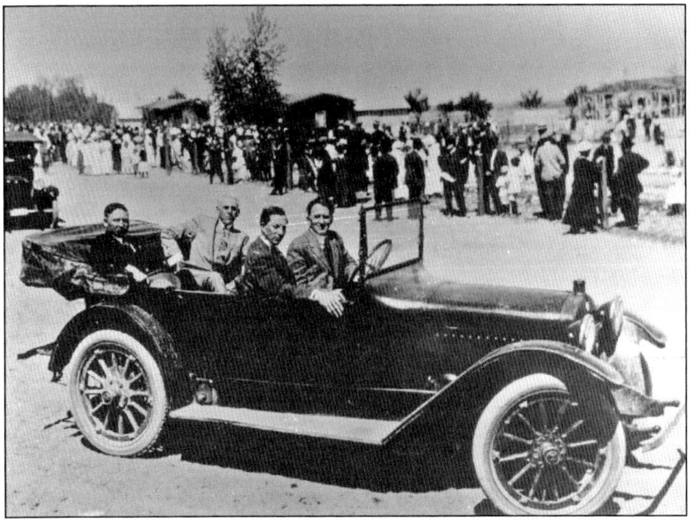

Job Harriman, pictured in the front passenger seat during a Llano parade, was a socialist lawyer who ran for governor of California (1898), vice president of the United States (1900), and mayor of Los Angeles. The people at Llano came from every walk of life, representing nearly every skill, profession, and level of prosperity. Anyone could join the colony if he or she was financially able to afford membership.

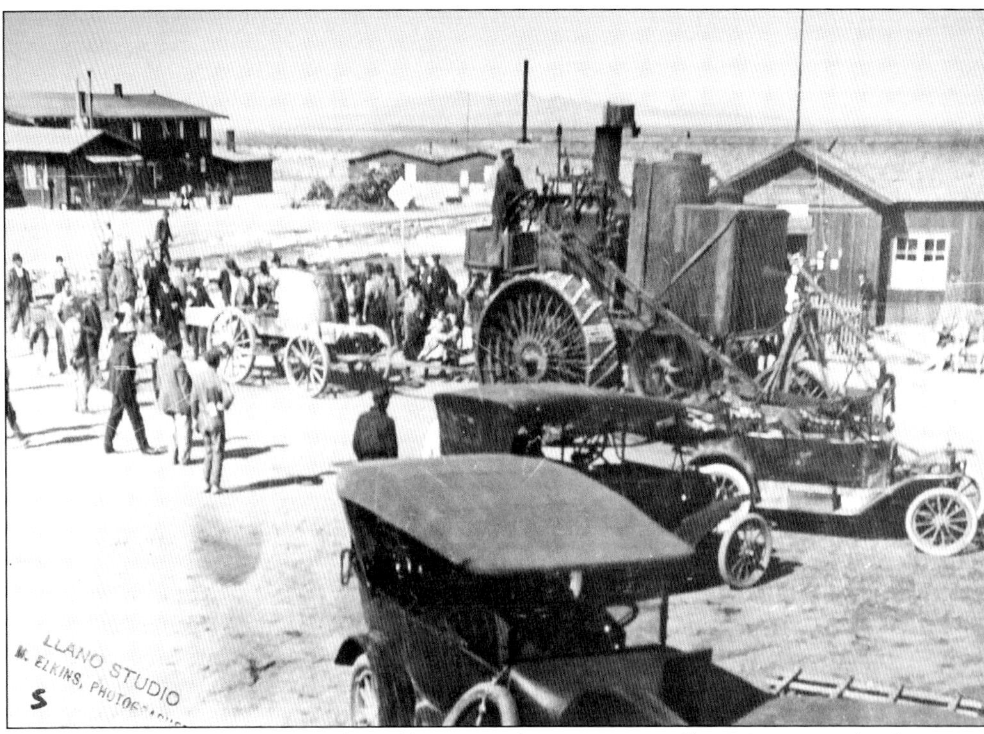

Llano had several firsts within the valley: a rug factory, a sawmill, a Montessori kindergarten, the first constructed motorized airplane (although it never flew), and an Esperanto language club. Bella Lewitzky, the doyenne of modern dance, was born here. Gregory Ain, a well-known architect, and Fred Moore, an Academy Award–winning Walt Disney artist-animator, all lived here. The first child born in Llano, a little girl, was named Llano.

After Frank H. Sweet's wife, Cora, died giving birth to their fifth child, Sweet decided to go to the Llano del Rio Colony in order to live and support his children, Alfred, Henry, Eula Lee, and Olga. Baby Cora did not go to Llano but lived with relatives. Al worked at the sawmill while young Henry helped in the bakery after school. (Courtesy of Cora Sweet McCrumb family.)

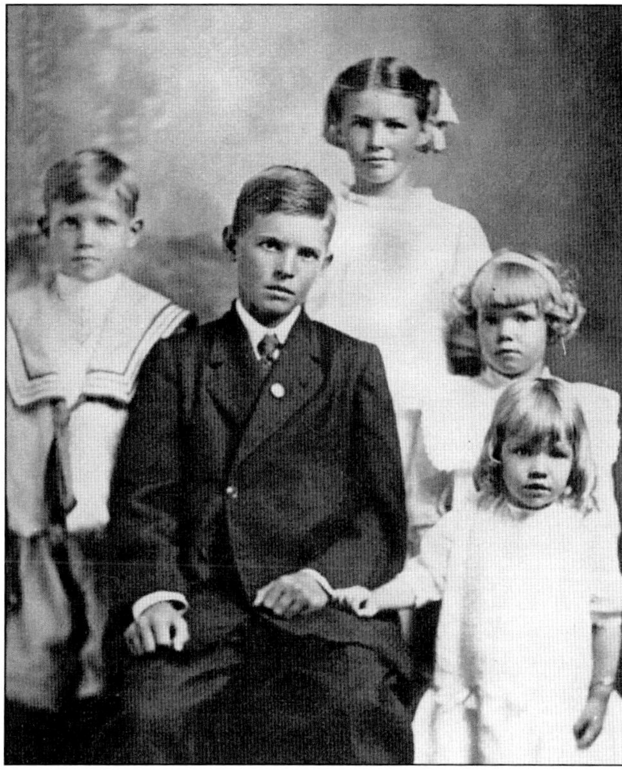

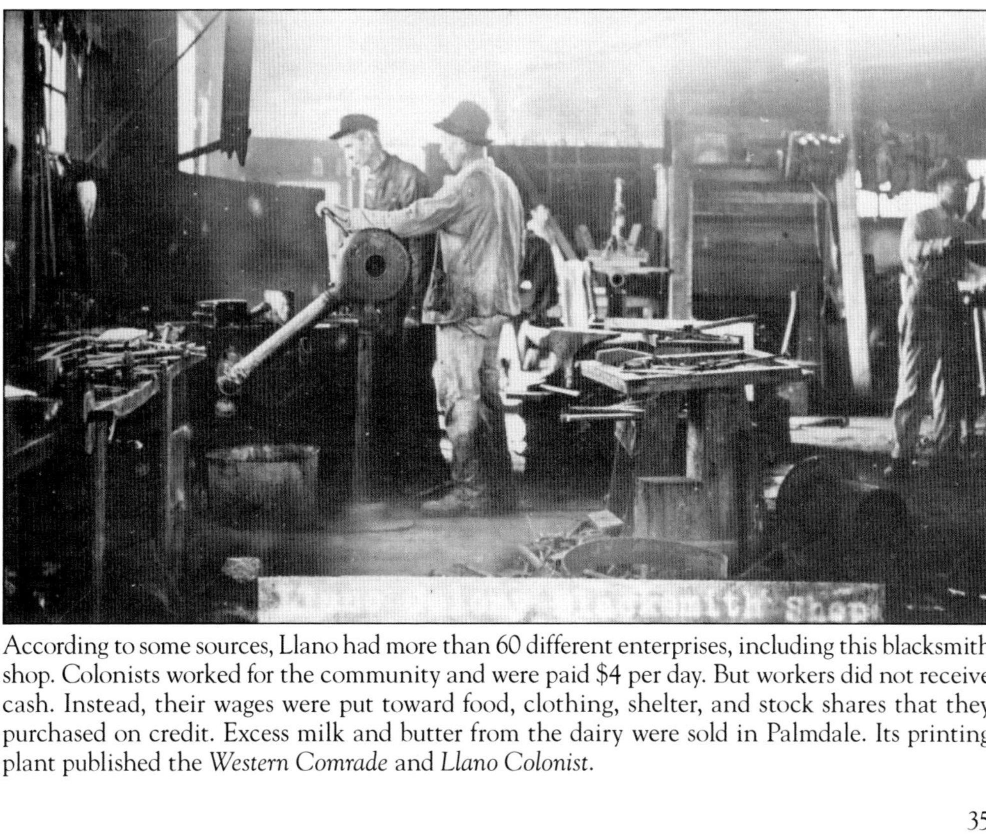

According to some sources, Llano had more than 60 different enterprises, including this blacksmith shop. Colonists worked for the community and were paid $4 per day. But workers did not receive cash. Instead, their wages were put toward food, clothing, shelter, and stock shares that they purchased on credit. Excess milk and butter from the dairy were sold in Palmdale. Its printing plant published the *Western Comrade* and *Llano Colonist*.

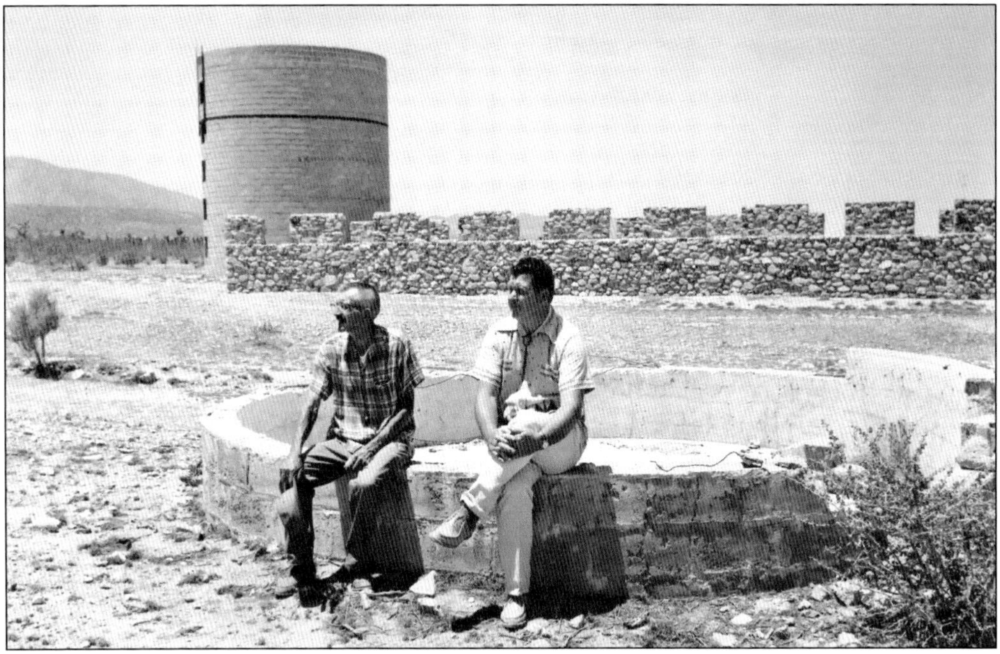

Life was not easy in Llano del Rio Colony. The small homes were made of adobe or were crude tents, which were constantly ripped apart from strong winds. After four years in the Antelope Valley, the colony succumbed to numerous problems, and most colonists moved to New Llano in Louisiana. C. K. Eklund, a former resident (left), and local historian Glen Settle are visiting some of the colony's ruins in 1964.

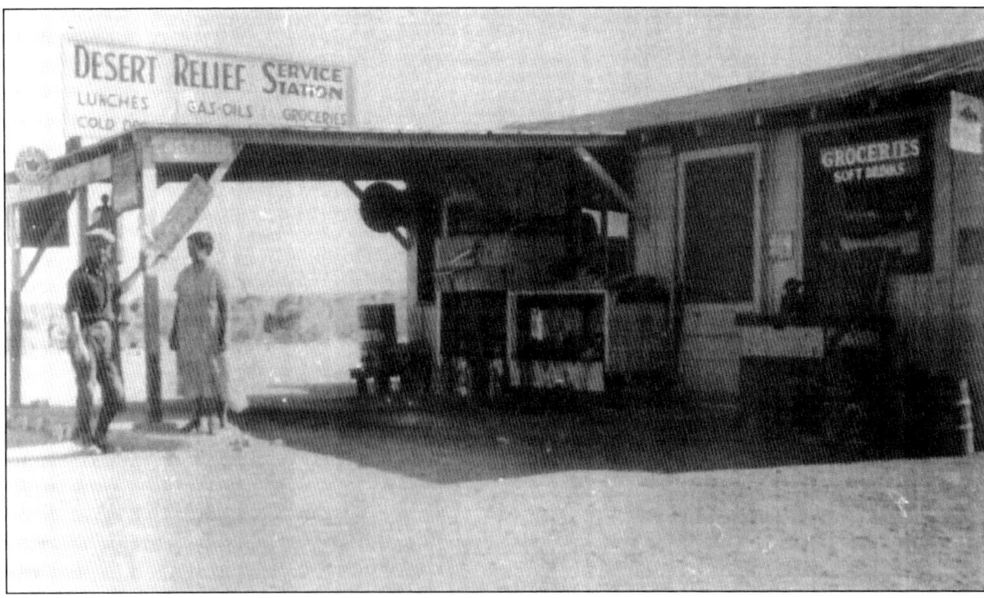

Besides the people residing at the Llano del Rio Colony, there were many farmers and ranchers living around the area not associated with it. Later writer Aldous Huxley was a resident. Lydia and Fred Nixon settled in Llano. They had a general merchandise store at 165th Street East on Pearblossom Highway. They had three daughters: Bessie, Pearl, and Gladys. Bessie married Dan Ledbetter in 1923. (Courtesy of the Ledbetter children.)

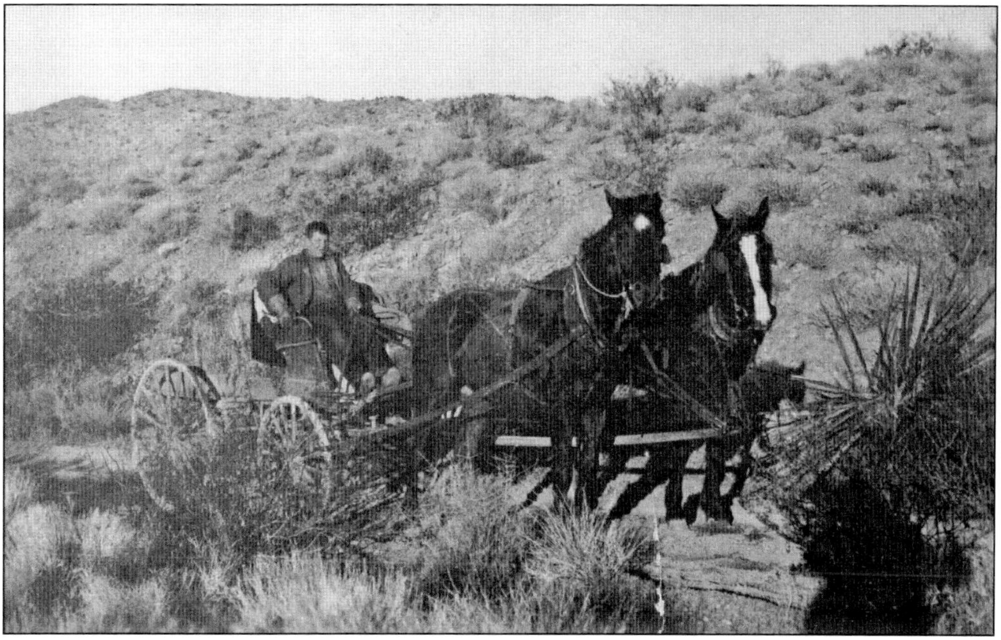

Dan Ledbetter's family moved from Burbank to the Llano area in 1915. A former deputy sheriff from Los Angeles County, Dan came here in 1922 when he transported prisoners and supplies back and forth from Los Angeles to road camps. The prisoners were building the roads from Llano to Big Pines. The Ledbetter family was very involved with horse events, including various parades and rodeos. (Courtesy of the Ledbetter children.)

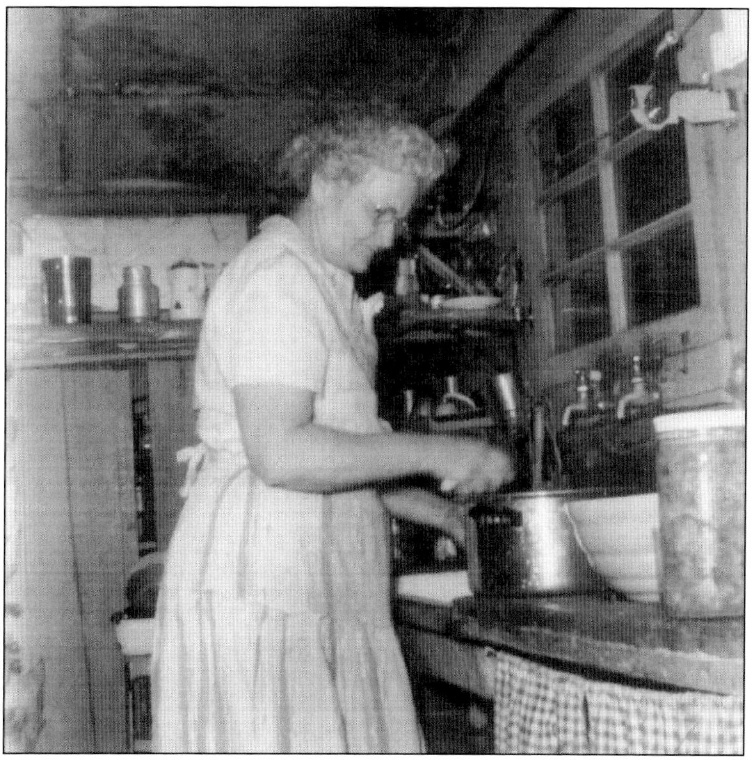

Bessie Ledbetter is shown in the family's kitchen. The Ledbetters had four children: Roger, Sallie, Lydia (Cozby), and Bessie. Bessie was also the Llano postmistress in their general store as well as the local tax assessor. Sallie married Barney Thatcher, who came to Pearland, an agricultural pear-growing area near Palmdale, around 1930. Sallie is a well-known artist whose depictions of the valley are greatly admired. (Courtesy of the Ledbetter children.)

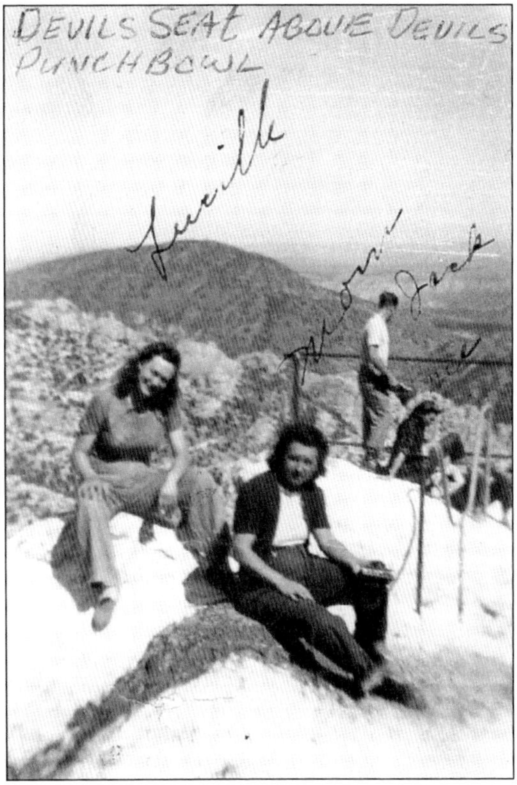

Members of the Sweet family and friends are relaxing after hiking to the Devil's Punch Bowl, a spectacular historic and unique geologic site located on the San Andreas Fault. Pioneers enjoyed its great natural beauty. It was dedicated as a Los Angeles County Regional Park in December 1963. The master of ceremonies was Mary Swan, a past president of the Pearblossom Chamber of Commerce. (Courtesy of Cora Sweet McCrumb family.)

Tucked into the foothills of the San Gabriel Mountains in a small area between Juniper Hills and Llano is Valyermo. Around 1808, the small Native American village of Muscupian (Am'utskupiat) was located here. The Valyermo Ranch receives its water from Big Rock Creek. Howard Shoemaker came here during the late 1880s. Mrs. Holmes and her son, Fred, are shown by their adobe house in June 1900.

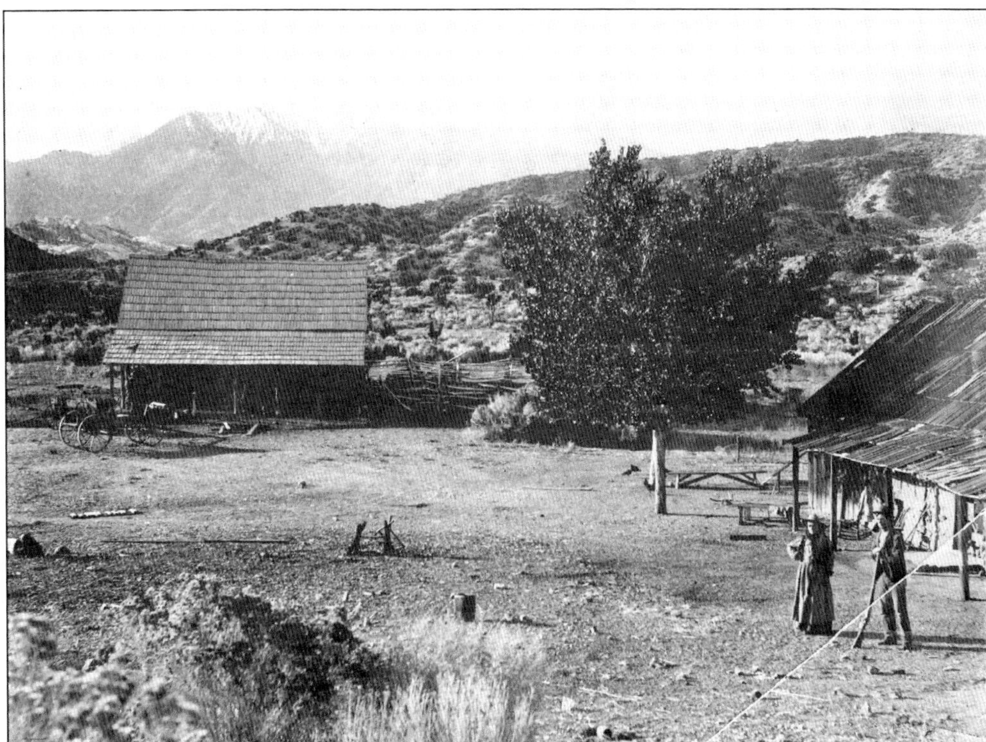

Before 1910, there were only a handful of ranchers in this area. During the early decades of the 20th century, fruit cultivation—pears, apples, and cherries, among others—and ranching expanded in the Valyermo area. In 1912, the area had an official post office. Shown here are, from left to right, Valyermo area residents Howard Shoemaker, Fred Holmes, Harry Heath, and daughter in 1908.

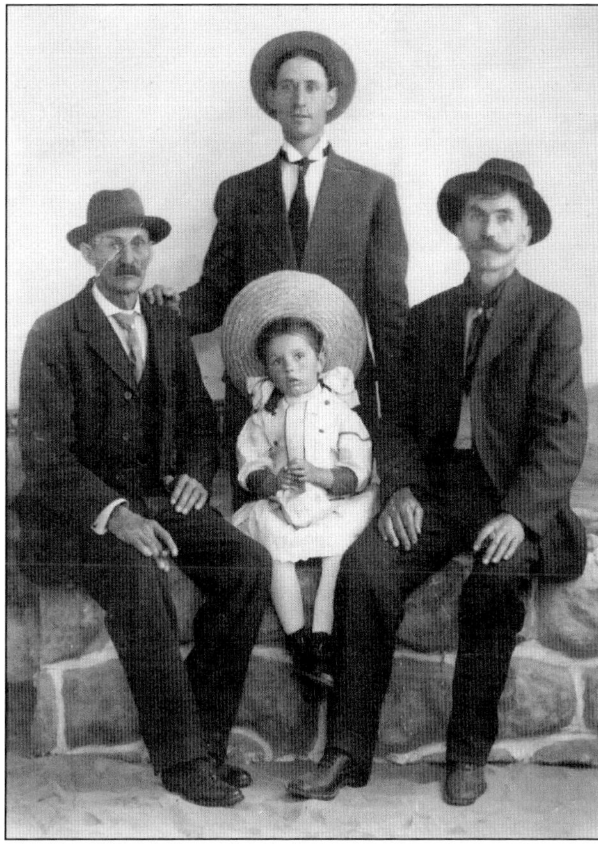

Dr. Cadwallader Evans later purchased 800 acres of land in the Valyermo area, including the Valyermo Ranch. As a wedding present in 1910 to his daughter, Dorothy, he gave her and her world-renowned geologist husband, Dr. Levi Noble, a portion of the ranch. Sweet family members are shown in front of the Valyermo Ranch house during the 1920s. (Courtesy of Cora Sweet McCrumb family.)

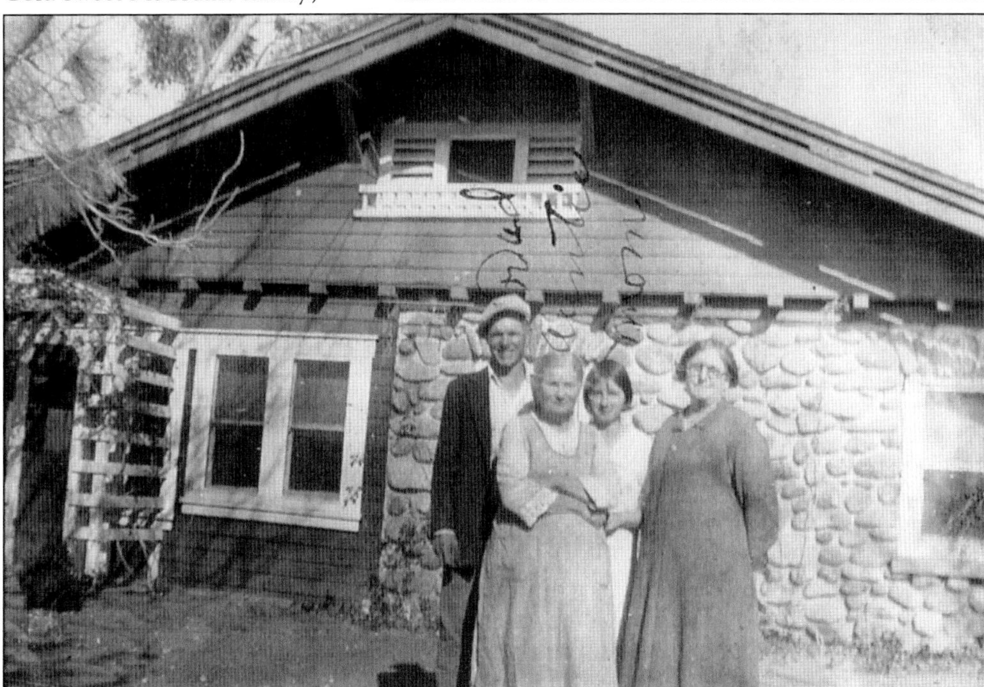

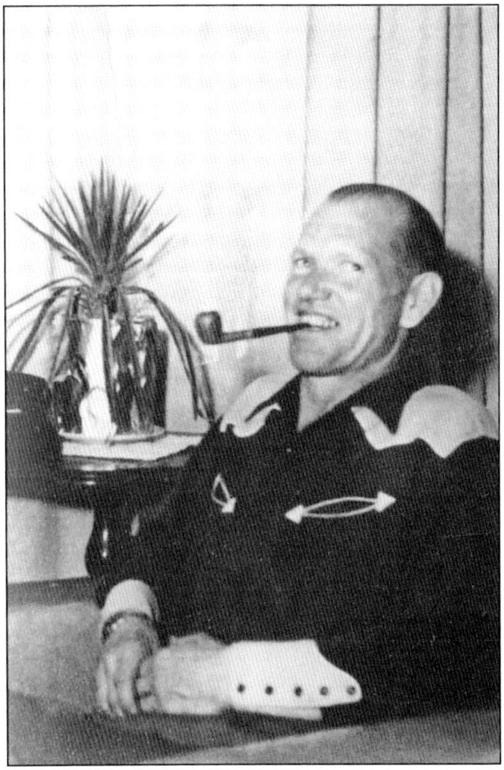

After the collapse of the nearby Llano del Rio Colony, young Henry "Hank" Sweet (shown here in 1952) returned to the area with his sick father, Frank. Henry began working on the Valyermo Ranch and eventually became its manager, overseeing its operations. Several generations of the Sweet family lived and worked at the Valyermo Ranch. Sweet descendants still reside in the valley. (Courtesy of Cora Sweet McCrumb family.)

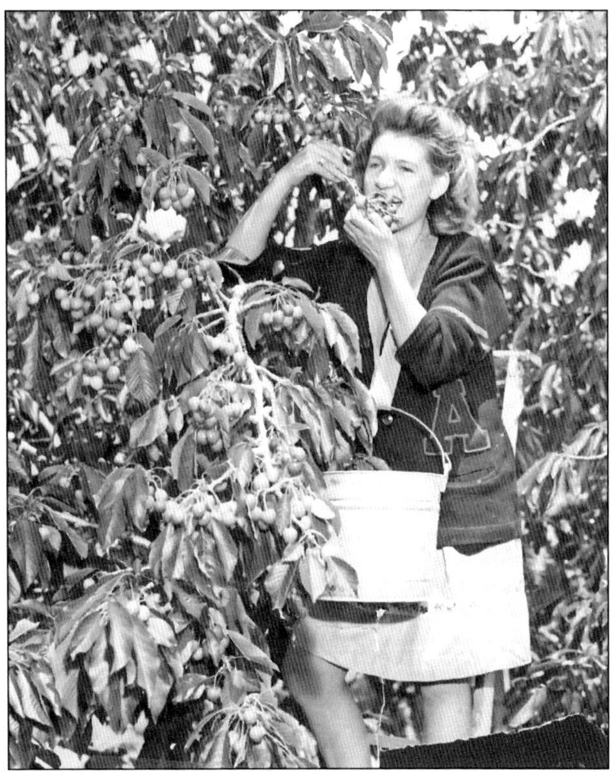

In 1911, the Valyermo Ranch had the first electricity in the area, which was provided by two large generators. At a staggering cost in 1911, the ranch also had the area's first telephone. Cora Sweet McCrumb loved growing up on the ranch. Wearing her husband James's Antelope Valley High School sweater, Cora is picking and tasting some of the ranch's delicious cherries in 1947. (Courtesy of Cora Sweet McCrumb family.)

Dorothy Evans's father gave her and Levi a wedding present of property in either the future Long Beach oil fields, downtown Hollywood, or a portion of the Valyermo Ranch, which sat upon the San Andreas Fault. They selected Valyermo with no regrets. Dr. Levi Noble, shown here as a young boy, became the nation's leading expert on the San Andreas Fault's structure and geological behavior. (Courtesy of Cora Sweet McCrumb family.)

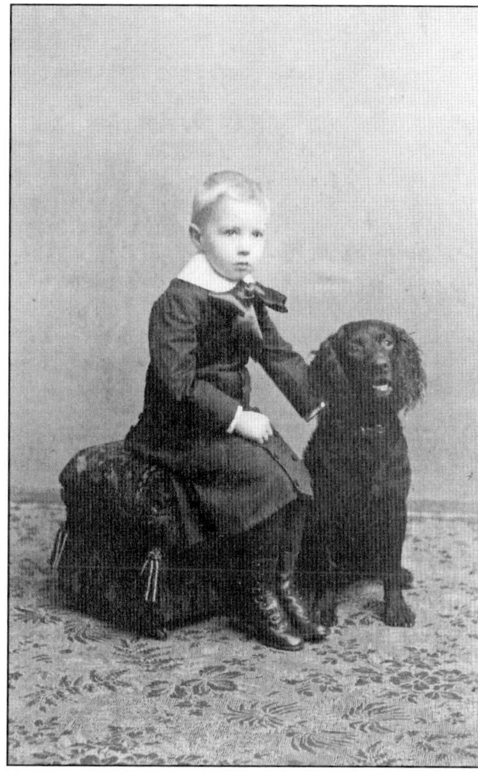

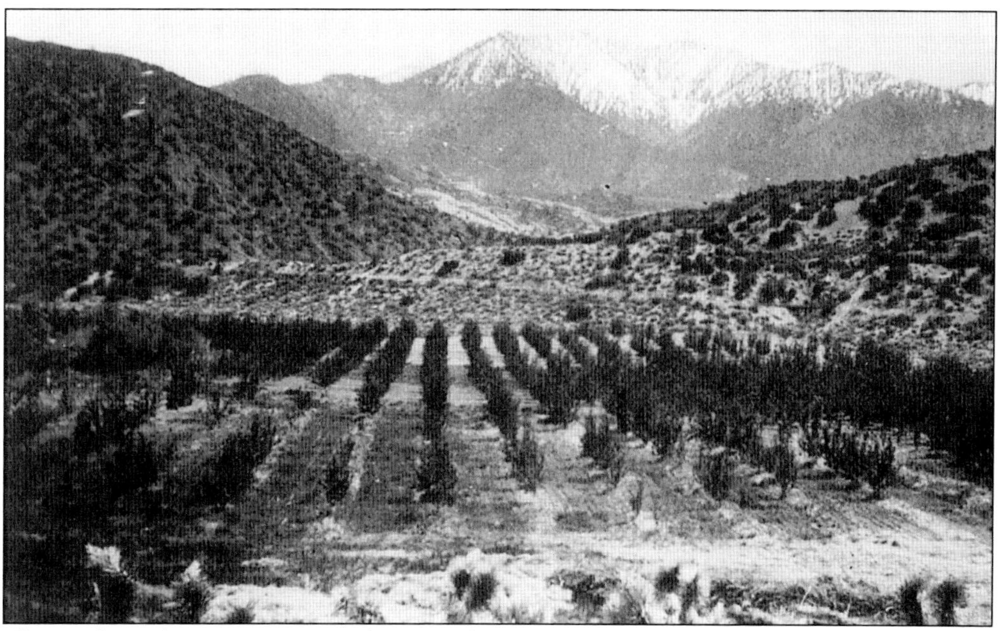

The ranch's early owner, W. C. Petchner, was born in a covered wagon en route to California. He later became a lawyer in the Antelope Valley. He also wrote poems about the Antelope Valley. It is thought that he may have named the area in 1909. The name Valyermo is a combination of two Spanish words, *val* for *valle* ("valley") and *yermo* ("barren"). (Courtesy of Cora Sweet McCrumb family.)

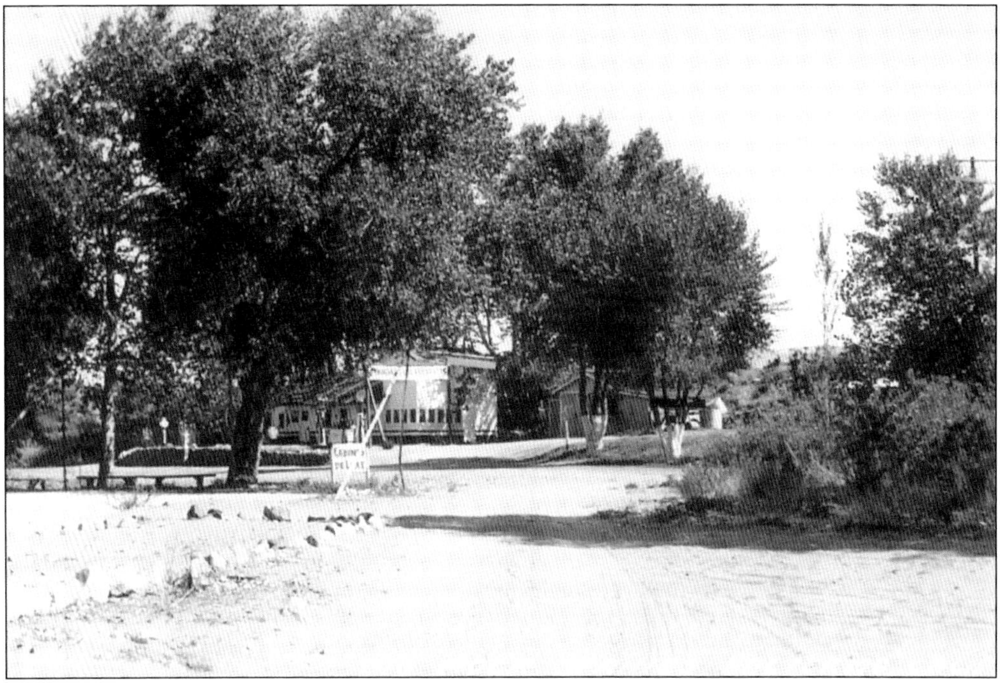

Dr. C. Evans built Valyermo's first post office and general store in late 1911. Dorothy Noble became the community's postmistress. A new general store was built in 1926. By 1935, Cecil and George Brandenberg purchased the Valyermo-Big Rock Springs Store, which also had a tennis court and a campground. During the Depression there was a tent city in the area for traveling fruit pickers. (Courtesy of Cora Sweet McCrumb family.)

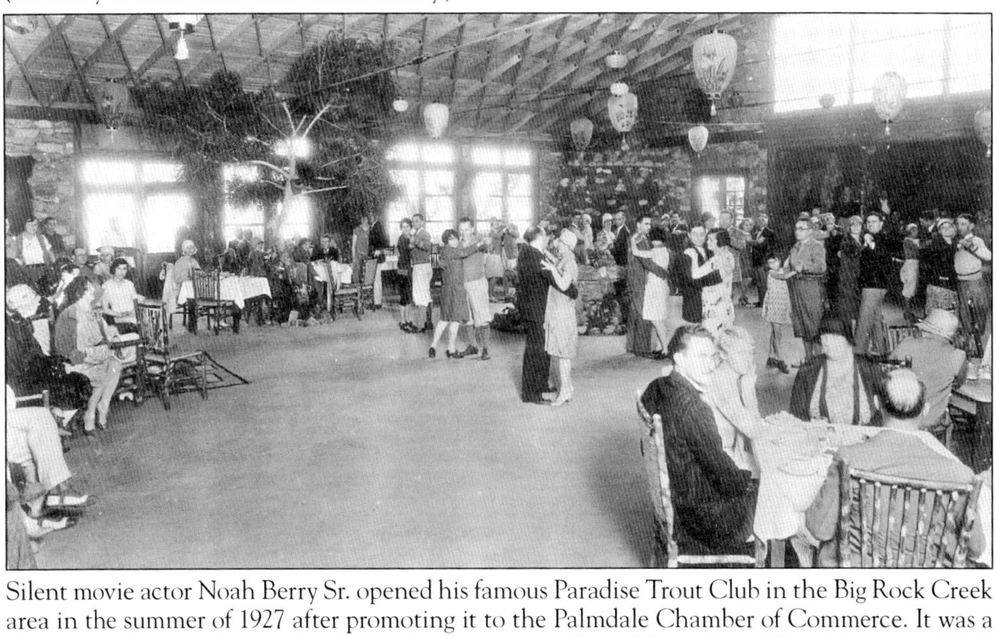

Silent movie actor Noah Berry Sr. opened his famous Paradise Trout Club in the Big Rock Creek area in the summer of 1927 after promoting it to the Palmdale Chamber of Commerce. It was a favorite rendezvous for many Hollywood movie stars and notables such as Gloria Swanson, Clark Gable, Johnny "Tarzan" Weissmuller, Joseph Kennedy, and Charlie Chaplin, among others. Valley residents also enjoyed the club's dances and various activities.

Five

Resting in Old Palmdale

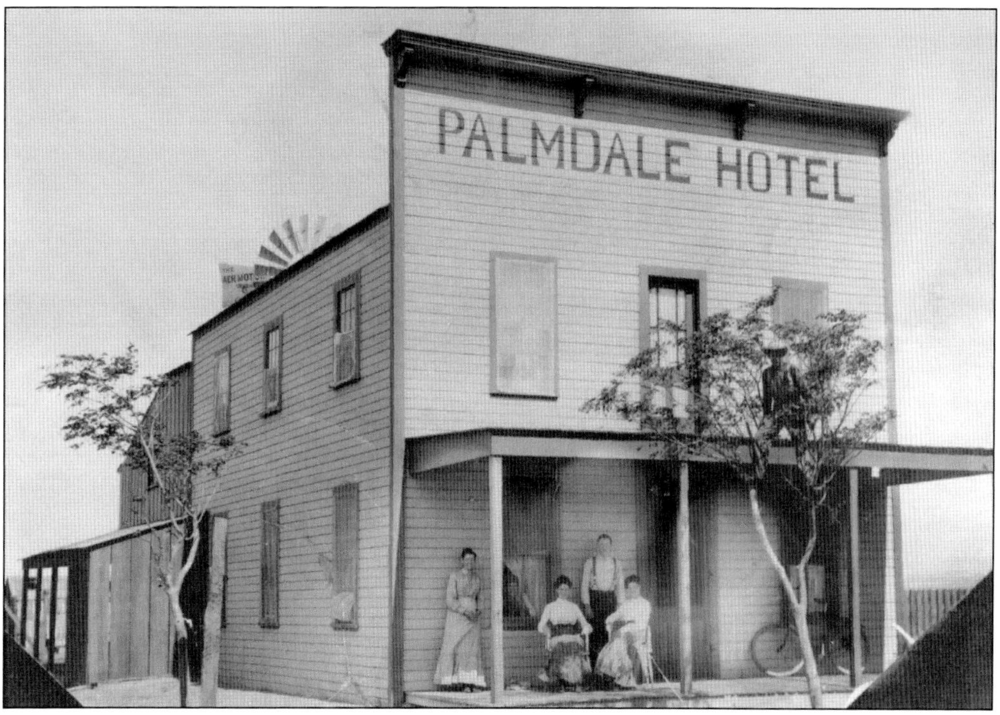

In April 1892, the Palmdale Hotel opened for business. Always a hub of activity, it was located at Eighth Street East and Avenue Q-7. The hotel's wooden back addition was supposedly shipped here piece by piece from Santa Monica around 1898. This 1903 view of the hotel shows, in addition to the hotel's owners or guests, a young Clyde Primmer in the tree. (Courtesy of Walt and Mickey Primmer.)

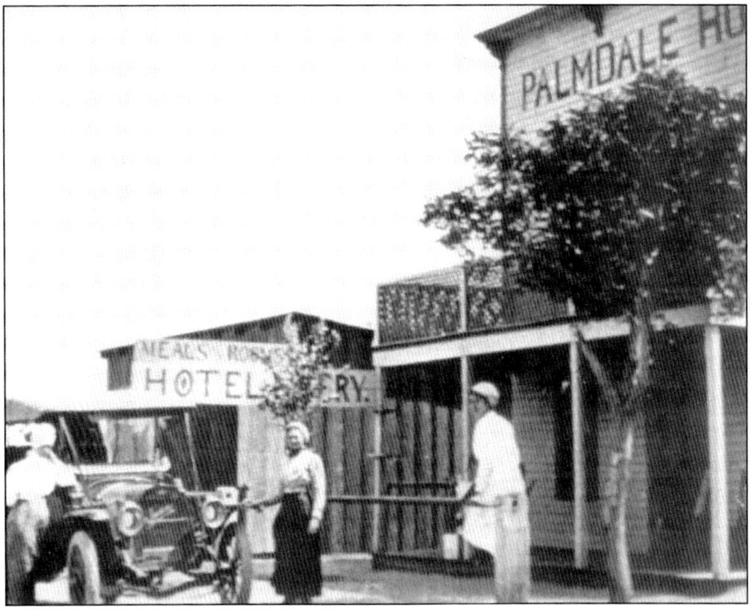

A very homey hotel, the Palmdale Hotel was one of the first buildings in New or West Palmdale. In the early days, room and board at the Palmdale Hotel was a $1 per day. Like all hotels, it had many proprietors through the years; some of them included Mrs. Baseler, Mrs. Goodrich, Esther Primmer, Mrs. E. J. Glasow, Mrs. Alfred Meek, and Rosa Brians.

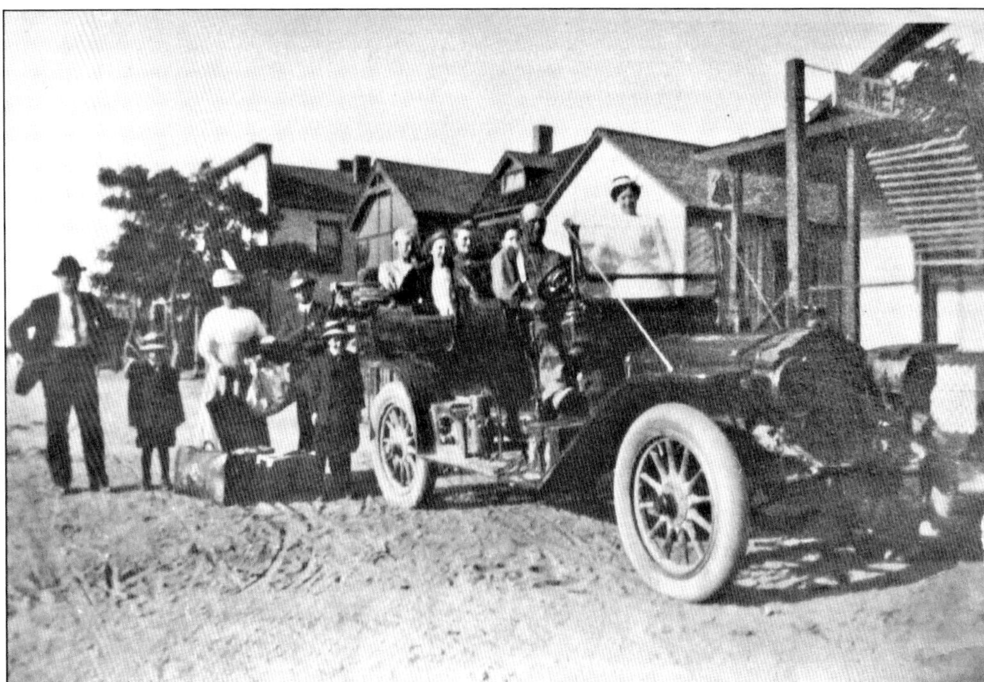

The hotel's last proprietor was Helen Wykoff, who owned it for 39 years until 1978. The Palmdale Hotel, later renamed the Pearland Hotel, was damaged by fires in 1979 and in 1981. The damage was too great, and it had to be demolished. This pioneer hostelry (*c.* 1910) should not be confused with the Hotel Pearland that was located on Forty-seventh Street East near Avenue S in the Pearland area.

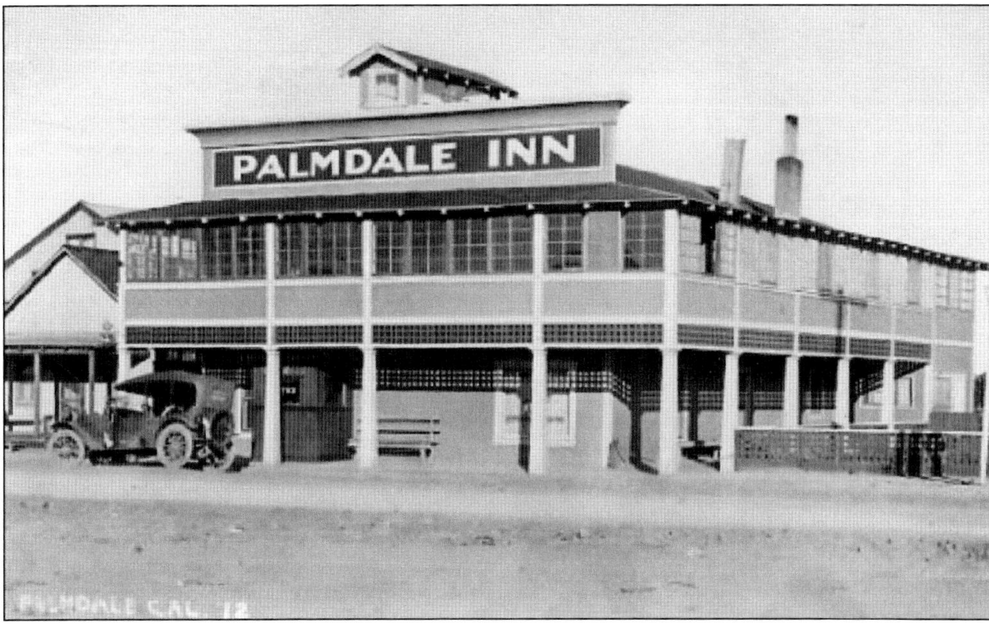

The Palmdale Inn opened for business in June 1914. It was owned by a Palmenthal pioneer, Hannah Nagel, and under the management of Eliza Moore, who came here in 1911. The inn stood at the busy intersection of present-day Sierra Highway and Palmdale Boulevard, on the northeast corner. By the 1920s, the inn was a large, two-story cement building with 20 rooms. (Courtesy of WAVHS.)

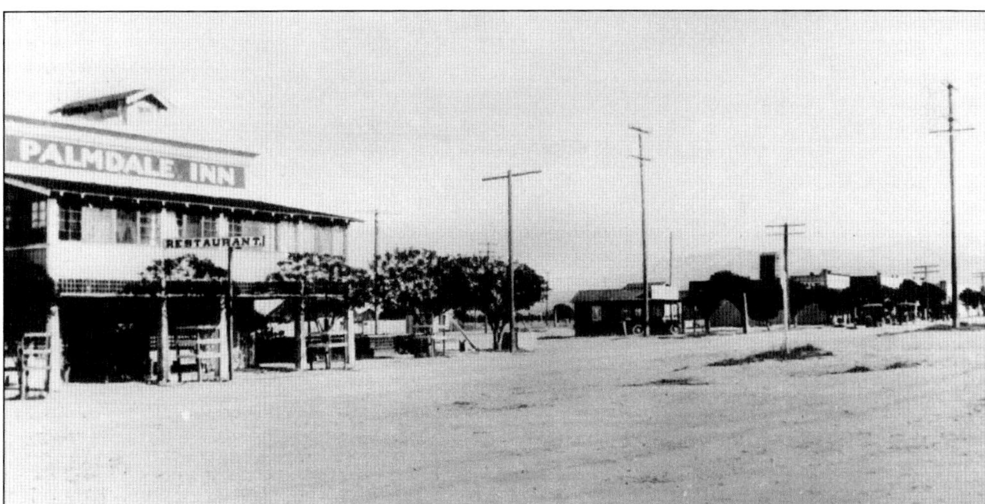

The inn was a very popular spot and became well known for Eliza Jane "Mother" Moore's pear pies and, later, fried chicken dinners. The inn's dining room could seat up to 100 guests. Visitors would come up from Los Angeles just to devour the pies. During the 1920s, it advertised: "Good beds and good eats. Hot and cold water. Prices Reasonable." This view dates to 1918.

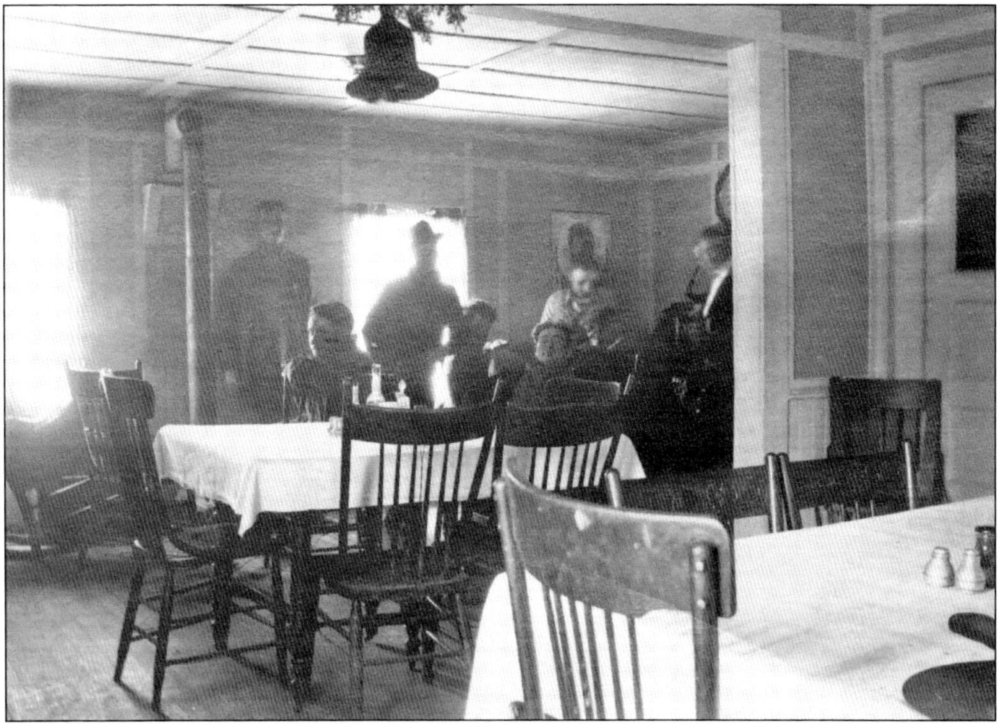

During the 1920s and early 1930s, many movie crews and stars stayed at the inn, including James Stewart, Shirley Temple, and even Rin Tin Tin. Local service clubs and organizations also met here. Many community dances were presented here. The Moores sold the inn to Howard Bland in 1924. Some other owners and managers included Mr. B. Sherick, Mr. and Mrs. McKee, actor Don Ameche's father, Felix, and Jack Crawford.

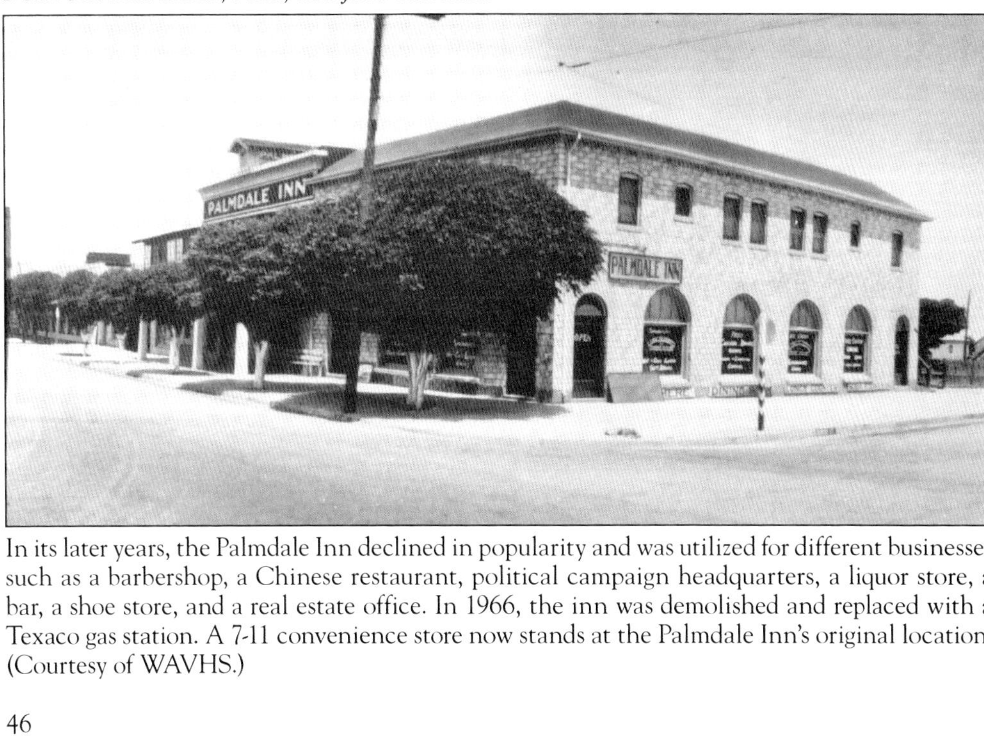

In its later years, the Palmdale Inn declined in popularity and was utilized for different businesses such as a barbershop, a Chinese restaurant, political campaign headquarters, a liquor store, a bar, a shoe store, and a real estate office. In 1966, the inn was demolished and replaced with a Texaco gas station. A 7-11 convenience store now stands at the Palmdale Inn's original location. (Courtesy of WAVHS.)

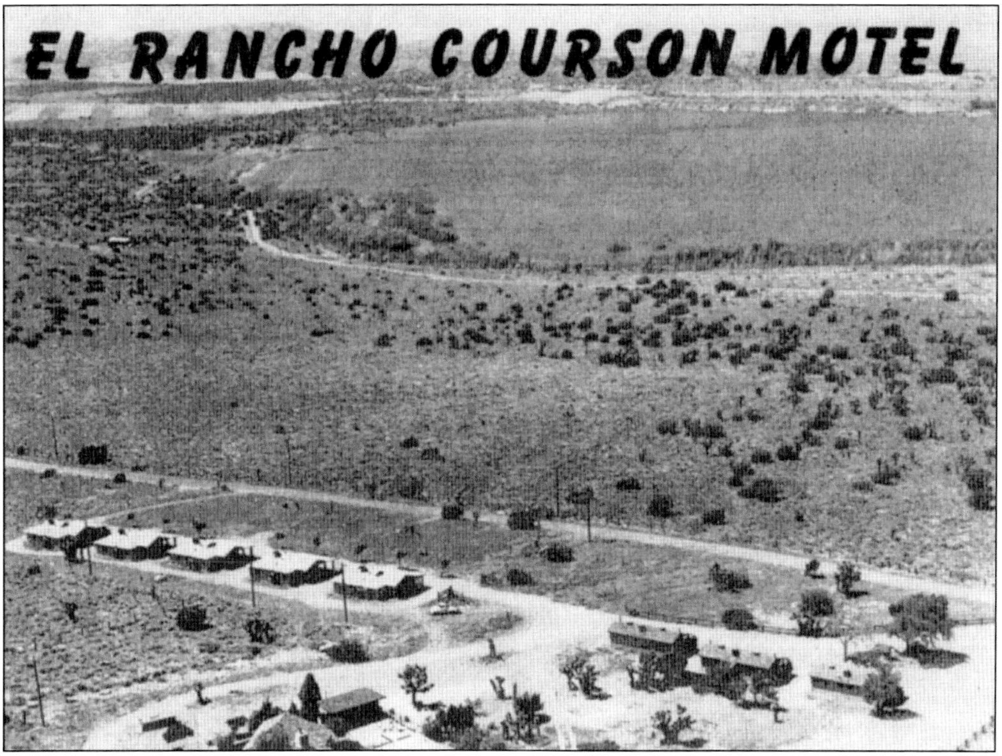

Mel Courson, a former banker and vaudeville performer, and his wife, Mary, came to the valley in 1941. With $3,000, they built the valley's first motel (with 12 rooms), El Rancho Courson, off Sierra Highway near Palmdale. It was a popular hotel with actors, as well as Howard Hughes. In honor of his community and civic activities, Palmdale Park was renamed Melville J. Courson Park in 1952.

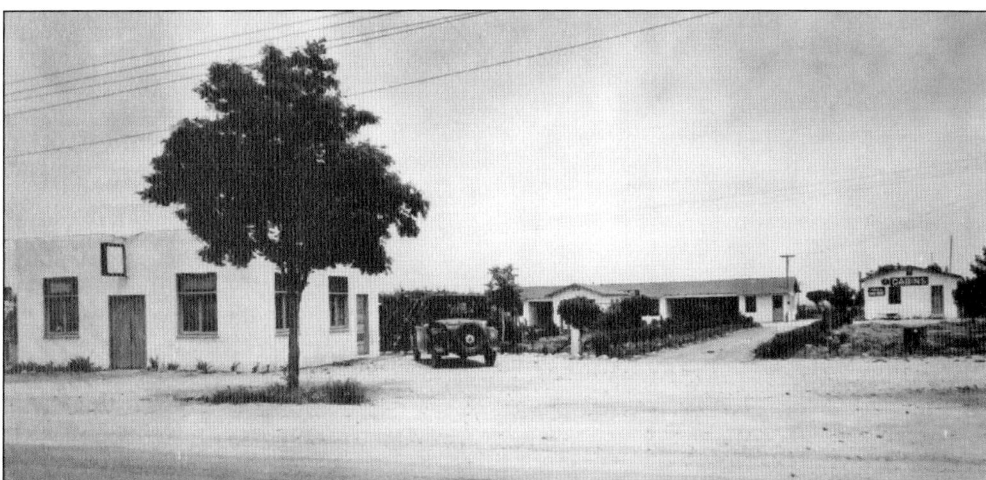

Domenic Massari, "Mr. Palmdale," was an original member of the Palmdale City Council (1962) and a former mayor. One of his early jobs included working as a cook at the Palmdale Inn preparing spaghetti. In 1930, he leased the land just north of where the former Palmdale Plaza was located. He built a service station here as well as cabins for travelers (at right-hand corner). (Courtesy of Larry Chimbole.)

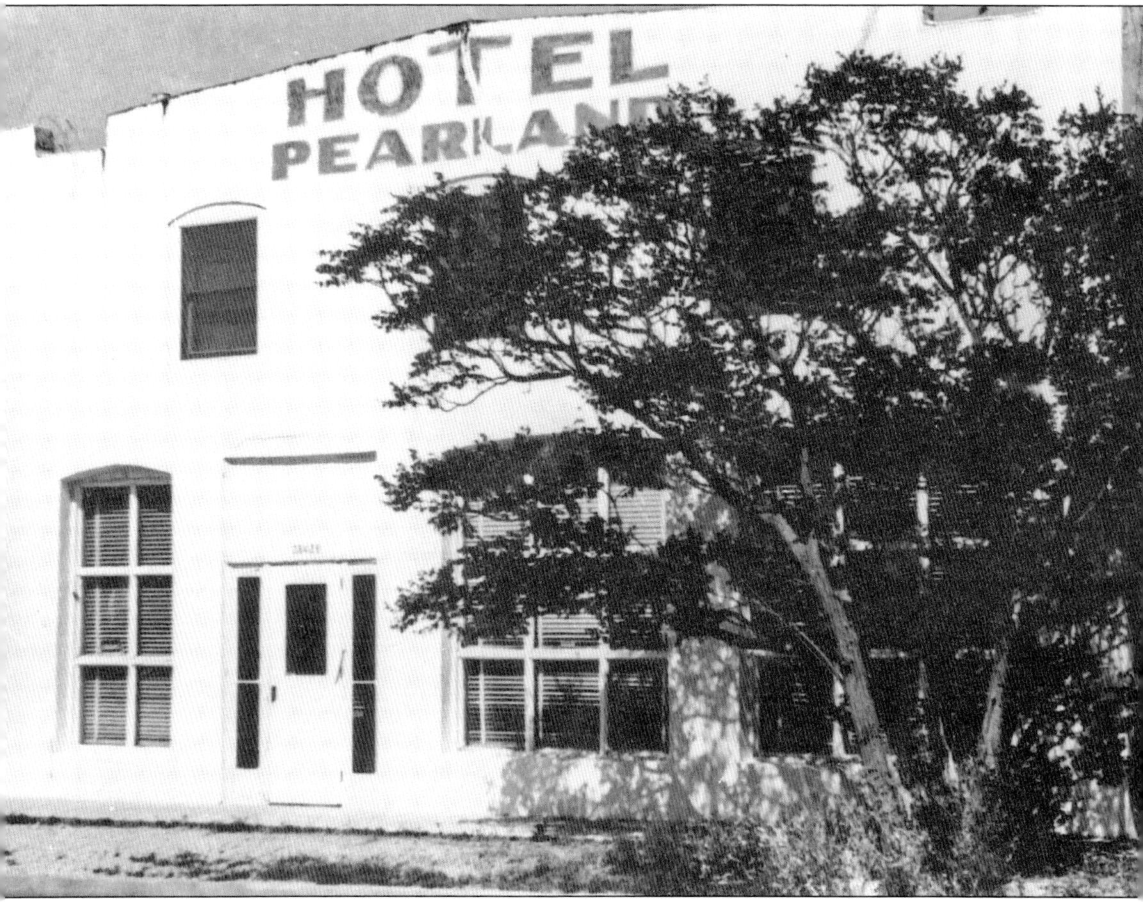

Located southeast of Palmdale, Pearland was a short-lived agricultural area during the 1910s and early 1920s. It was located between Fortieth and Fiftieth Streets East and just north and south of Pearblossom Highway. It consisted of only a few buildings at the intersection of Avenue S and Forty-seventh Street East. William McAdam purchased land around there and then sold 5-acre parcels. During the mid-1930s, five acres of land could be irrigated for $3 per month. Pears were grown here in the 1920s, but a pear blight near the end of the decade caused many families to turn to raising poultry. Other prominent families in the area included the Starks, Elliotts, and Wykoffs. Palmdale's DryTown Water Park, located at Fortieth Street East and Avenue S, was once the site of pear orchards belonging to the Kregbaum family. At one time, Peter McLoomis owned the small general store at the Hotel Pearland on Forty-seventh Street East; he lived upstairs. This structure was built in the 1920s. It was demolished in the early 1990s.

Six

MAKING A LIVING

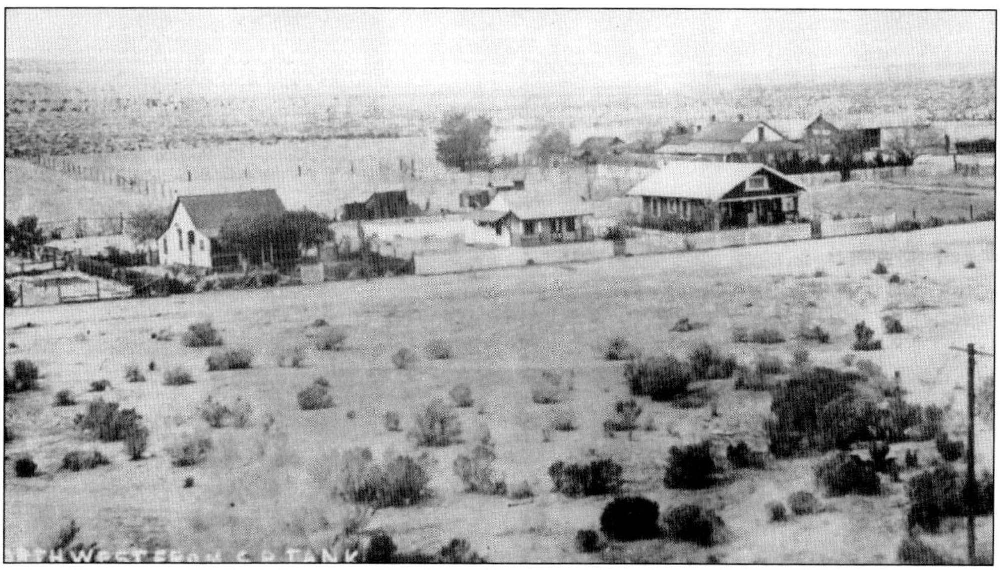

This 1918 view of Palmdale was taken from the railroad water tower looking northwest. The *Palmdale Post* reported that in 1923, Palmdale consisted of a post office, two cafés, pipe yards, a public hall, a blacksmith, a meat market, four garages, an athletic club, an ice plant, a tailor shop, a weekly newspaper, a fruit warehouse, a modern drugstore, a lumberyard, an aviation field, and more.

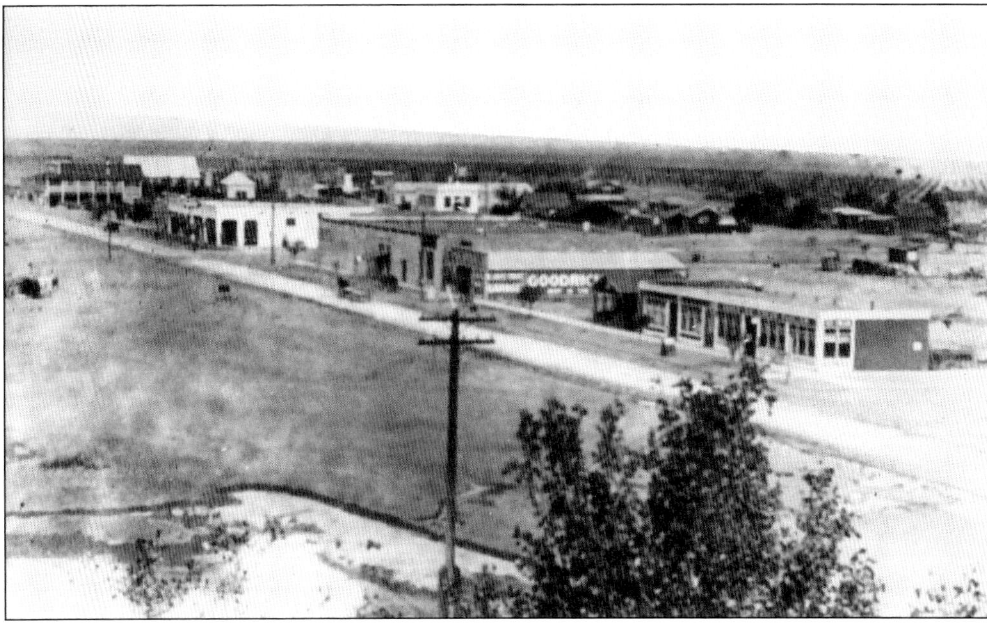

This view of Palmdale's business district in 1918 was taken from the railroad water tower, looking northeast. At the far left corner is the Palmdale Inn. There are garages, the post office, and general merchandise stores on two Sierra Highway blocks. Palmdale would later boast additional businesses such as a movie theater, automobile agencies, a branch of the Los Angeles County Library, and a bank. (Courtesy of WAVHS.)

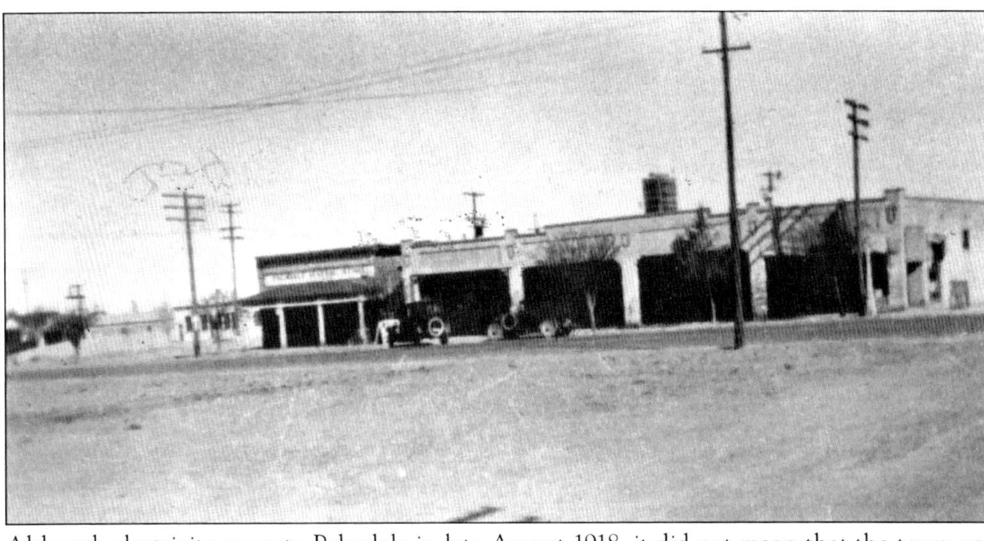

Although electricity came to Palmdale in late August 1918, it did not mean that the town was completely illuminated with electricity in private residences, businesses, or the streets. That would still take several years to accomplish. Electricity first illuminated the Palmdale Inn, the Cottage Hotel, the Antelope Valley Bank, and library. It only took one year, however, for Southern California Edison to ask for a rate increase. (Courtesy of WAVHS.)

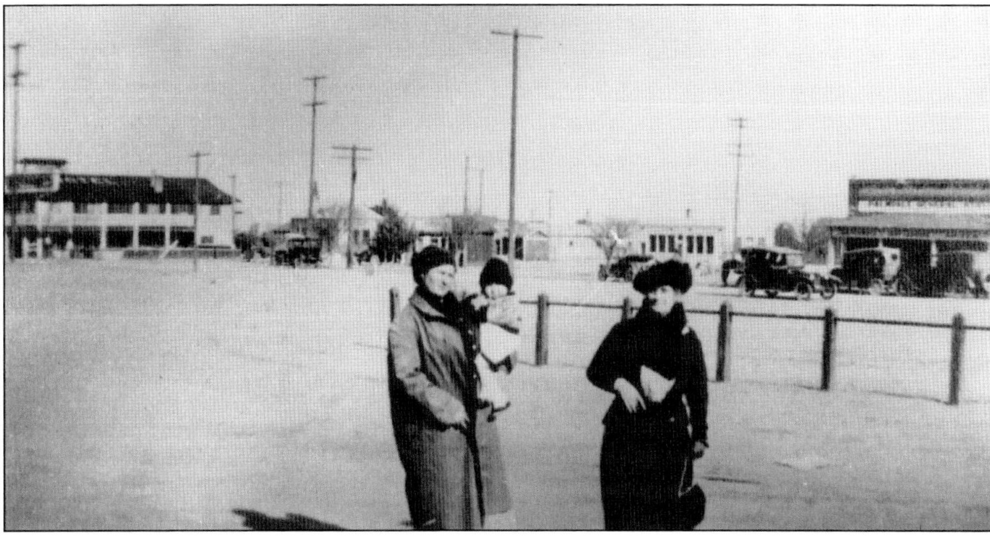

Mrs. Isaac Wilkins (left) is holding her son, Larry, before going shopping. The Palmdale Inn is located to the left while the Palmdale General Store is to the right. During Prohibition, an underground tunnel was constructed along Sierra Highway near Palmdale Boulevard for hiding and transporting illegal alcohol to the cellars of several adjacent businesses. Large stills were also built in the foothills near Littlerock. (Courtesy of WAVHS.)

Jarvis Phillips was an important community leader during the 1910s and 1920s. His real estate office (1915), which was located near the southeast corner of Sierra Highway and Palmdale Boulevard, also housed the library and telephone office. A street called Jarvis was named after Phillips but is now the continuation of East Avenue Q-9, a short block west of the railroad track. (Courtesy of Palmdale City Library.)

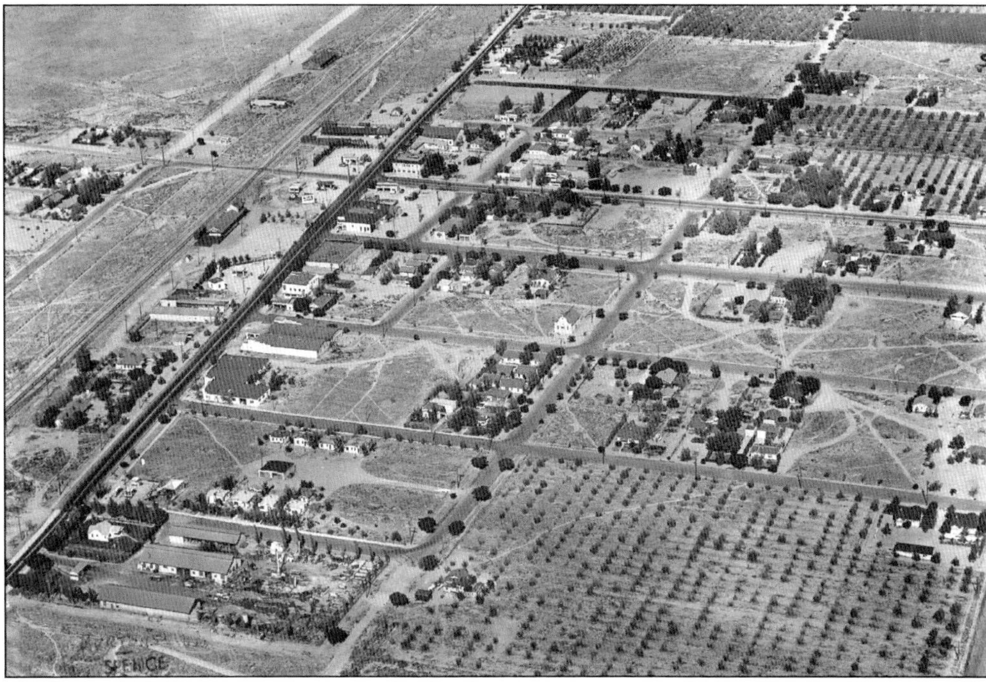

This 1937 aerial view of Palmdale shows that it was still a very small town with many fruit orchards. The Palmdale Inn is located northeast of the train depot. Across from the inn is the Antelope Valley Lumber Company, also known as the Antelope Valley Lumberyard. East of the inn is the bank and a variety store. The buildings in the lower left area comprise the Los Angeles County Road Maintenance Yard. (Courtesy of *Antelope Valley Press*.)

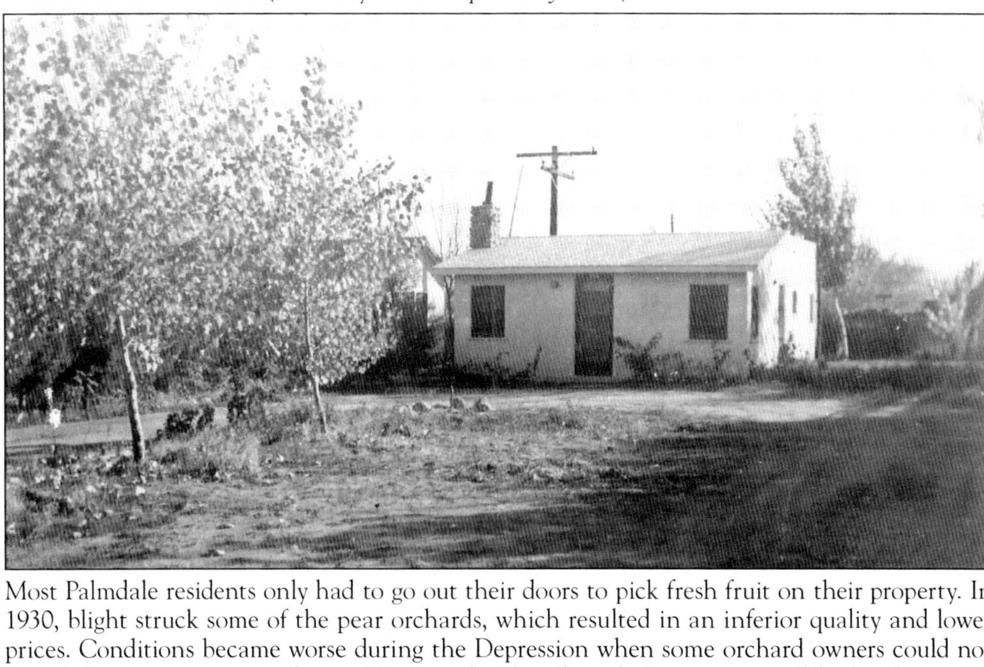

Most Palmdale residents only had to go out their doors to pick fresh fruit on their property. In 1930, blight struck some of the pear orchards, which resulted in an inferior quality and lower prices. Conditions became worse during the Depression when some orchard owners could not pay their mortgages or get loans. Many orchardists lost their property and had to leave the Antelope Valley.

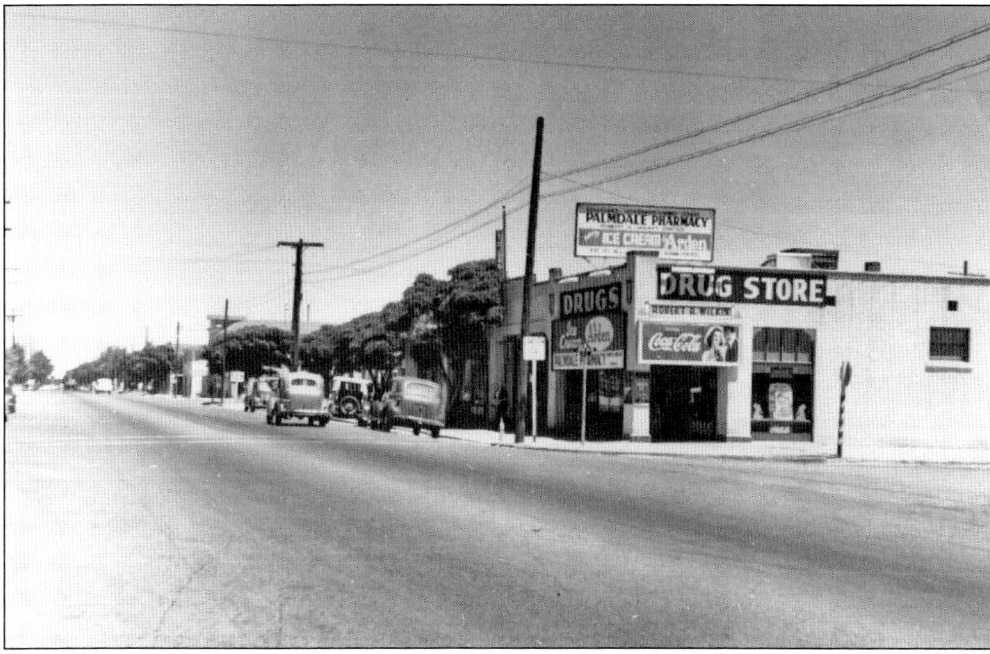

The first Palmdale Pharmacy was owned by J. E. Jones in 1916. During the Christmas season, people were urged to shop locally and not in Los Angeles. Fred Fehrensen purchased the property next. Children liked going there on Fridays for a free ice cream cone. A popular gathering spot in the 1920s, it was located at the northeast corner of Sierra Highway and East Avenue Q-9. (Courtesy of WAVHS.)

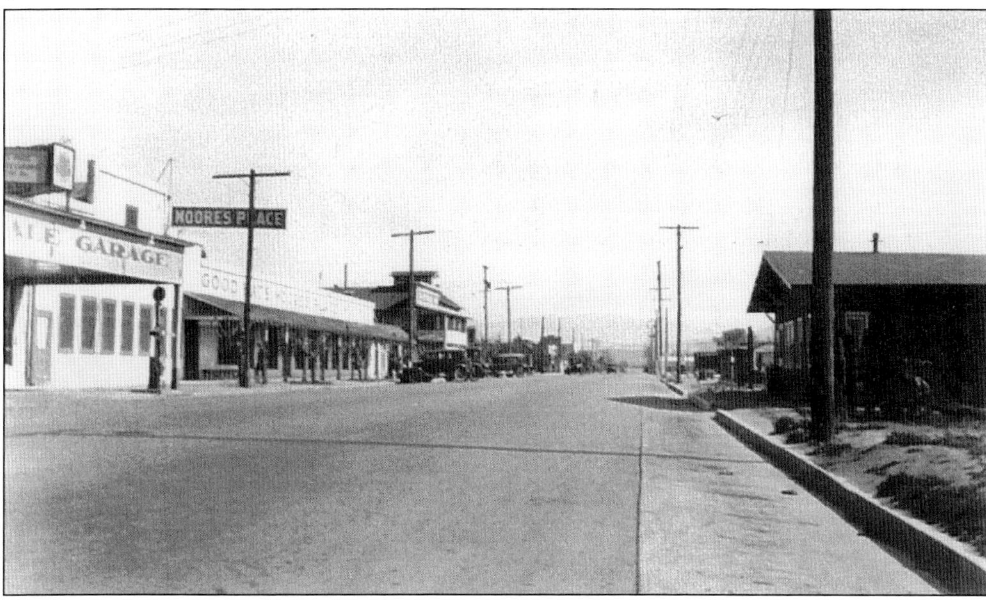

This photograph was taken on Sierra Highway (1931), one block north of Palmdale Boulevard. Looking south, on the right is Antelope Valley Lumberyard and across from it is a garage, Moore's Place, and the Palmdale Inn. Different Moores were engaged in various businesses, including general stores, garages, and hotels. The Moore building also rented to barbers. In 1916, Palmdale had the valley's first female barber, Miss L. R. Barr. (Courtesy of WAVHS.)

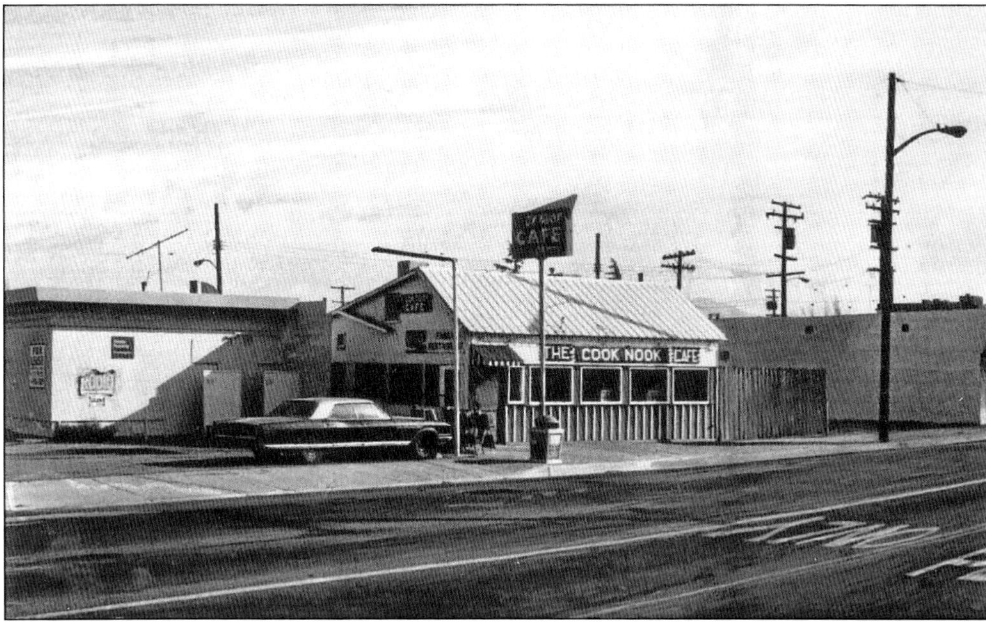

This 1960s view was taken on Sierra Highway, south of Palmdale Boulevard. The Cook Nook Café, also known as Mac's Cook Nook, was located in the vicinity of the Palmdale City Library and Civic Center. C. Webster was the manager in 1947. It was open 24 hours a day, and its prime location attracted many motorists. The younger crowd considered it a great spot for a tasty snack after a movie. (Courtesy of Palmdale City Library.)

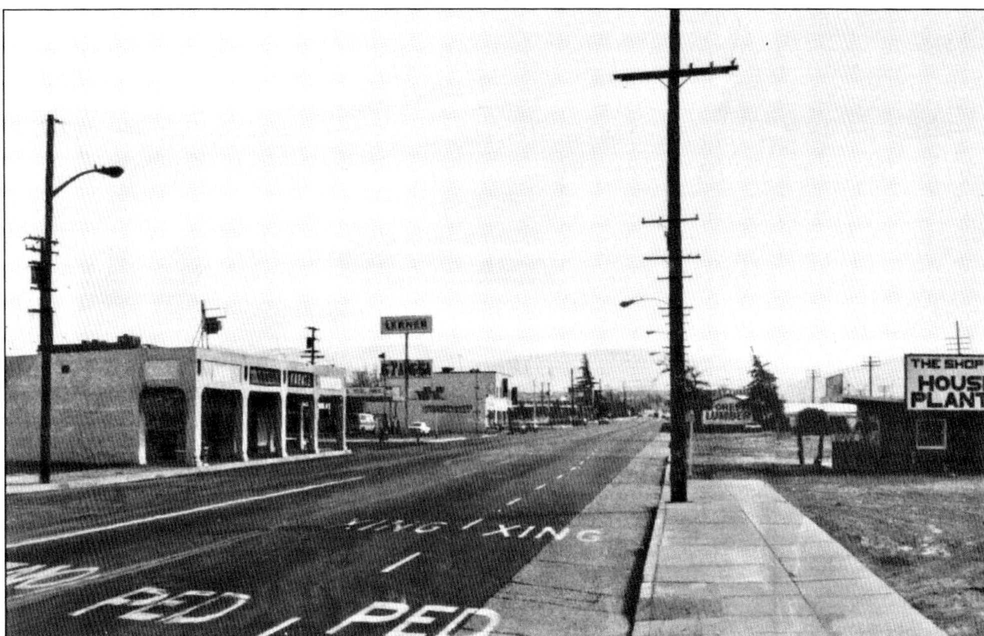

This photograph is a little farther south on Sierra Highway. The complex on the east side dates to the late 1910s and early 1920s. South of the plant shop is Forest Lumber, which was originally the Palmdale Lumber Company. During the 1960s, Lerner Gas Station was selling gas for 55¢ per gallon. (Courtesy of Palmdale City Library.)

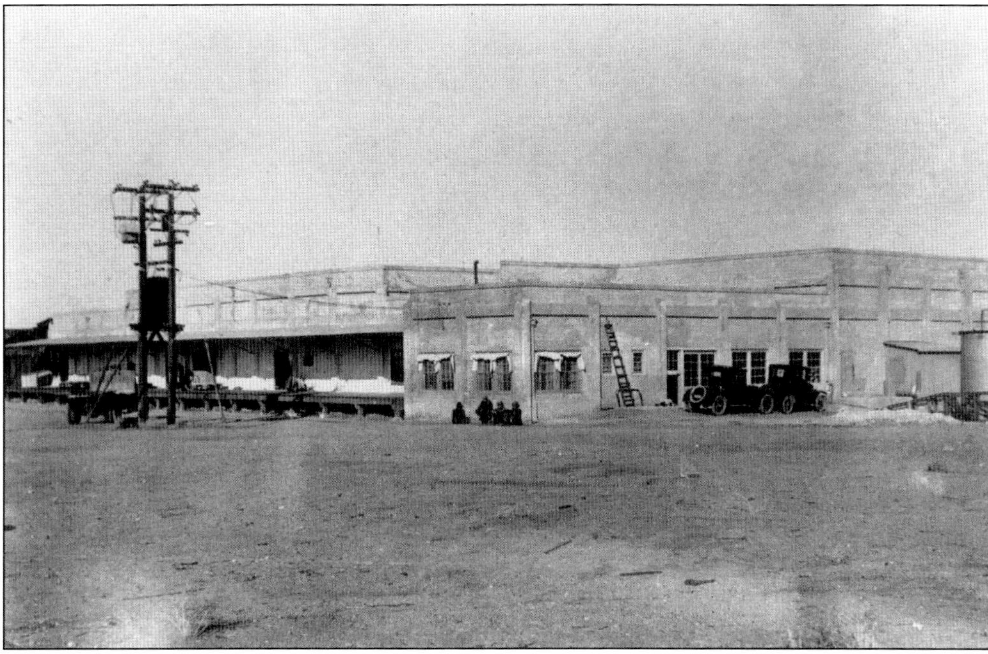

The Palmdale pre-cooling/ice and cold storage plant was built in 1918 by J. E. Jones and E. Davis, after the arrival of electricity. It provided vital services for the area's booming pear industry. It turned out almost 4 tons of ice every 24 hours. Located at the southeast corner of Sixth Street East and Avenue R, this building is now the Bekins-Antelope Valley Van and Storage Company. (Courtesy of WAVHS.)

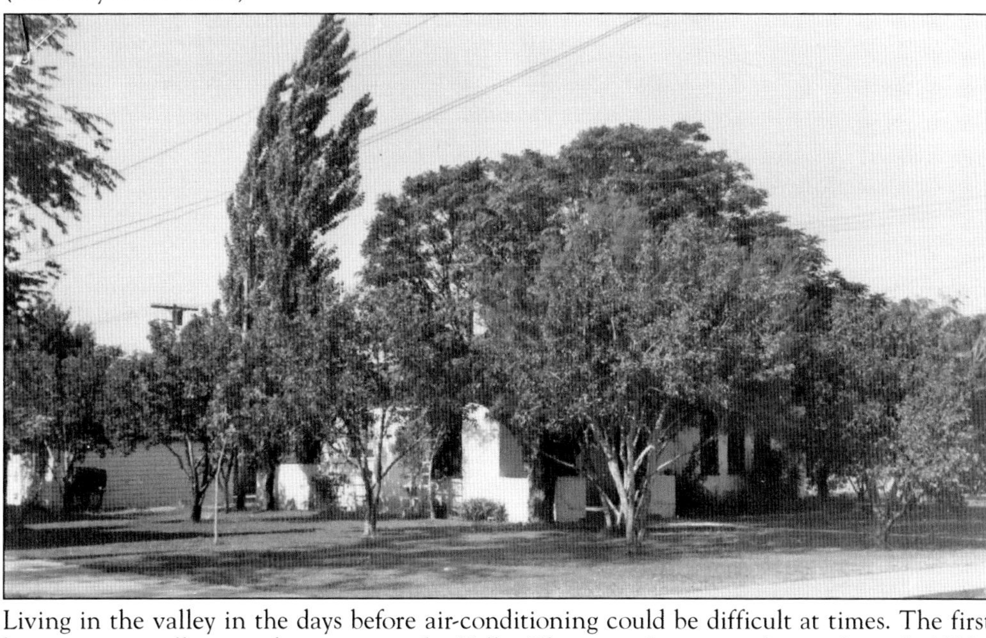

Living in the valley in the days before air-conditioning could be difficult at times. The first business to install air-conditioning was the Valley Theater in Lancaster during the early 1930s. Markets were next. Some residents said they visited a market's freezer section just to cool down. Another way to beat the heat was to have lots of shade trees surrounding one's house, like B. M. Starksen's Palmdale home pictured above.

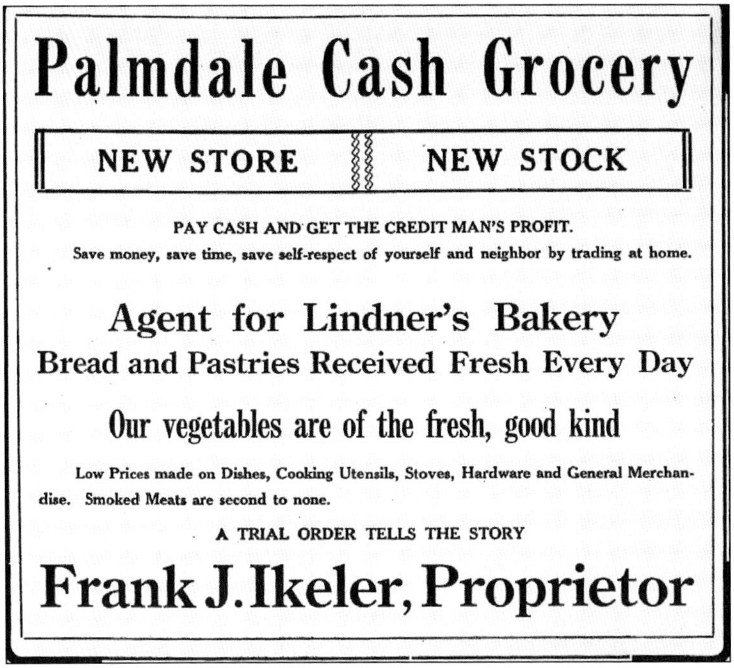
Palmdale Cash Grocery
NEW STORE
NEW STOCK
PAY CASH AND GET THE CREDIT MAN'S PROFIT.
Save money, save time, save self-respect of yourself and neighbor by trading at home.
Agent for Lindner's Bakery
Bread and Pastries Received Fresh Every Day
Our vegetables are of the fresh, good kind
Low Prices made on Dishes, Cooking Utensils, Stoves, Hardware and General Merchandise. Smoked Meats are second to none.
A TRIAL ORDER TELLS THE STORY
Frank J. Ikeler, Proprietor

Frank Ikeler had a grocery store next to the Richfield station. He was in the grocery business for more than 30 years. He was married to Clara Ritter, an original Palmenthal family member. As a volunteer fireman, he had one of Palmdale's first telephones—number three. It was not always easy being a storekeeper. Ikeler once got into a fight with an armed vagabond over a 5¢ packet of matches.

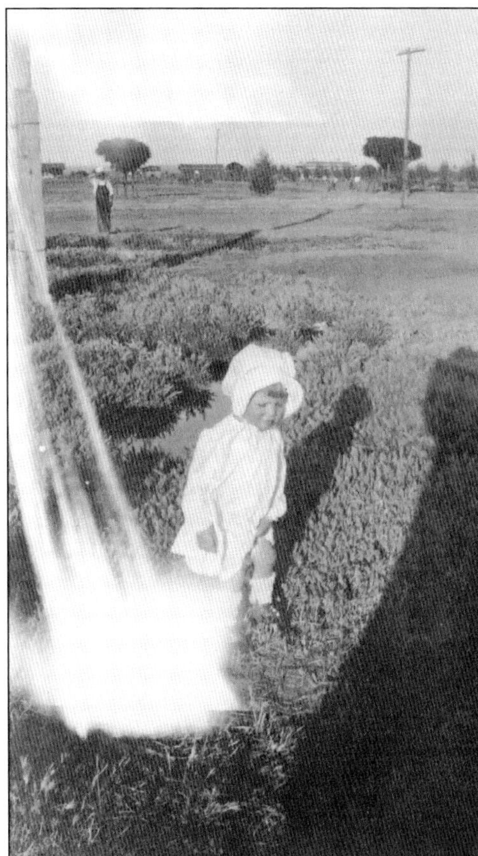

Frank and Clara Ikeler's daughter, Mildred, is enjoying herself on the family's property. One of her fondest childhood memories of old Palmdale was when every morning all the schoolchildren lined up in front of the school, saluted the flag, and marched to the rooms, with the Victrola playing "The Star-Spangled Banner." As a teenager, she enjoyed hiking in the foothills west of old downtown Palmdale.

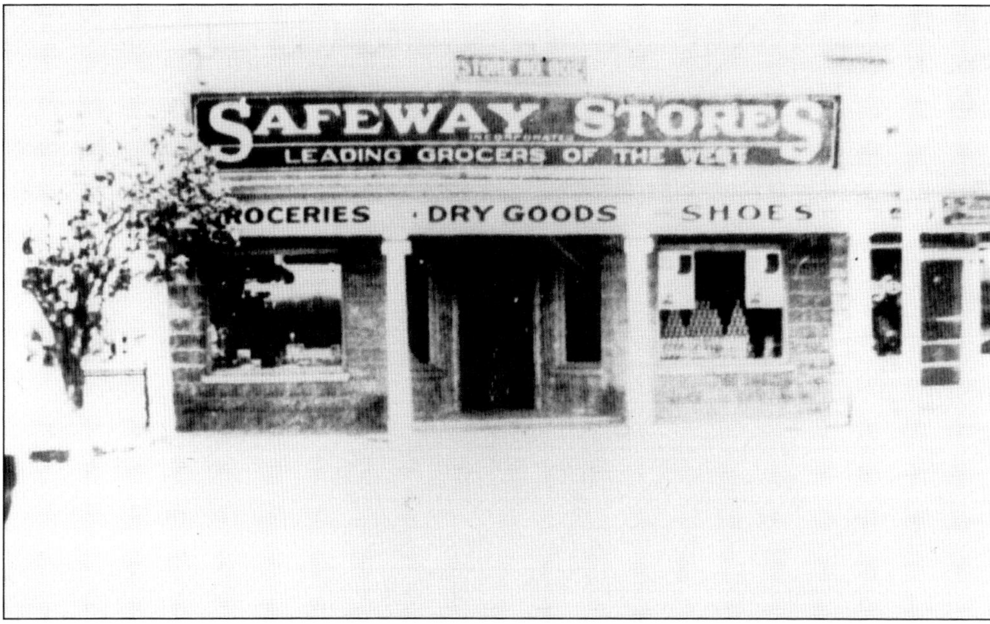

The first chain store to come to Palmdale (aside from gas stations like Richfield) was Safeway in June 1926. The company purchased the Frank Ikeler and Will Ritter grocery store and hired J. D. Cunningham, Stroud McBride, and Lonnie Hood. A. W. Wilson was the manager for both the Palmdale and Lancaster stores. Afterwards Ikeler built a men's furnishing store next to the post office. (Courtesy of WAVHS.)

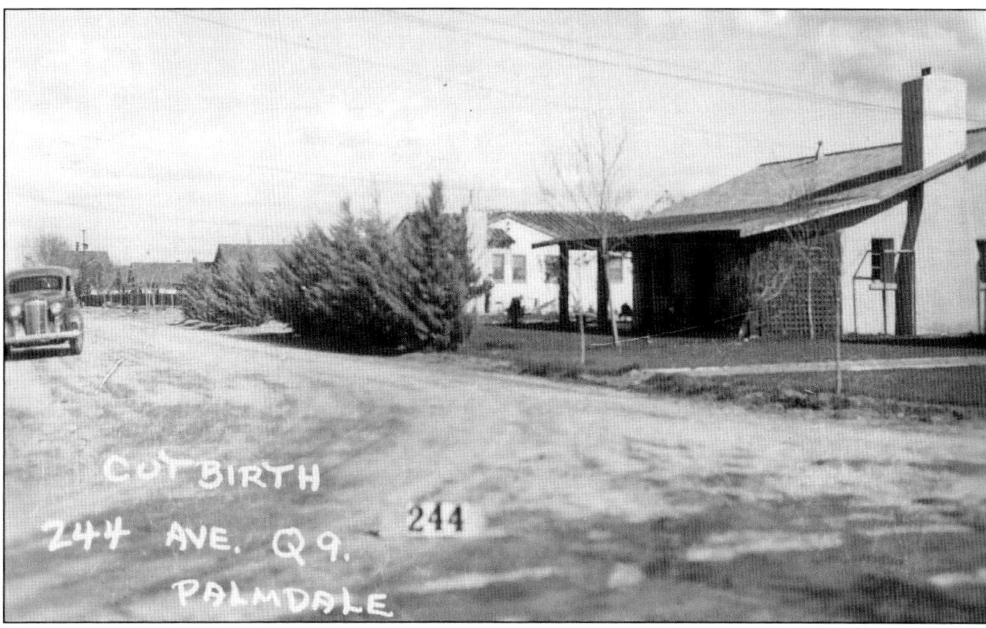

Living adjacent to downtown Palmdale made shopping quite easy. During the early 1930s, Rev. Jessie Wilson's son, Craig, built four adobe houses in Palmdale, including this one. There were several other adobes built in Palmdale and the Littlerock areas; some are still standing today. Craig Wilson was also president of the Fin and Feather Club, president of the Palmdale School Board, and a director of the Antelope Valley Fair Board.

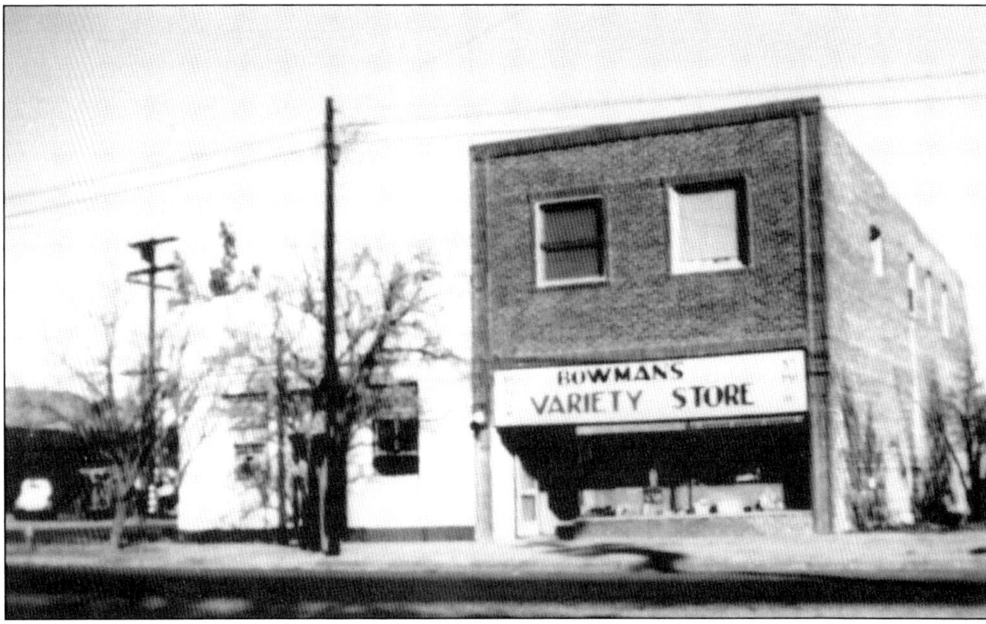

The building on the left was the Antelope Valley Bank and then the Bank of America. The other edifice was Bowman's Variety Store and later Moulton's Hardware. These structures still stand, although the right one is now only one story. They are located on the northeastern corner of Palmdale Boulevard and Eighth Street East. Some early bank employees were Frank Reynolds, Charles Williams, and Emma Orr.

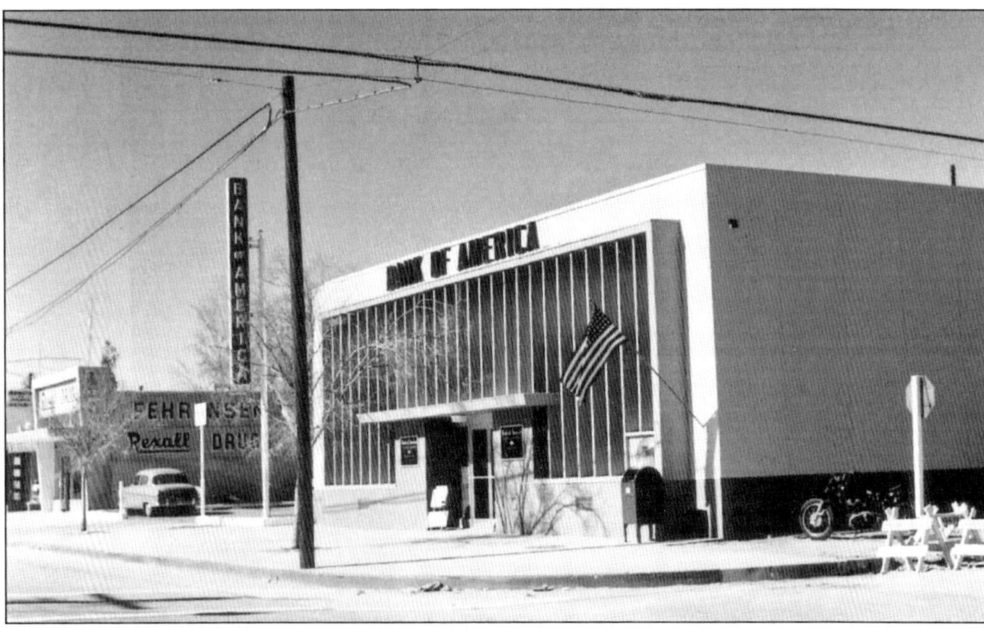

Old Palmdale did not have a bank, and even years later, a visiting Lancaster bank employee would handle the residents' financial transactions once a week. In August 1915, Palmdale's first bank, the Antelope Valley Bank—not to be confused with the present-day Antelope Valley Bank branch—opened at Center Street and Antelope Avenue. The Palmdale Lumber Company made the first deposit. (Courtesy of Palmdale City Library.)

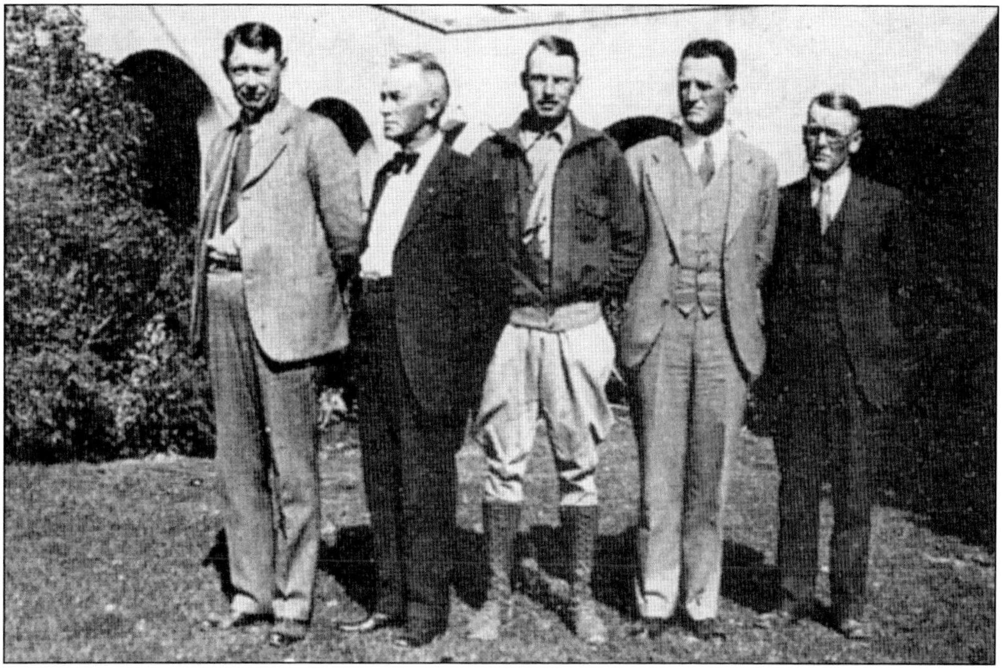

William J. McAdam Sr. moved to the valley in the early 1900s. He was a prominent insurance agent, orchard grower, and real estate broker. He was also a member of the A. V. Union Joint High School Board of Trustees (1931) who are, from left to right, G. Hill, William McAdam, Dr. Savage, Grant Shockley, and J. Maxwell. In 1960, a Palmdale park was dedicated in his name.

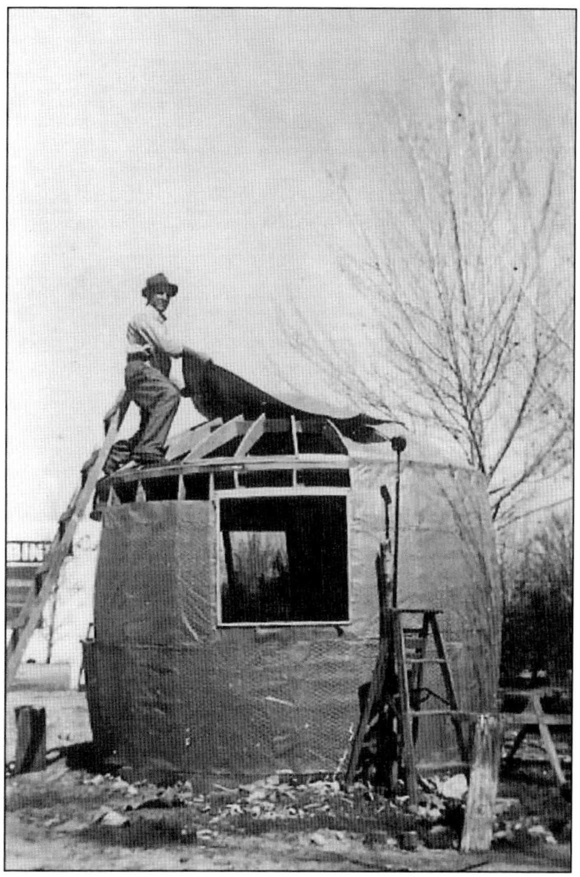

Domenic Massari fell in love with Palmdale in 1929. He served as a council member, the city's second mayor, helped establish the annual Lilac Festival, and assisted in the construction of St. Mary's School. He is seen here building a giant orange fruit juice stand on his property, which was located near the present-day Palmdale Children's Library. His wife, Teresa, was responsible for selling the juice. (Courtesy of Larry Chimbole.)

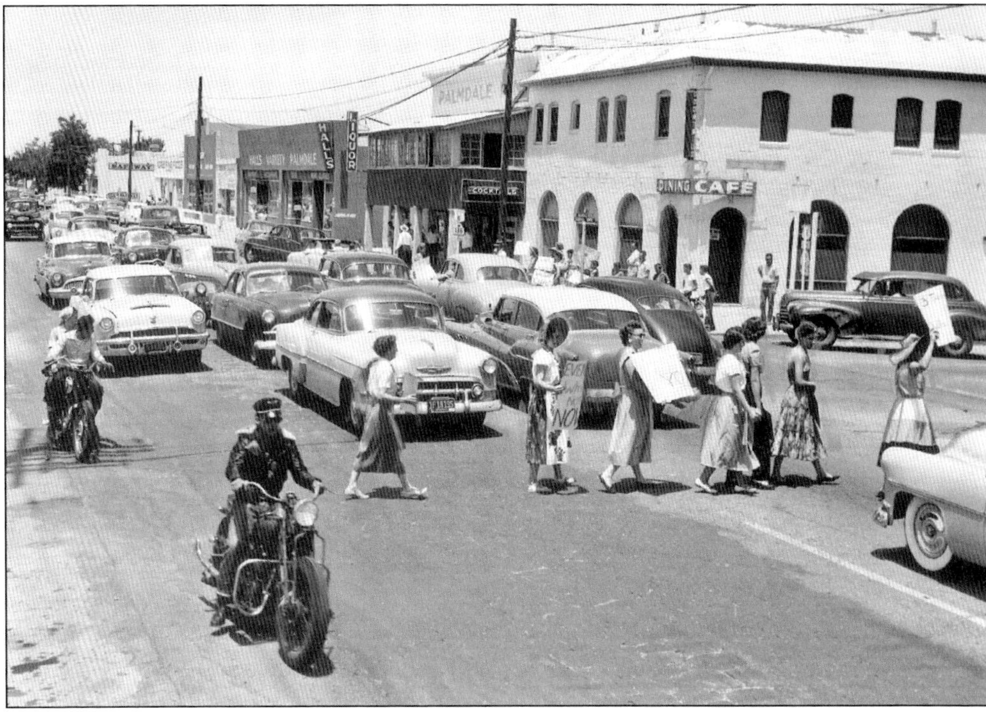

In May 1954, members of Palmdale's Junior Woman's Club and others formed a picket line and walked back and forth at the deadly intersection of Sierra Highway and Palmdale Boulevard to get the community's first traffic signal. They stopped traffic for several hours but were successful. Judge Keller was also very helpful in this cause. (Courtesy of *Herald-Examiner* Collection/Los Angeles Public Library.)

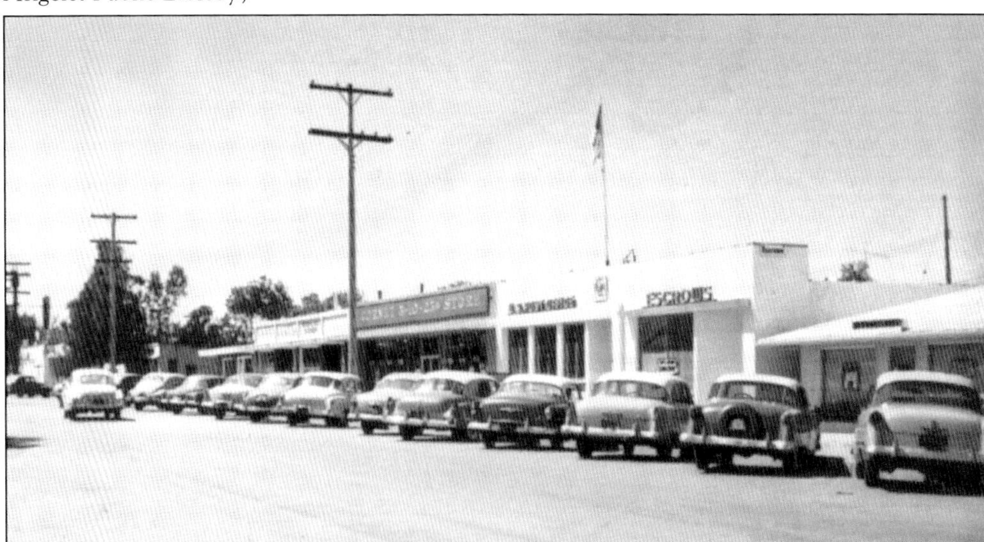

This older shopping area of Palmdale on East Avenue Q-9 still exists. It is located directly east of the Palmdale Library. During the 1950s, it was the site of the post office. Earlier post offices were located in various stores and businesses on Sierra Highway. Genevieve Frahm became Palmdale's postmistress in 1919 and did not retire until 1959.

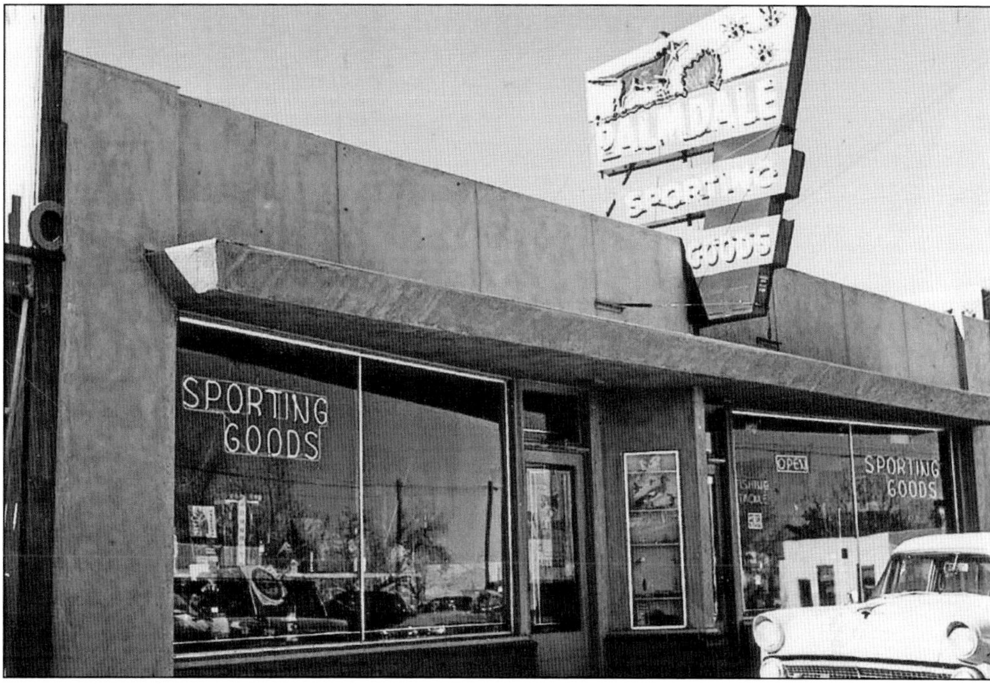

During the early 1950s, with the development of the aircraft industry and USAF Plant 42, many newcomers arrived in Southeast Antelope Valley. They soon discovered that the region offered many recreational activities and the Palmdale Sporting Goods Store suited all their sporting needs. Before this type of specialty store, residents would purchase their sports items in Ikeler's or Moore's general stores. (Courtesy of Palmdale City Library.)

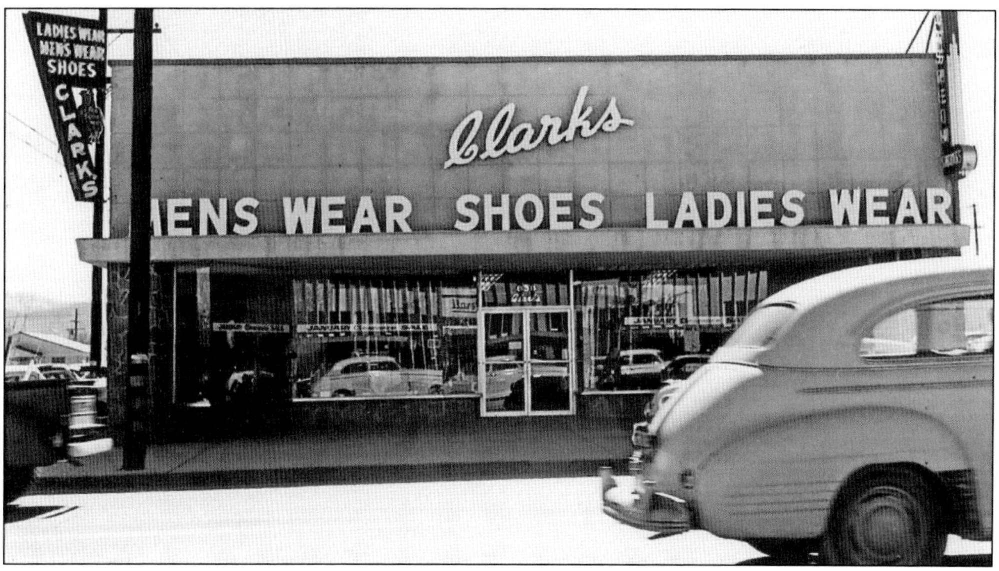

In 1947, Clyde and Lorna Wallace opened the first men's ready-to-wear shop on Sierra Highway in a small section of the White Spot building. Not long after, as Palmdale was growing, new clothing stores such as Clarks appeared. J. Shelton Gordon, a building contractor, constructed many 1940s and 1950s structures in Palmdale. He was also president of the chamber of commerce in 1953. (Courtesy of Palmdale City Library.)

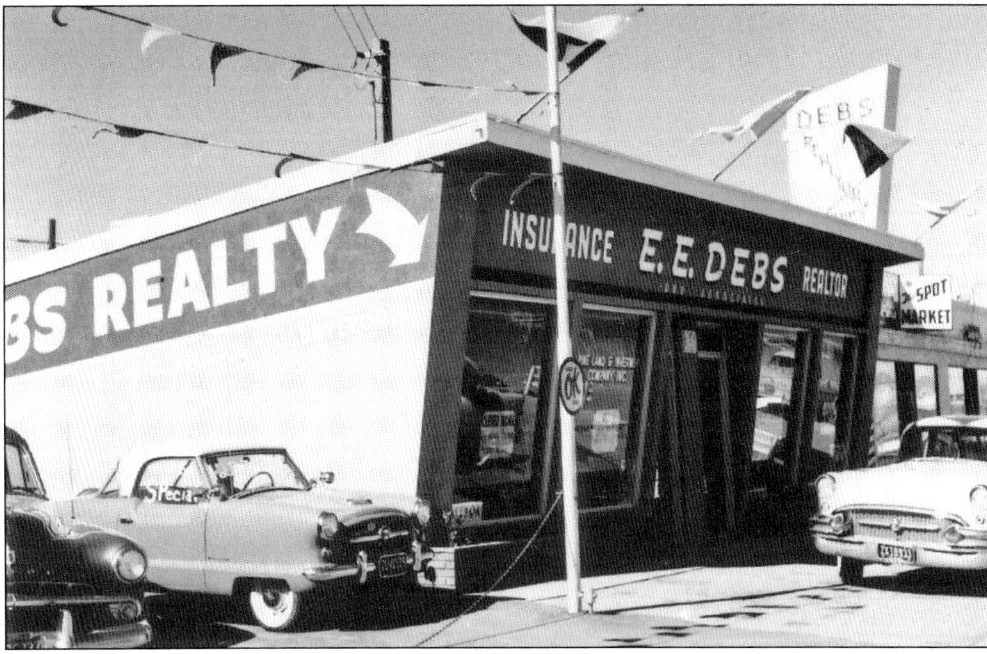

The Southeast Antelope Valley has experienced its ups and downs in the real estate market. After the introduction of electricity in 1918, many workers came to the area for jobs. Construction of the Littlerock Dam in the 1920s also created a regional boom. When the Depression arrived, it was not until after World War II that Palmdale's population steadily grew. (Courtesy of Palmdale City Library.)

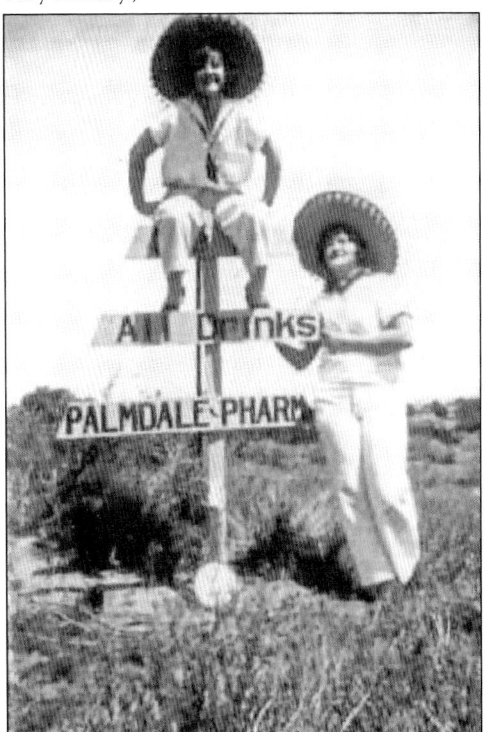

The sign indicating the way to the Palmdale Pharmacy made sure visitors would take the correct route. Advertisements for Palmdale and surrounding areas were quite glowing in old newspapers. One of the first publications devoted completely to publicizing Palmdale was *Romance and Drama in the Valley of Sunshine—Being a Story of Old Palmdale.* It was published by the Palmdale Fruit Land Company in 1914. (Courtesy of Dayle DeBry.)

In December 1896, the *Los Angeles Times* noted that Palmdale would soon have a telephone line. However, the first telephone did not materialize until 1908 in the Cottage Hotel (shown here) with two subscribers. By 1921, there were 35 telephones. In 1929, telephone service was expanded to a 24-hour basis, with two switchboards located in rented quarters on Sierra Highway. In 1942, a new building was erected on Palmdale Boulevard.

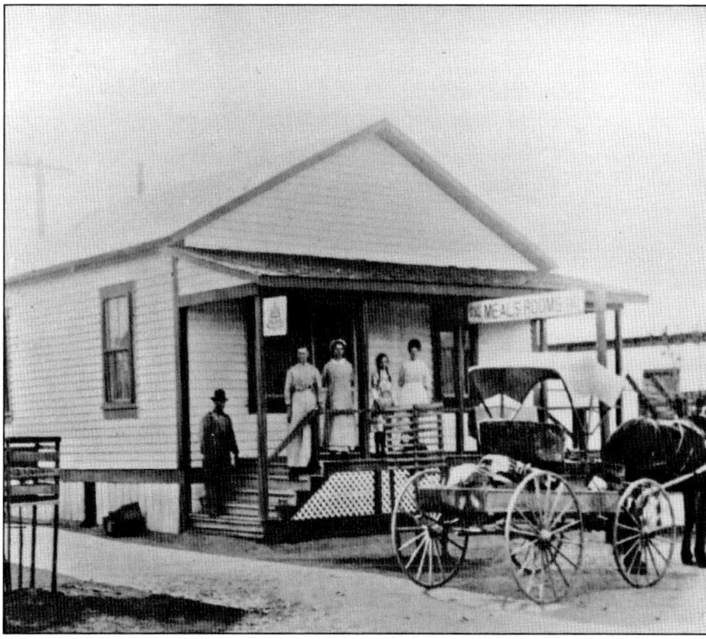

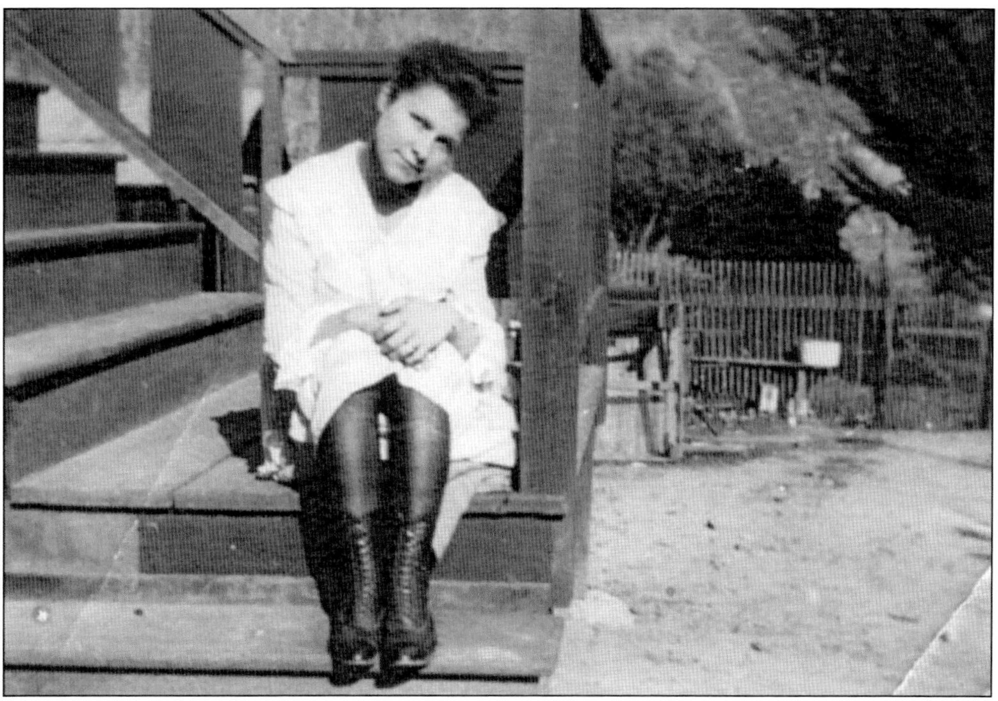

The Pacific Telephone Exchange included the communities of Palmdale, Littlerock, Pearblossom, and Acton. The career of a telephone operator was one of the few technically oriented jobs available to women during the 1910s and early 1920s. Ruth Settle, the sister of Maude (pictured here), was an early operator. Some women who worked as operators included Ruth Varner, Viola Wells, Mrs. Phillips, Marion Blanchard, and Mrs. Stroud McBride, among others.

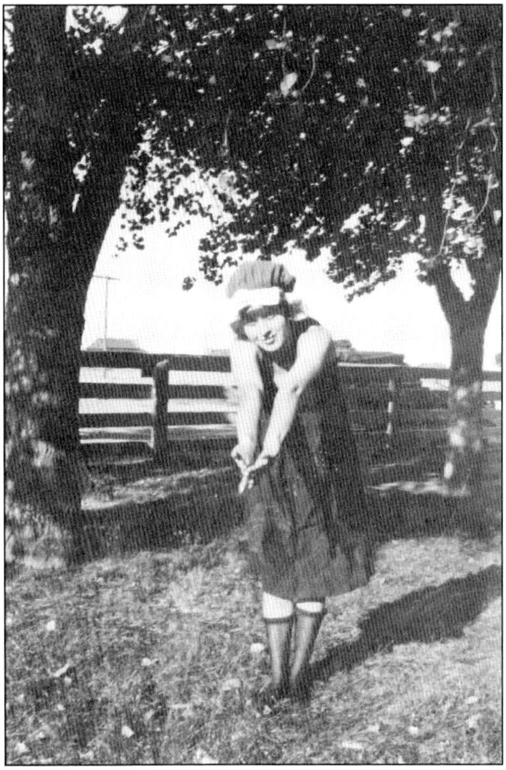

Pictured in the Settle family's backyard in Palmdale, bathing beauty Lillian Lorenz was also a telephone operator. In 1925, telephone bills had to be paid on the 20th of each month; there were no extensions. If the bill was not paid, the telephone was disconnected on the morning of the 21st and only reconnected for a fee of $1, which had to be paid before services could be continued.

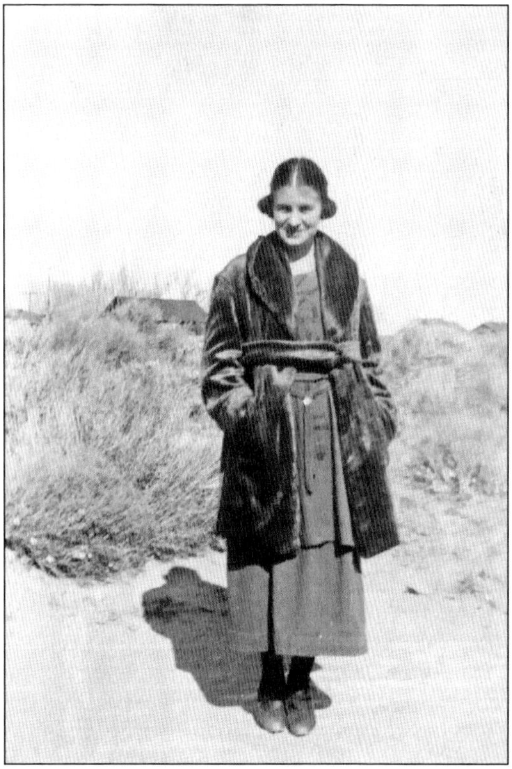

In 1891, George Clark was old Palmdale's first professional photographer. He took studio photographs and pictures of special events like Fourth of July celebrations. In 1896, Clark also ran the Palmdale Hotel. P. A. Rowland was a Palmdale photographer during the 1920s. He took the high school's graduating class photographs in 1925. Mabel Jones (1918) looks happy to have her photograph taken in Palmdale.

Women always want to have their hair done, even when times are tough. Mabel Jacobs opened what was probably the first Palmdale beauty parlor in September 1924. The salon was known for good service and low prices. In 1926, Emily Johnson owned the Palmdale Beauty Shoppe. In these beauty shops, the customers—like Mabel Jones—not only had their hair styled but also caught up on the latest gossip.

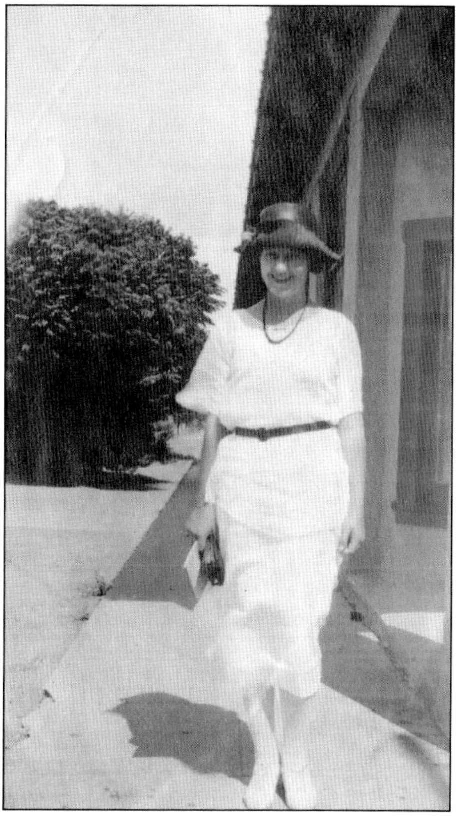

Palmdale Plaza (top), Palmdale's first major shopping outlet, opened in the late 1950s. Located between Sierra Highway and East Avenue Q-6, the one-story commercial center had a J. C. Penney, an F. W. Woolworths, a grocery store, the Palm Theatre, and other smaller businesses. The Palmdale Plaza, except for the former market, which became the Hammack Youth Center, was razed after the opening of the Antelope Valley Mall. (Courtesy of WAVHS.)

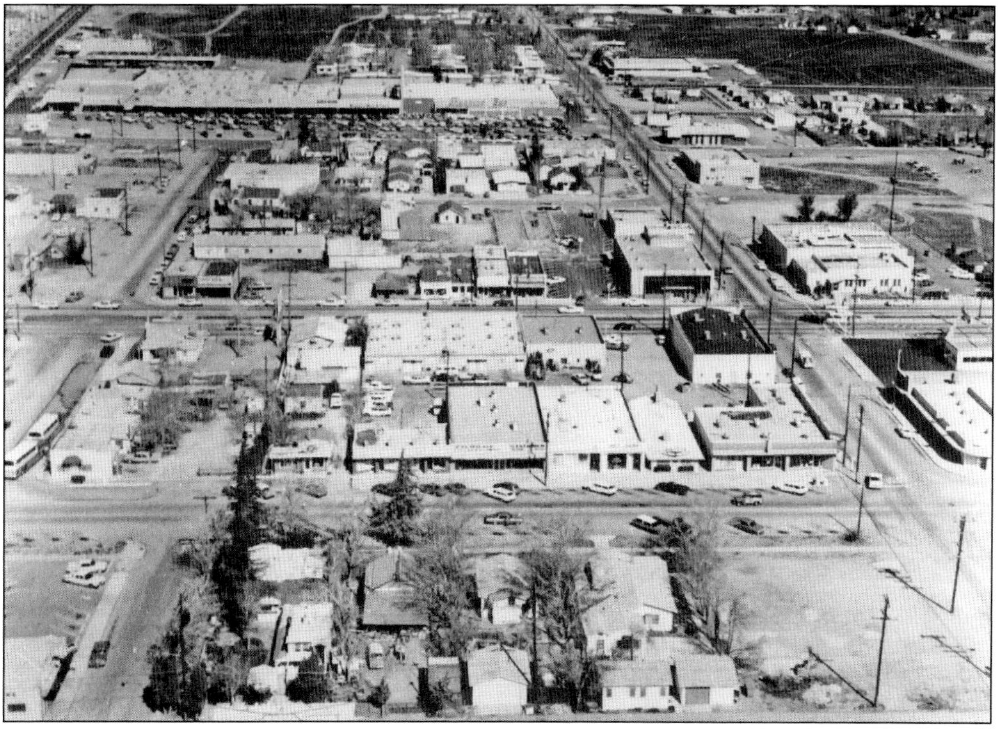

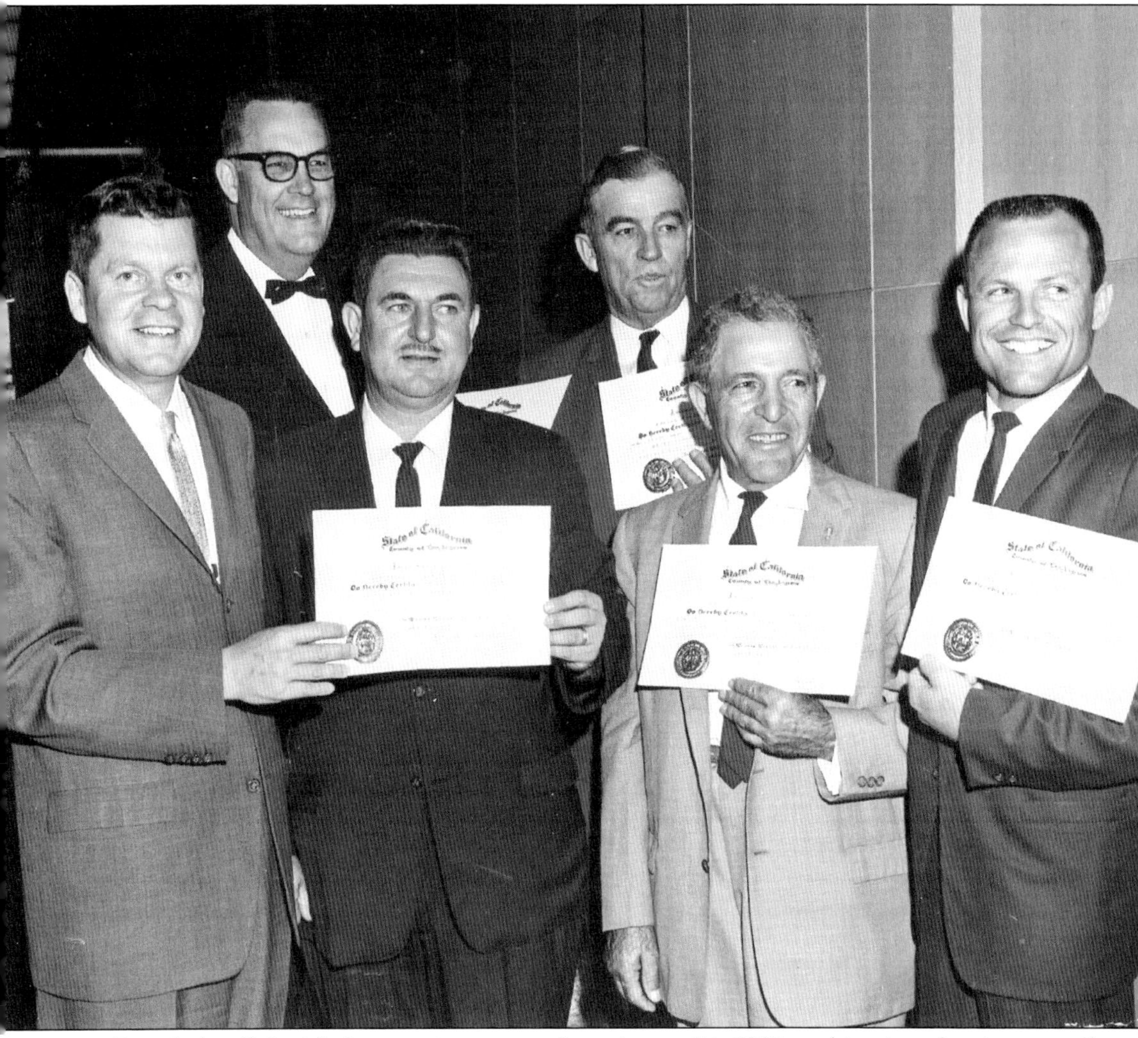

Even before Palmdale became incorporated on August 24, 1962, and instituted a city council, local people always performed their civic duty for the community. As soon as women received the right to vote, Cleopatra Dudley began working at local election precincts. Although Palmdale did not have an official mayor until the 1960s, pioneer Oscar Newquist was called the "Mayor of Palmdale" in 1915 by "Palmdalites." He was also referred to as one of the "Four Fathers of Palmdale" in 1917. In 1957, Larry Chimbole moved to Palmdale and almost immediately became involved in the community's civic affairs. The owner of several hardware stores, Chimbole worked with the "Fifty Grand Men" program, which led the way to Palmdale's incorporation. Chimbole was Palmdale's first mayor. He was also involved with the annexation of Plant 42 to Palmdale. Los Angeles County supervisor Warren Dorn and the new city of Palmdale council members in August 1962 are, from left to right, Dr. Lester Nichols, Larry Chimbole, Marlin Gilbreath, Domenic Massari, and Vice Mayor Richard Linaker. (Courtesy of *Antelope Valley Press*.)

Seven

Schools, Churches, Cemeteries, and Military

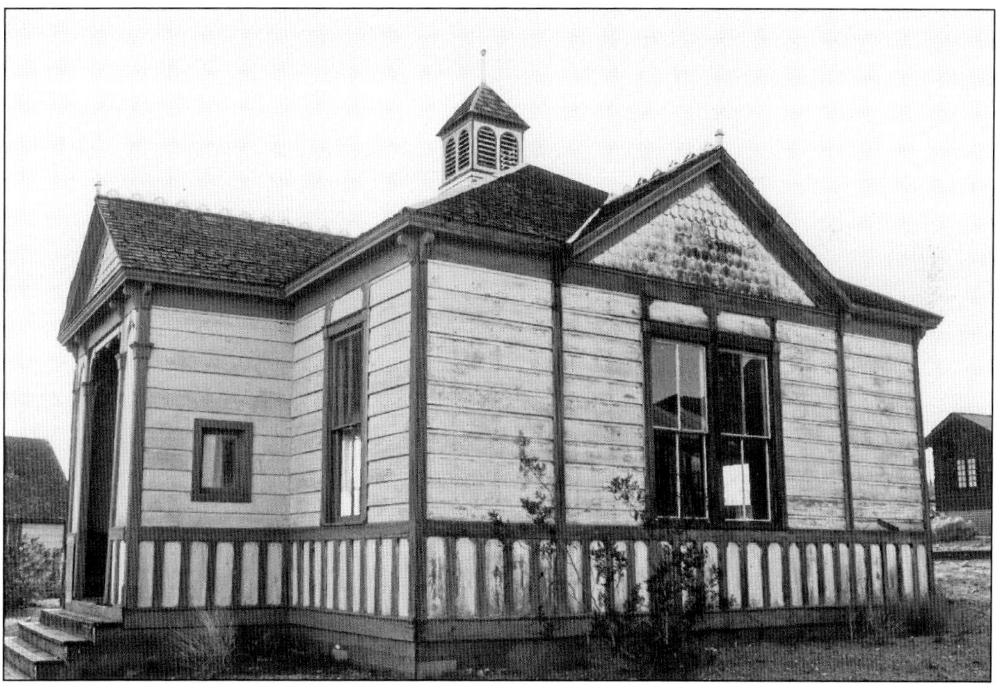

Charles Hahn and Henry Godde built Palmenthal's one-room schoolhouse, which was erected at approximately Avenue R-8 and Twenty-seventh Street East. As the town's population dwindled, in 1910, a decision was made to close down the school and sell it. It was moved to Lancaster, and years later Glen and Dorene Settle saved it (1960s). Today the school, now a small museum, has a new home at McAdam Park.

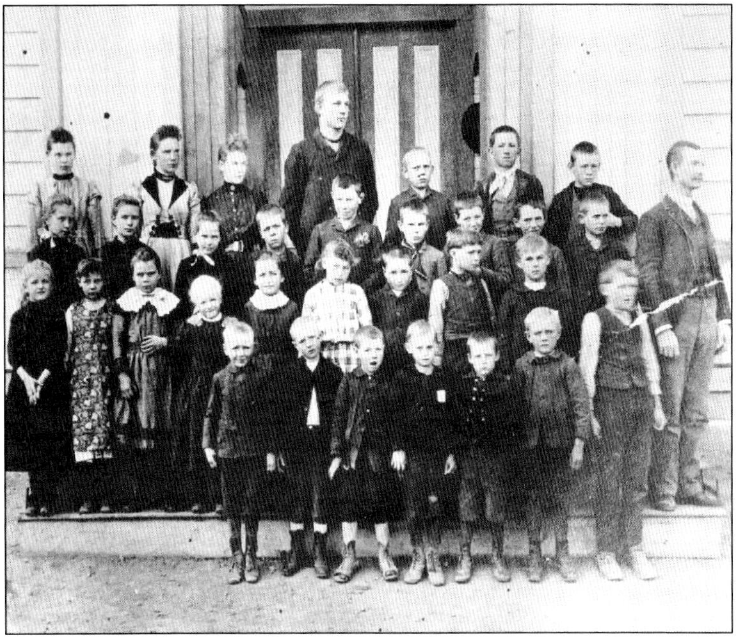

The schoolhouse (c. 1888) opened with 30 students and Henry T. Shirley as the first teacher. Shirley, who taught for two terms, earned $65 a month. This picture shows all eight grades. After a visit to the school, the local newspaper editor described that "the scholars all seemed clean, studious, and attentive." In addition to this school, there was also a German language school held in the Lutheran church.

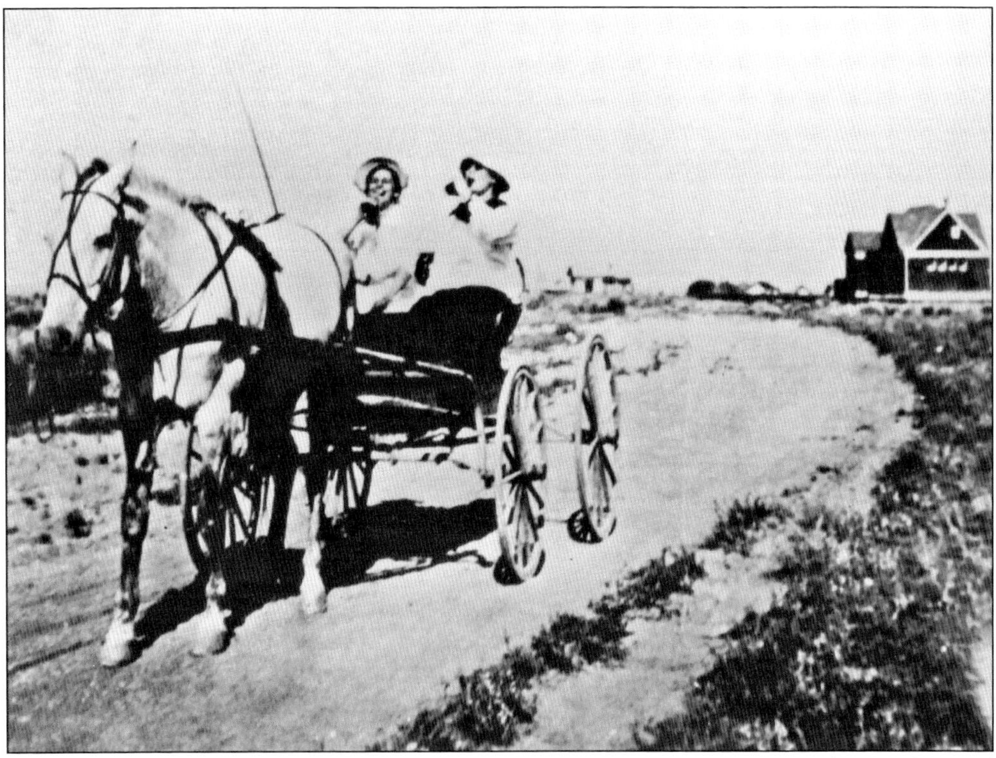

Paul Schoeller's nieces, pictured here c. 1915, are enjoying a soda while taking a ride near the New/West Palmdale School (at right), which was built near Sixth Street East and Palmdale Boulevard. The two-story, brick school opened in 1908. Clara Johnson, the first teacher, taught 56 students by herself for some time before a second teacher, Rose Gemmill, was hired. Later J. Calverland, Leona Ellington, and Gwendolyn Sargent joined the teaching staff.

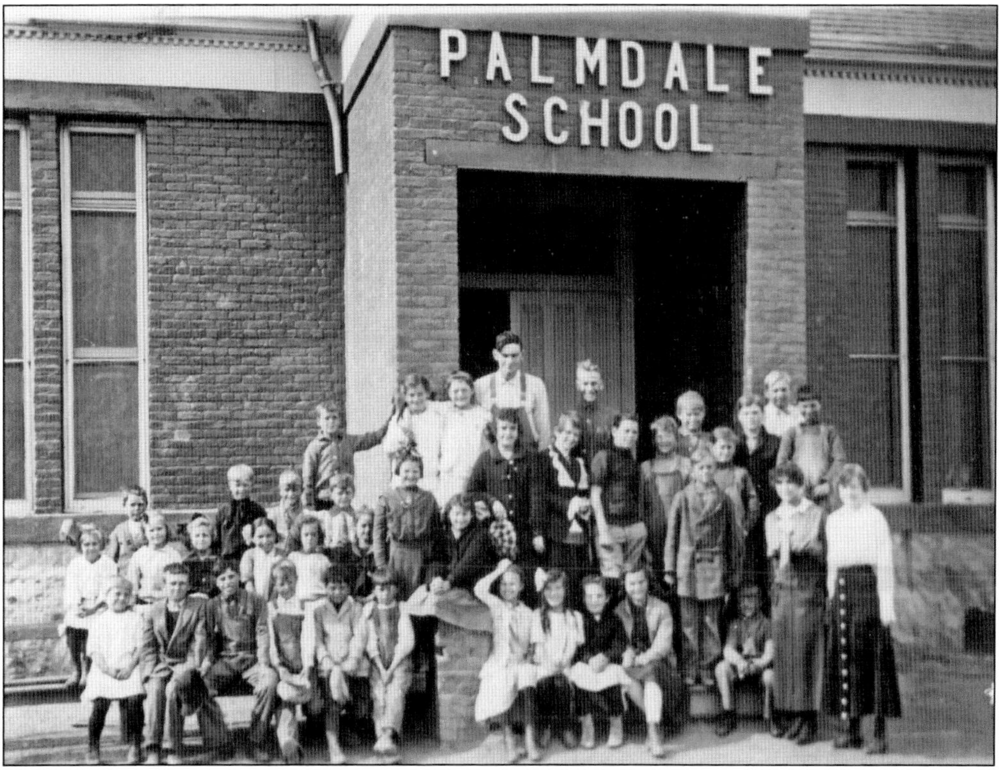

This is the entire student body at the school around 1916. The school closed in 1917. For the move into the new school, the teachers had the students walk in parade fashion holding their books and supplies. It was very cost effective. When it was no longer utilized as a school, it became a printing plant, a cement pipe yard, the blacksmith's home, a laundry, and a pear-packing shed.

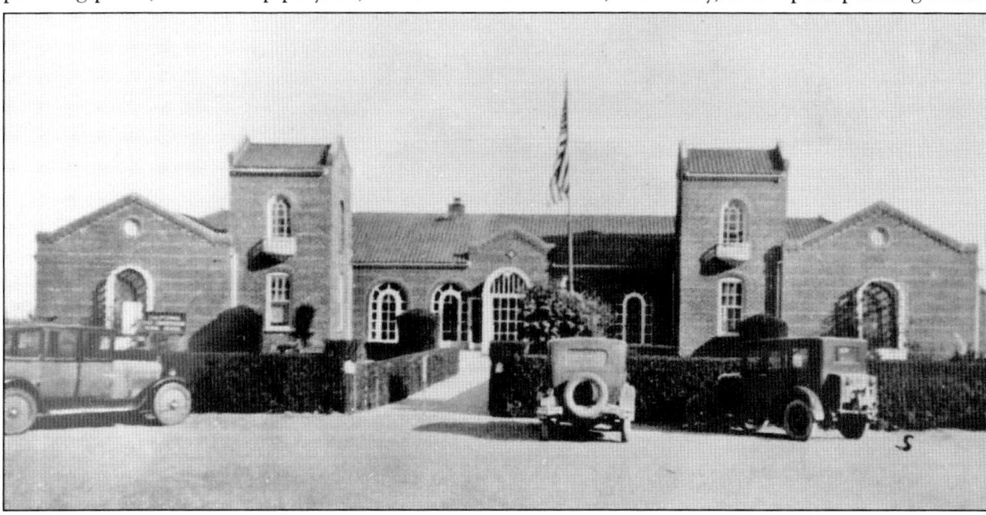

In 1917, for the sum of $10, the Palmdale School District was granted the deed to land between Tenth and Eleventh Streets East between Palmdale Boulevard and Avenue Q-12. A focal point for the community, the new brick Palmdale Grammar School consisted of a large central room that served as an auditorium, lunchroom, and gym; two small conference rooms and two classrooms were at either end of the structure (1927).

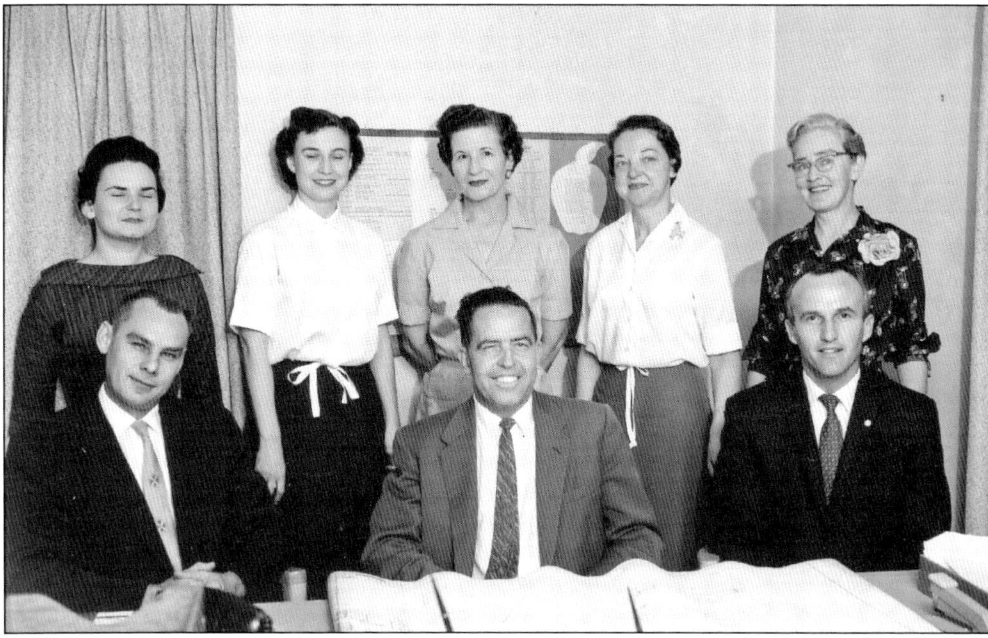

In 1933, the severe Long Beach earthquake was felt in Palmdale. The schoolhouse was condemned and replaced by a stucco school building at the same site. Roy Maryott (seated, center), a former A. V. High School teacher and vice principal, was hired as Palmdale School District superintendent in 1951, when Palmdale had fewer than 3,000 inhabitants and its one elementary school held 350 pupils. (Courtesy of *Antelope Valley Press.*)

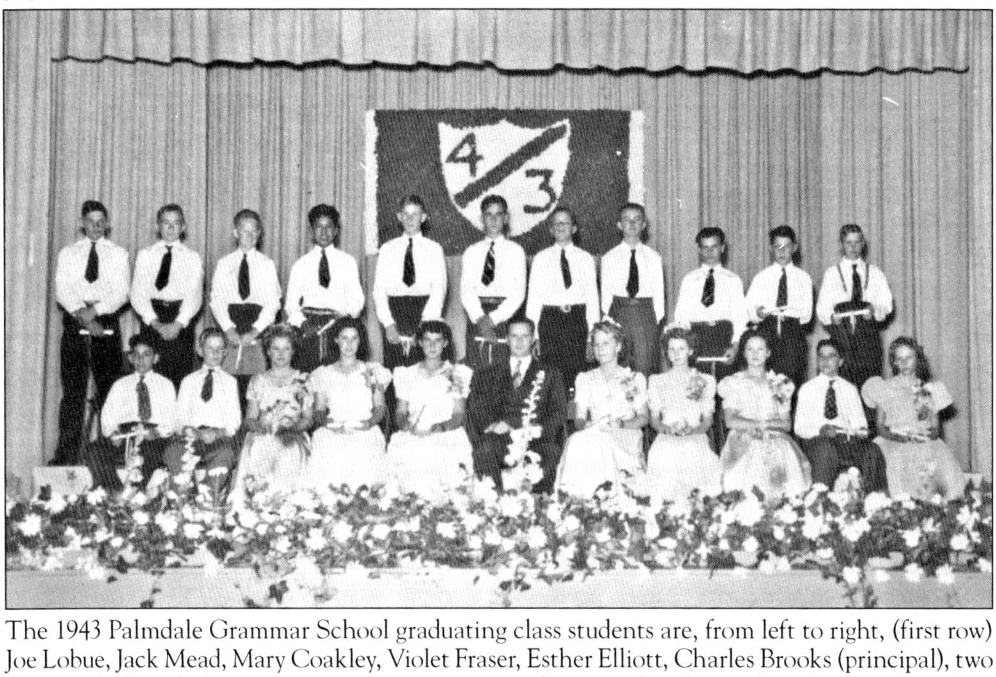

The 1943 Palmdale Grammar School graduating class students are, from left to right, (first row) Joe Lobue, Jack Mead, Mary Coakley, Violet Fraser, Esther Elliott, Charles Brooks (principal), two unidentified, Ophelia Montoya, Rocco Massari, and Rose Lulay; (second row) Lawrence Billet, Clifford Kimrough, Jim Barlett, Tony Custodio, Bob Nix, Roy Near, Sam Waddle, Ed Wilmont, Bob Prickett, Dick Moulton, and Dallas Brady. (Courtesy of Larry Chimbole.)

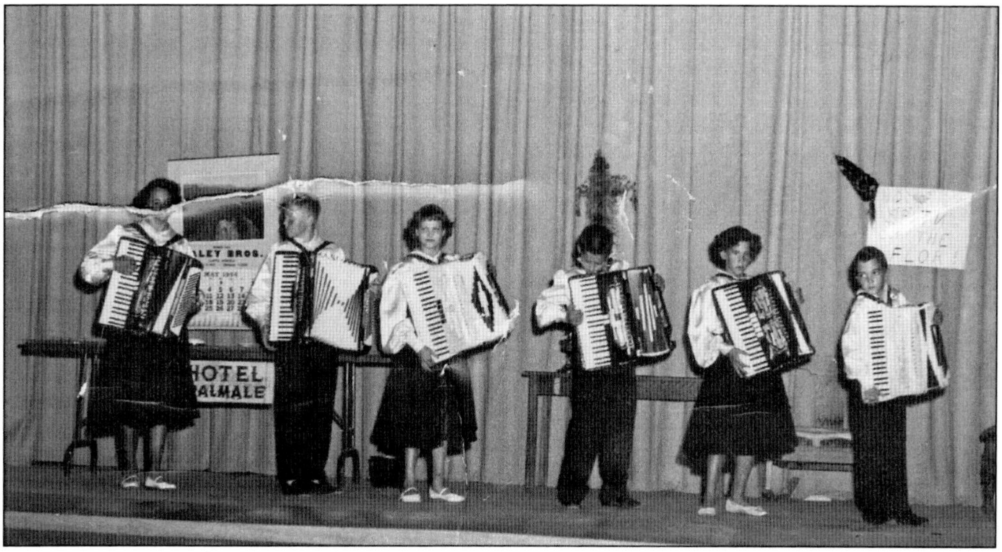

These young accordion players do not appear to be too nervous. The sign at the right reads "No Spitting on the Floor." Through the years, movies were shown locally at the Palmdale Community Church (1920s), the Palmdale Grammar School's large auditorium, the military base, the Palm Theatre, and the Palmdale Drive-in. Most rural schools would also at times show movies for the community. (Courtesy of Larry Chimbole.)

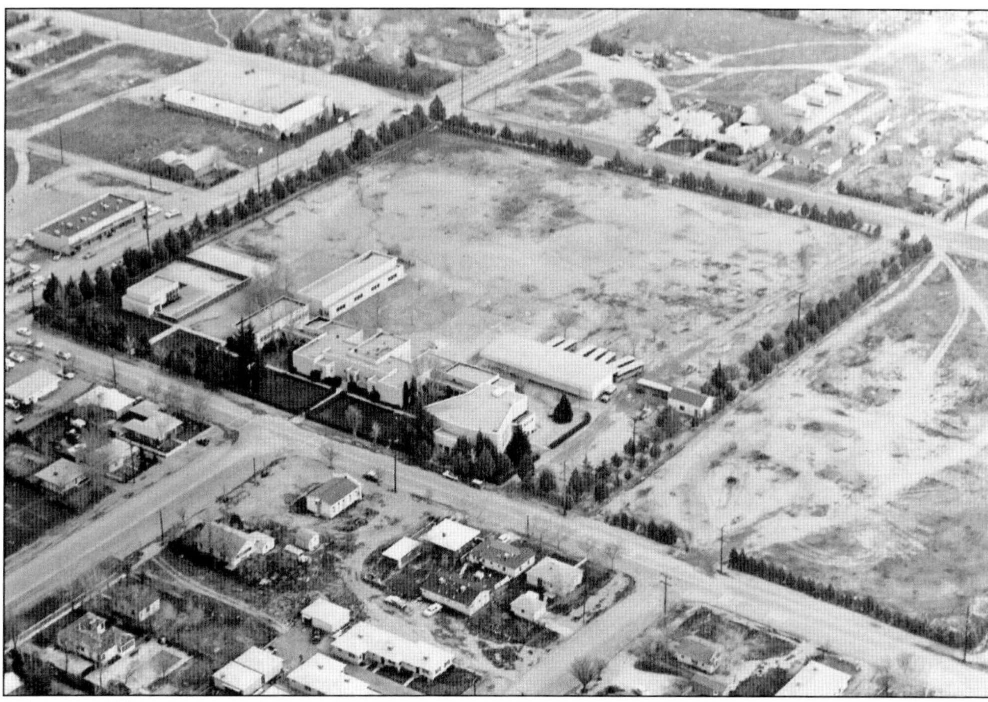

After World War II, and with the expansion of the aerospace industry, Palmdale's population exploded; new schools were needed. Sage School opened in 1955. In 1960, Palmdale Grammar School was renamed the Roy R. Maryott School, as Maryott had guided the district through a rapid growth period from 1951 until his death in 1960. Due to its age and funding problems, the Maryott School closed in 1981. (Courtesy of WAVHS.)

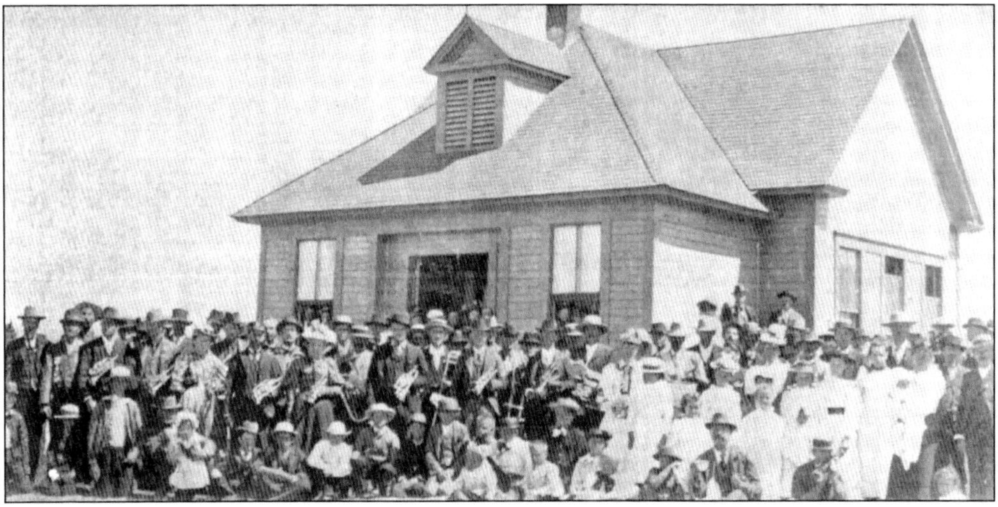

Before the Llano del Rio Colony of the 1910s, there was the older Quaker Llano Colony near the same area. With an estimated 100 residents in 1895, Llano supported a store, a post office, a school, and a doctor. The teacher was Mrs. Henry Shirley, the wife of the instructor at the old Palmenthal School. This picture, taken in 1895, shows a large group of picnic participants at the school.

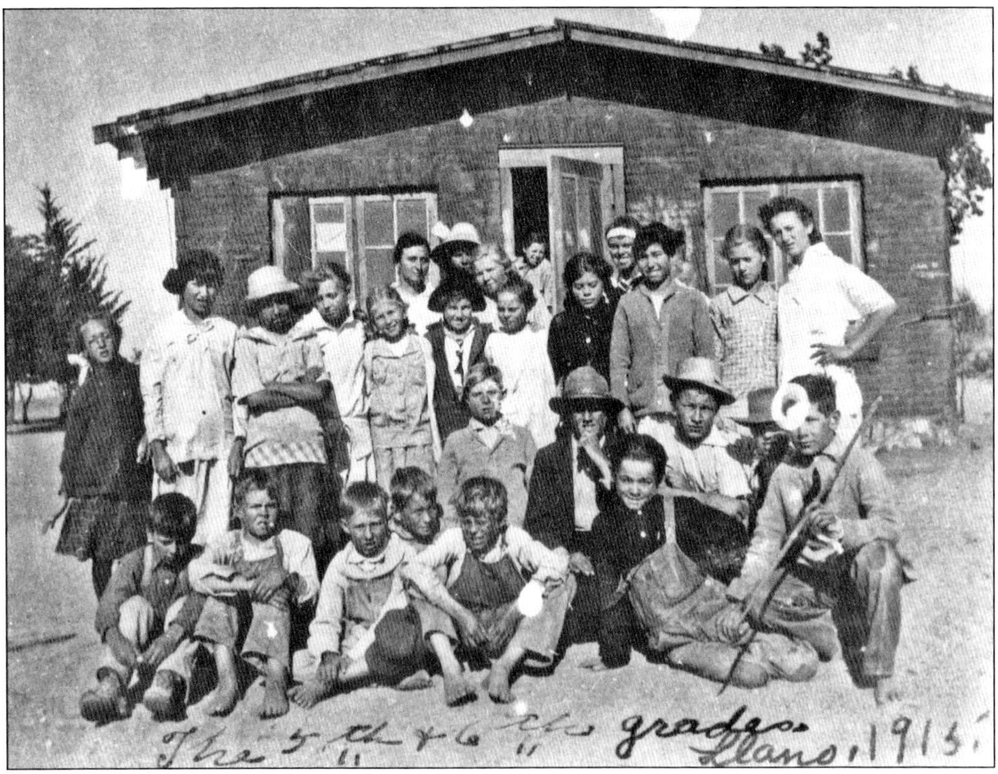

Llano del Rio schools ranged from a Montessori kindergarten (the second such school in California) to a community high school that only had two grade levels. The high school classes were held in the colony's hotel. The students attended school four hours a day, six days a week. Students could also attend an industrial school. This is the 1915 class comprised of students from the fifth and sixth grades. (Courtesy of WAVHS.)

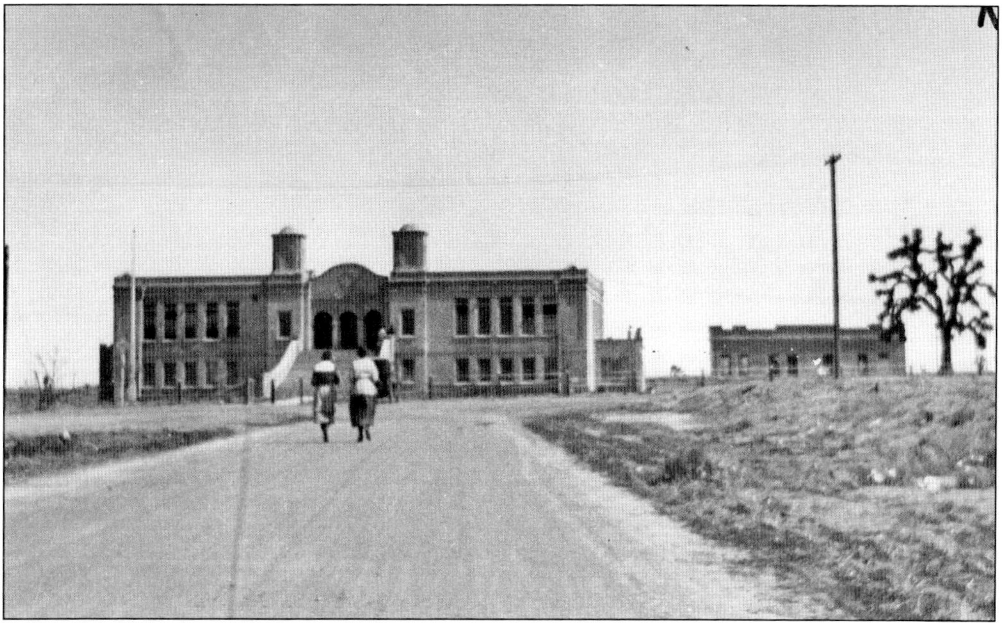

Before 1912, students in the high school grades had to board at schools outside the valley. The first high school was held in the Women's Independent Club building in Lancaster. The high school then moved into the former grammar school on Lancaster Boulevard near Beech Avenue. When A. V. High School opened September 20, 1915, it was in a new two-story structure. Enrollment totaled about 40 students, with a faculty of six.

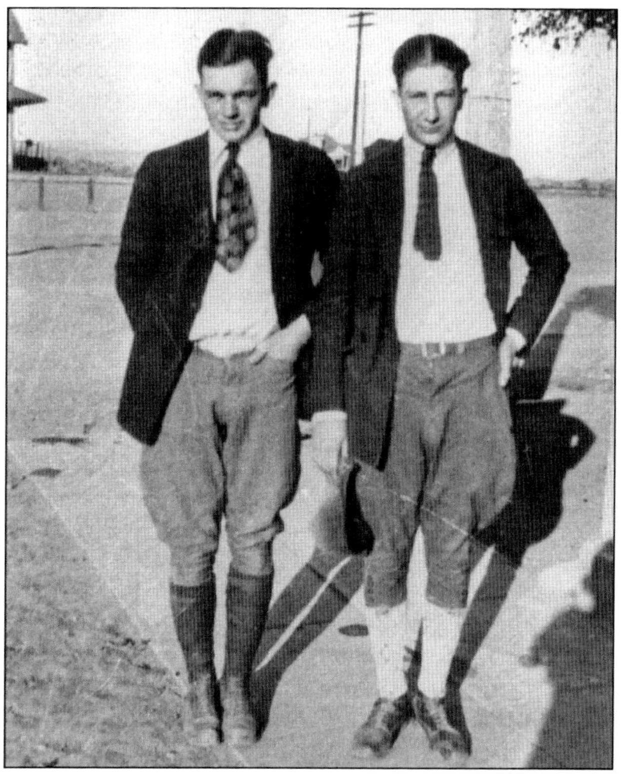

Fred Bradford and Fred Mower of Palmdale are waiting by the railroad depot for the A. V. High School bus to pick them up. Laura Mae and Ruth Lindsey lived at the high school dorm since the school was 12 miles away. The cost of room and board for one month was $18. During the 1920s, the girls were required to wear semi-uniforms, which consisted of skirts, blouses, and sweaters.

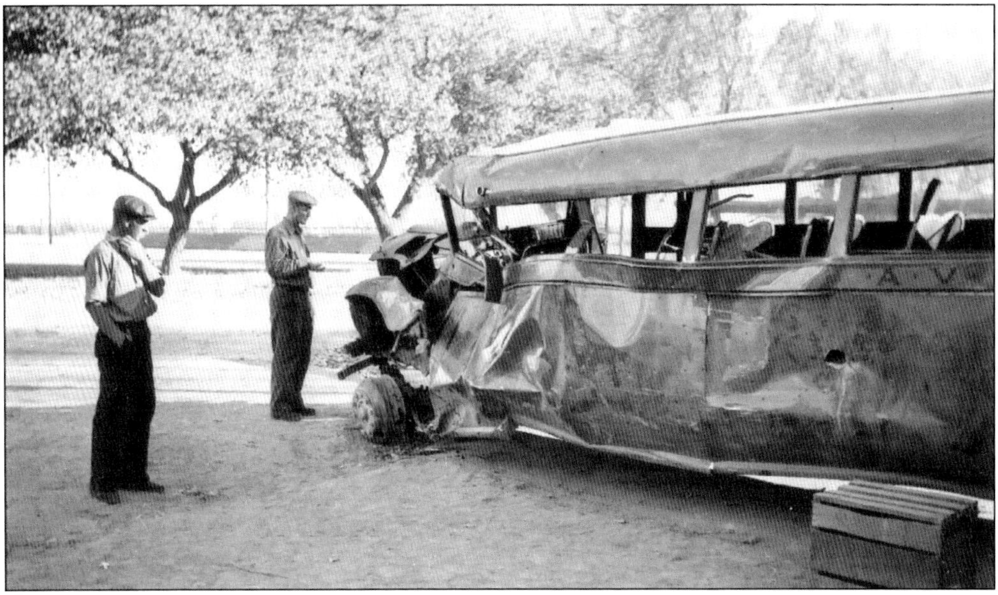

Many students had to travel 40 miles one way to the new high school. Bus transportation was provided but accidents happened, such as this one from the late 1930s. When floods and heavy snows occurred in the Littlerock area, grammar school children living in Valyermo and Big Rock Creek would sometimes spend the night at their bus driver's home since they could not get home safely.

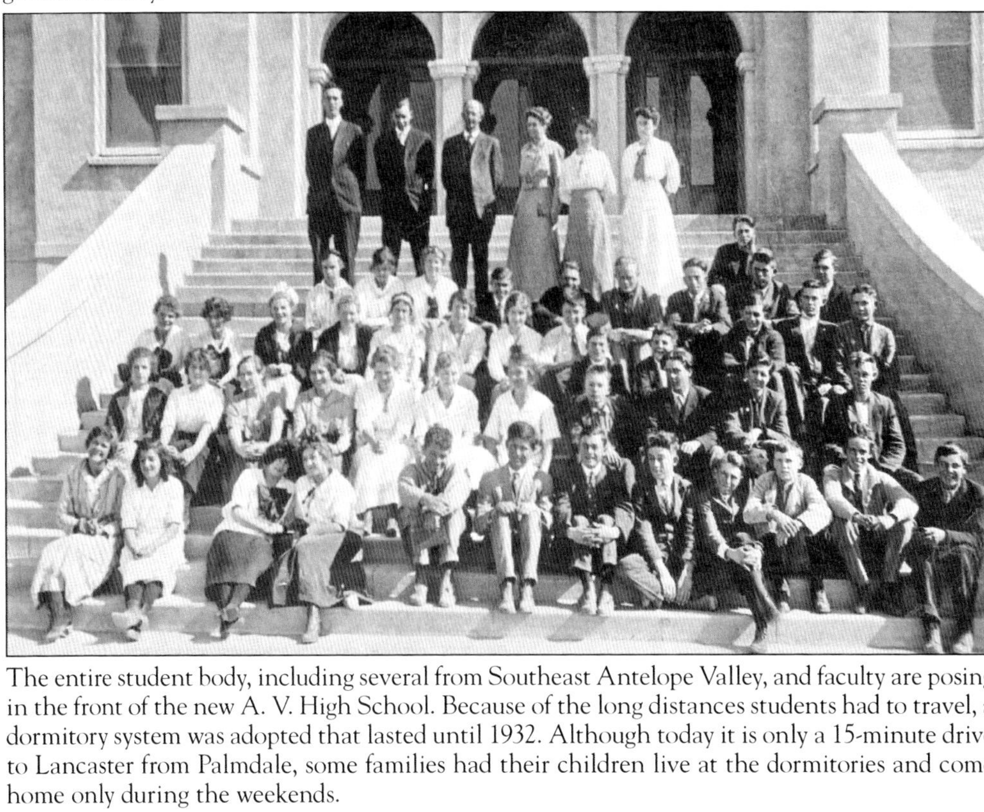

The entire student body, including several from Southeast Antelope Valley, and faculty are posing in the front of the new A. V. High School. Because of the long distances students had to travel, a dormitory system was adopted that lasted until 1932. Although today it is only a 15-minute drive to Lancaster from Palmdale, some families had their children live at the dormitories and come home only during the weekends.

Curtis E. Warren, a Palmdale resident, was an Antelope Valley High School teacher. He taught history, public speaking, and civics. By the early 1920s, he was the principal. In 1912, the trustees paid the principal $1,500 and an assistant $900 per year. Warren was paid a little more when he became principal. He left the valley and became the district superintendent in Santa Barbara and later in San Francisco.

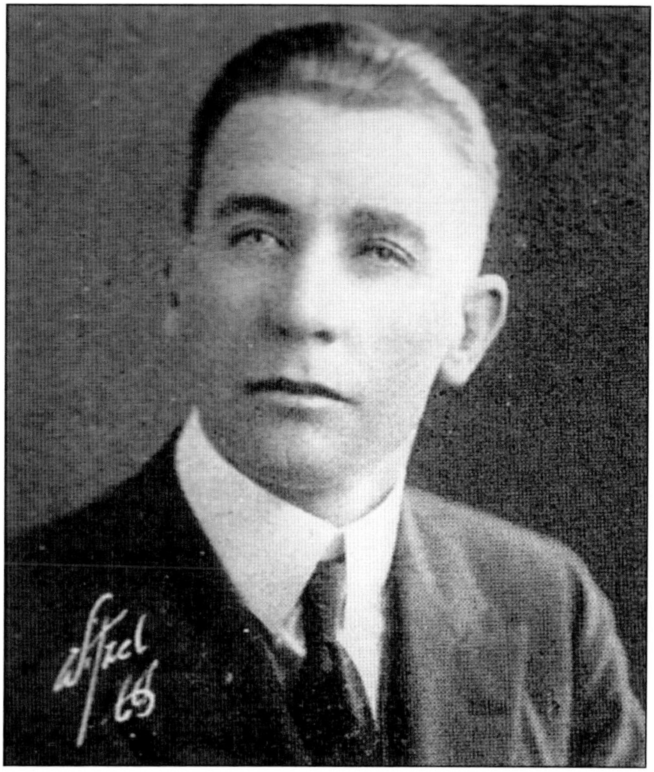

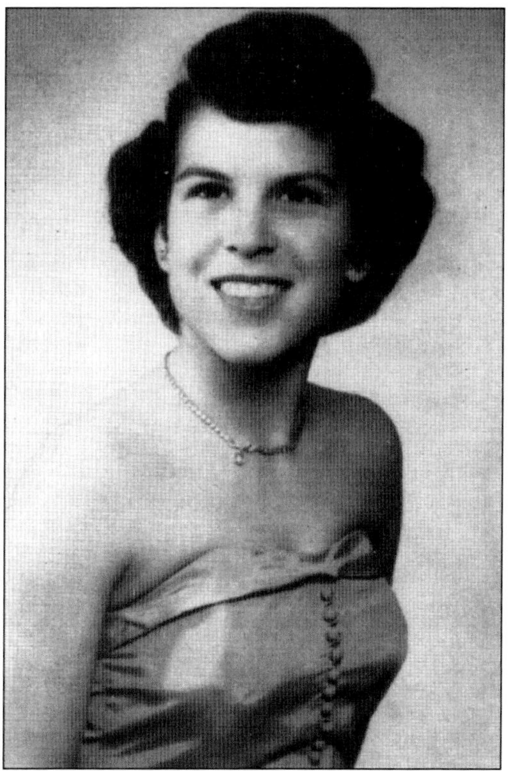

Palmdale resident Betty Valdez was selected as Antelope Valley High School's "Alumni Queen" in 1952. She was president of the Majorettes and a member of the "Big A." Pioneer Hispanics played important roles in Southeast Antelope Valley, from constables, orchardists, blacksmiths, miners, and aqueduct workers to farmers. The largest concentration of Mexican laborers, however, was with the Southern Pacific Railroad. Some also became section foremen.

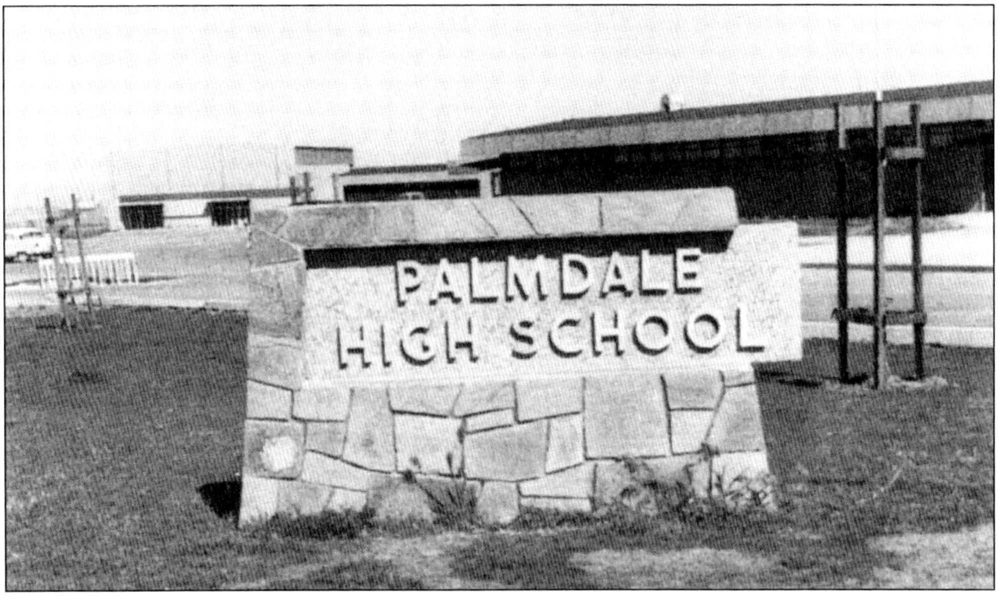

By 1952, as the region was growing, residents were asking: is Palmdale ready for a high school? A site search began and one was selected on Avenue R between East Twentieth and Twenty-fifth Streets. Construction by J. Shelton Gordon and others began in July 1955. On September 8, 1956, Palmdale High School opened its doors for the first time. (Courtesy of Palmdale High School.)

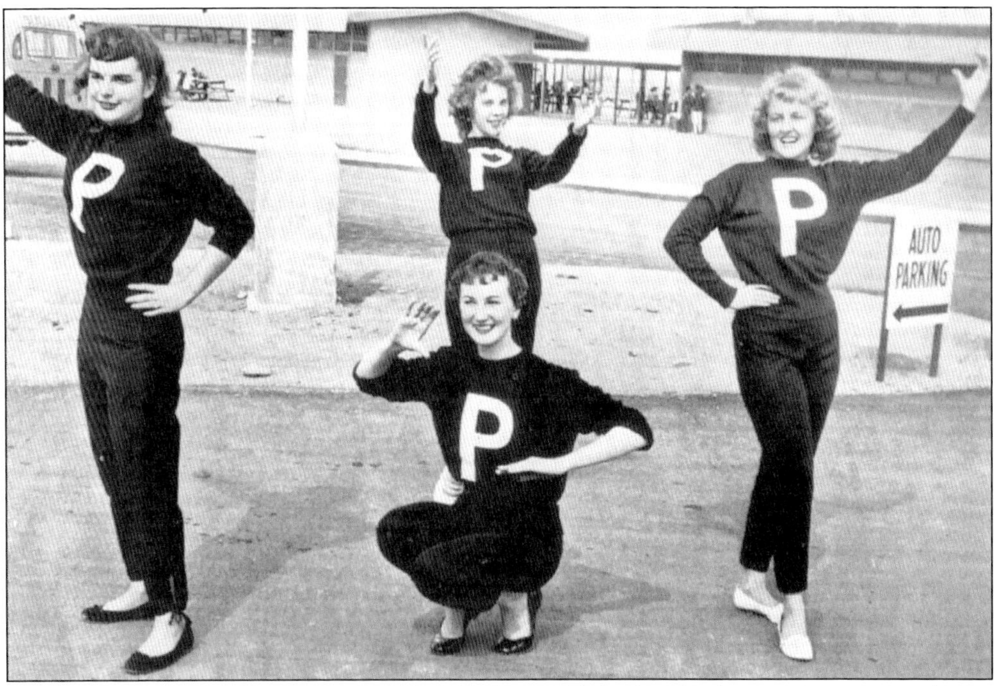

Palmdale High School was the second school to be established in the district. Approximately 500 freshman and sophomore students from the southern section of the Antelope Valley were enrolled. By midterm, the numbers increased to 600. Team spirit was important for the new school. The cheerleaders are, from left to right, Sandy Ingles, Klo Ann Williams (front), Carol Robertson, and Martha Schweich. (Courtesy of Palmdale High School.)

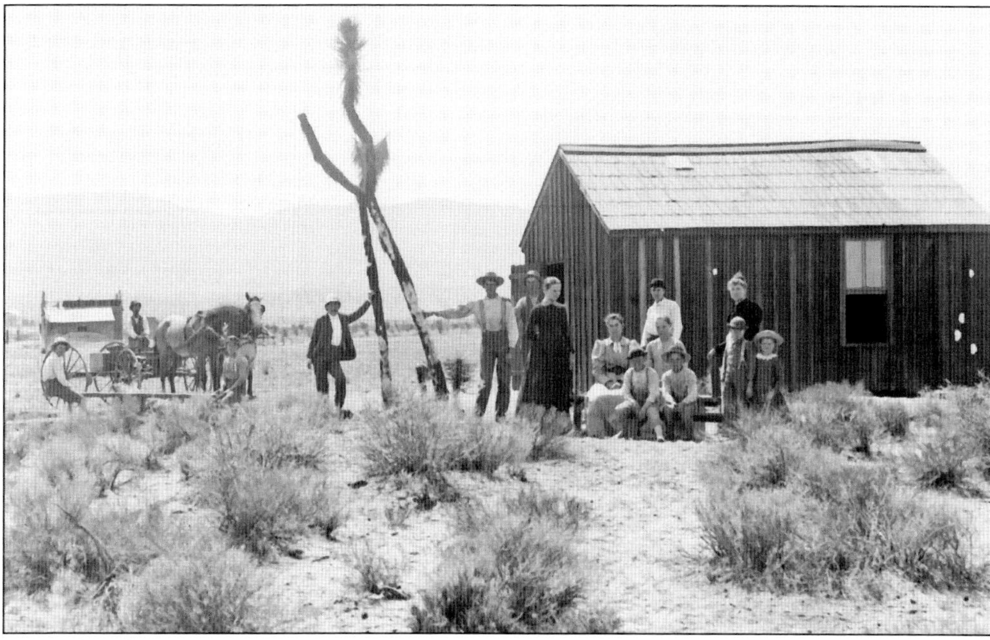

This schoolhouse is thought to have been located near Littlerock. According to pioneers, the first Littlerock School was started in 1893; a fire nearly destroyed it in 1896. The school was discontinued and then revived, first in a tent and then in a packing shed (1912), with Mattie Stanton as the instructor. (Courtesy of University of Southern California, on behalf of the USC Special Collections.)

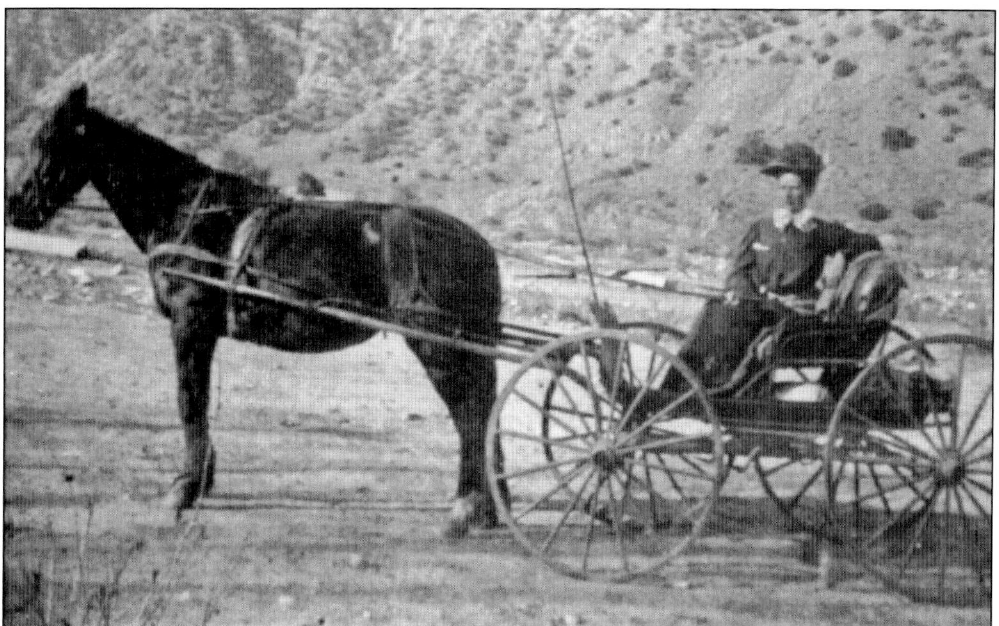

Rose Graves Kidd (*c.* 1905) was the wife of Emery Kidd, a leading cattleman. A very popular teacher, she taught at Big Rock, Almondale, Keppel, and Palmdale Schools. In the old days, she was often seen going to work in her horse-and-buggy rig; later she drove a Model T school bus. Members of the Kidd family still reside in the Antelope Valley.

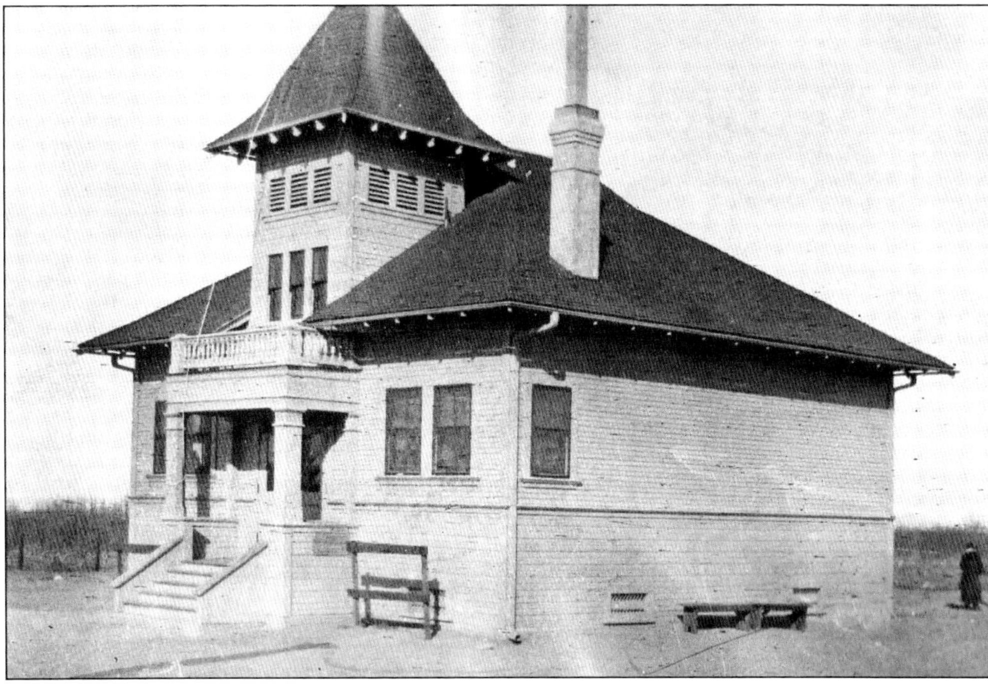

In 1912, an acre of land just north of Highway 138 on Seventy-seventh Street East, across the street from the Martin house, was purchased for a new school. The one-room school with a steeple opened in 1913; it was built at a cost of about $1,900. The old Littlerock Library was also located in this building. (Courtesy of Littlerock Library, County of Los Angeles Public Library.)

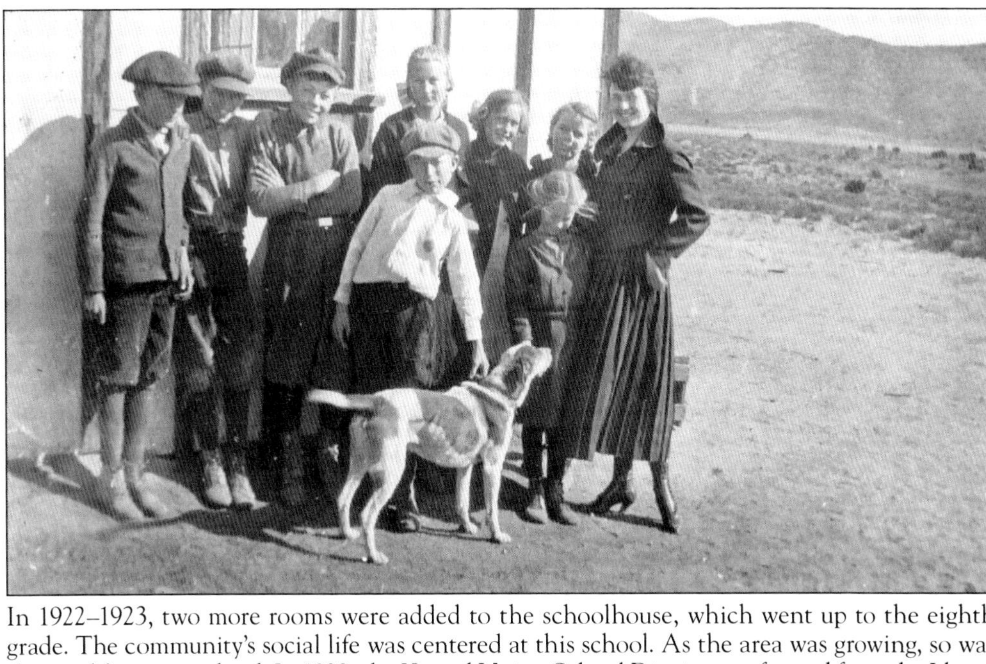

In 1922–1923, two more rooms were added to the schoolhouse, which went up to the eighth grade. The community's social life was centered at this school. As the area was growing, so was the need for a new school. In 1922, the Keppel Union School District was formed from the Llano, Almondale, Longview Schools, and the Alpine School District. (Courtesy of Littlerock Library, County of Los Angeles Public Library.)

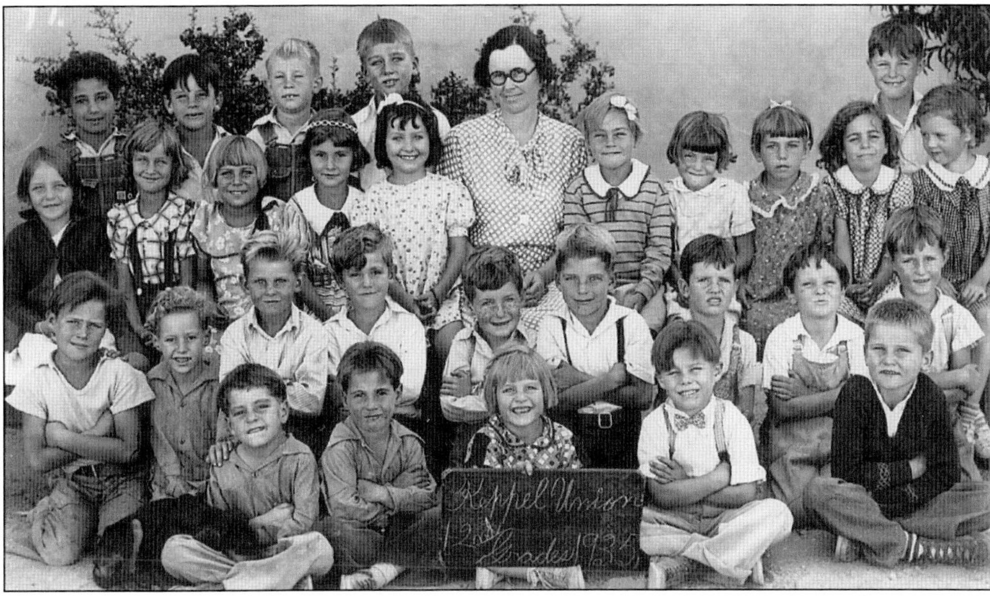

The new Keppel Union School, which was built in Littlerock on Pearblossom Highway, opened in 1928 at a cost of about $77,000. It was named after Mark Keppel, the superintendent of the Los Angeles County Schools. There were 65 pupils and three teachers. The district covered 305 square miles. Cora Sweet McCrumb is the little girl holding the 1935 class sign. (Courtesy of Cora Sweet McCrumb family.)

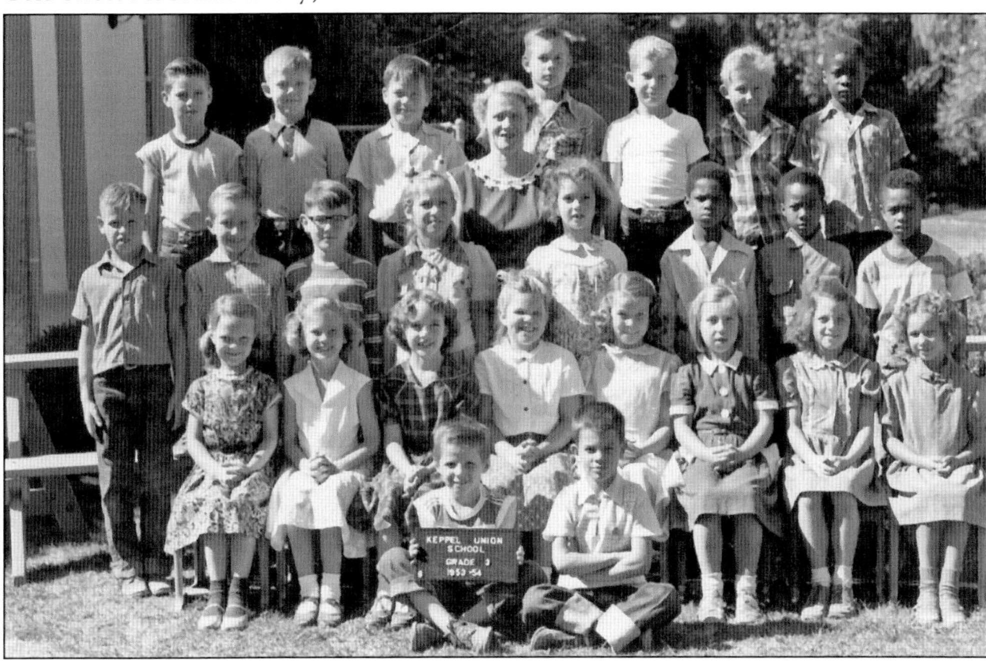

Henry Mentemeier helped build Keppel Union School, which is now Alpine Elementary. He hauled rocks and gravel from Little Rock Creek for the construction. He then went on to work as the school's custodian for 36 years until retiring. The schoolchildren remember him fondly. Phillip Snodgrass, who came to Littlerock in the early 1950s, is holding the class identification sign. (Courtesy of Charles Snodgrass family.)

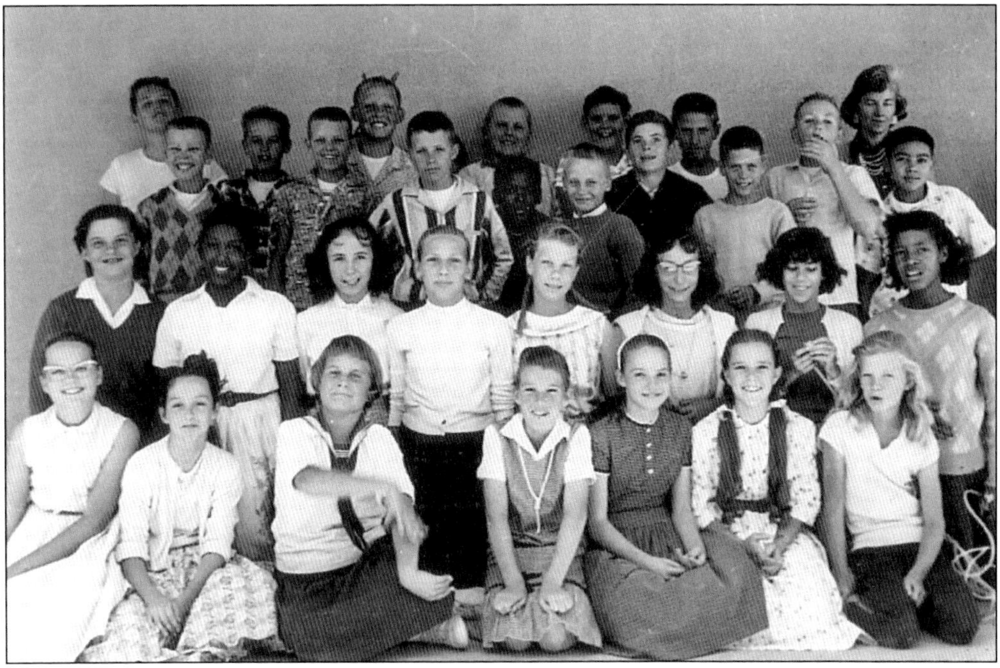

In 1959, an Alpine School class wrote individual essays. Dorothy Bones wrote: "I am 11 years old, and I have lived in Littlerock all my life and was born in Palmdale. I like Littlerock and hope to stay here as long as I can." Charles Snodgrass is in the last row, left of the boy holding his hand to his mouth. (Courtesy of Charles Snodgrass family.)

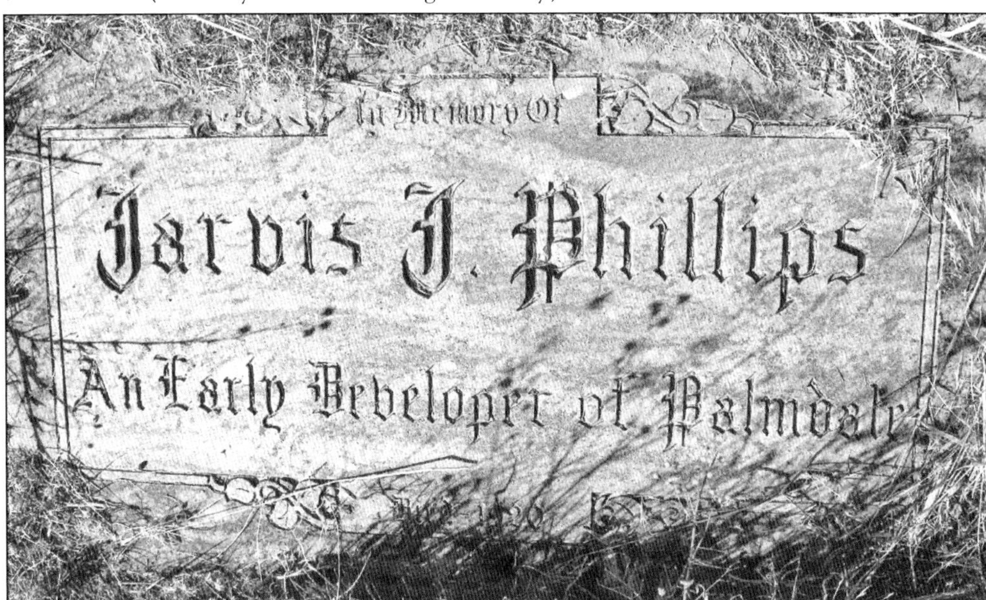

Located on Twentieth Street East, north of Avenue S, the Palmdale Cemetery is the final resting place for many pioneers. The only evidence of Palmenthal's existence today is the cemetery, the old schoolhouse, and some old canal ditches in the vicinity of Avenues R and S. This grave belongs to Jarvis Phillips, an early Palmdale developer. There are also many weathered wooden markers here. (Courtesy of the *Antelope Valley Press*.)

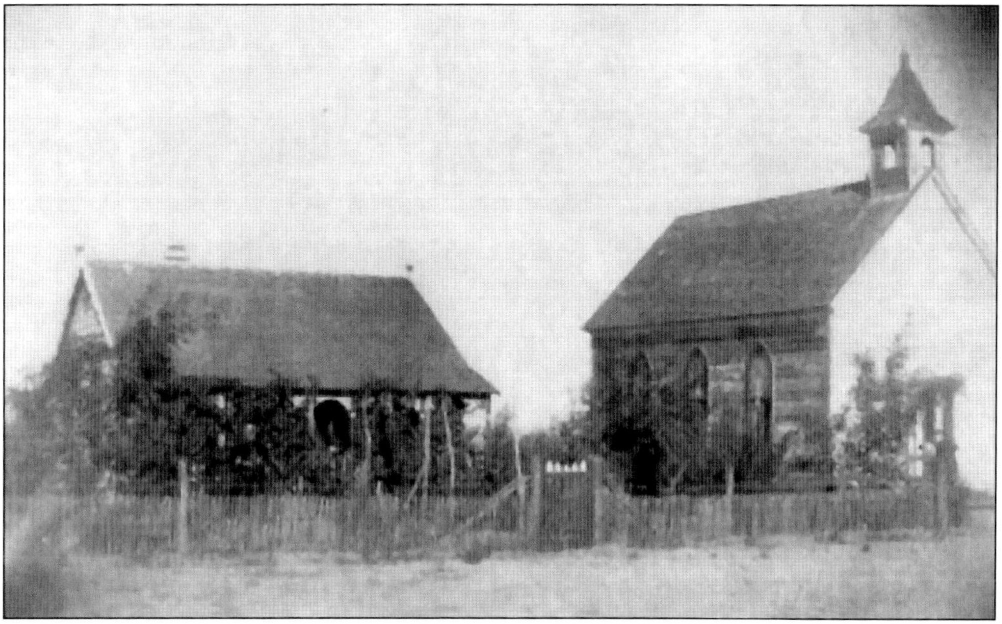

This is old "downtown" Palmenthal around 1889. It shows Rev. Christian Meyer's house and the Zion Evangelistic Lutheran Church. Before coming here, Reverend Meyer lived in South Australia, not far from another community called Palmenthal. He and his family are perhaps the only people to have lived in or visited two old Palmenthals. Meyer was pastor from 1888 to 1899. (Courtesy of Pacific Southwest District of Lutheran Church–Missouri Synod.)

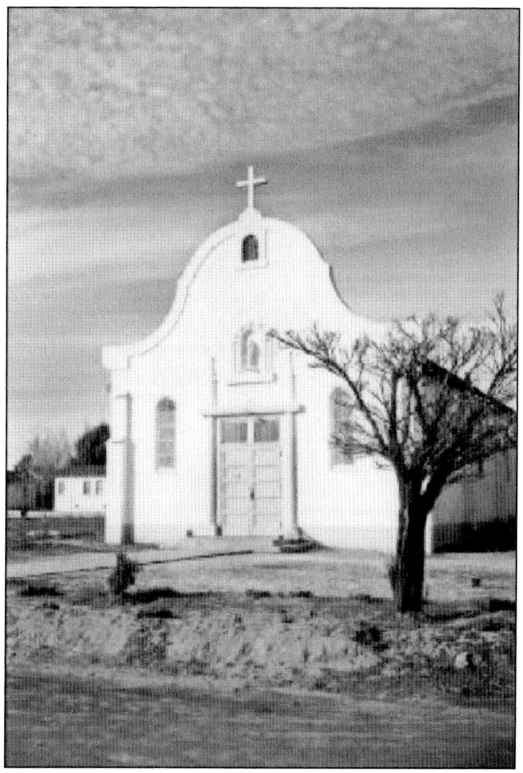

Located originally on the northwest corner of Ninth Street East and Avenue Q-10, St. Mary's Catholic Church was dedicated on October 10, 1924, by Los Angeles bishop John Cantwell. Before this time, priests would visit the community, or churchgoers attended mass in Lancaster. In 1906, Fr. Ralph Fuhr would visit Lancaster and Palmdale to conduct mass in German for non-English speakers. This view dates to 1947. (Courtesy of Dale DeBry.)

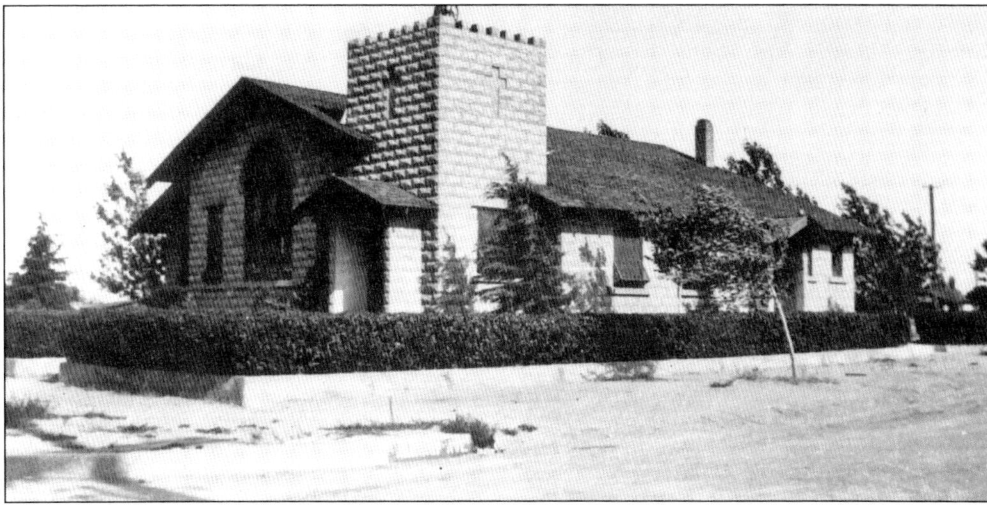

Palmdale's only other early church, the First Presbyterian Church, was located at what is now Ninth Street East and Palmdale Boulevard. It was organized on May 4, 1919. Rev. J. C. Wilson came to Palmdale in December 1919 and was the church's first pastor. It was the only Protestant church in Palmdale for years. It was known as the Community Presbyterian Church until 1952. (Courtesy of WAVHS.)

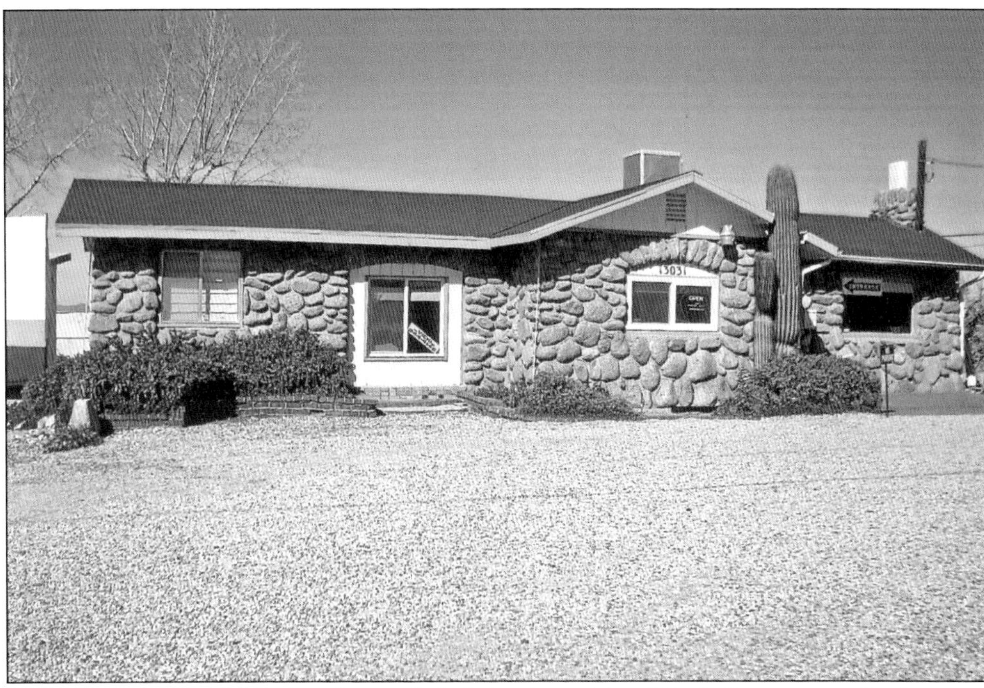

By 1951–1952, Palmdale's churches included the Assembly of God, Community Presbyterian, St. Mary's, the Foursquare Church, and the Holy Gospel Church. Littlerock had the Community Church, and the Union Church was established in Pearblossom. St. Andrew's Priory (now Abbey) relocated from communist China and moved to Valyermo in 1955. The Roberson real estate office in Pearblossom served as a Sunday school during the 1930s.

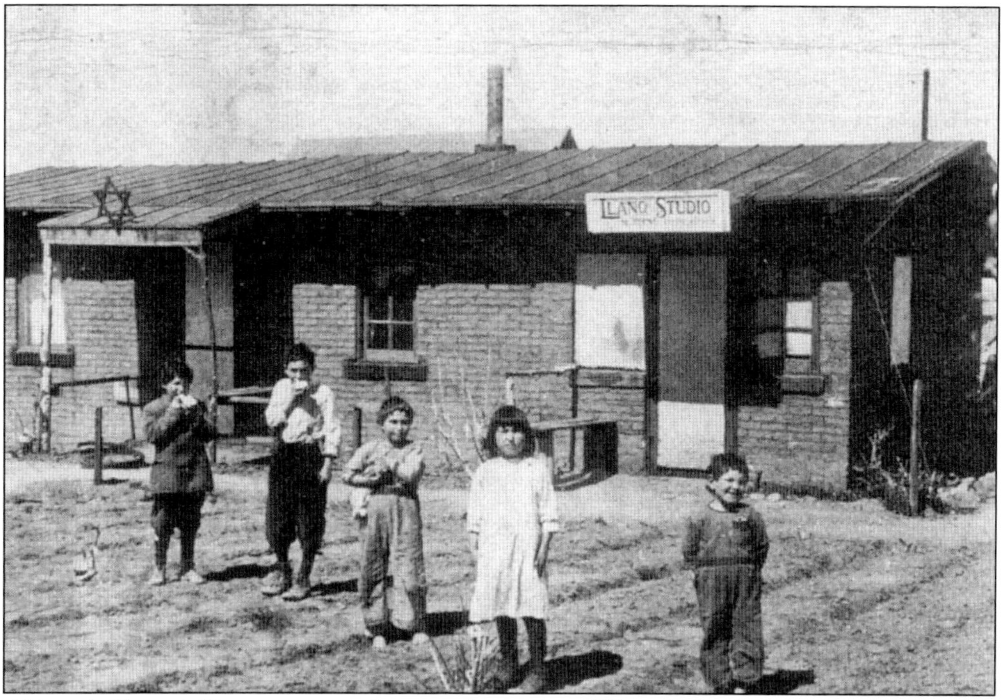

Although Llano del Rio was not a religious colony, Meyer Elkins let his faith be known by placing a Star of David above the doorway of his photography studio. This was probably the first time that a Star of David was placed on a building in the Antelope Valley. There were also other Jewish families who lived in the colony. (Courtesy of Phillip Elkins.)

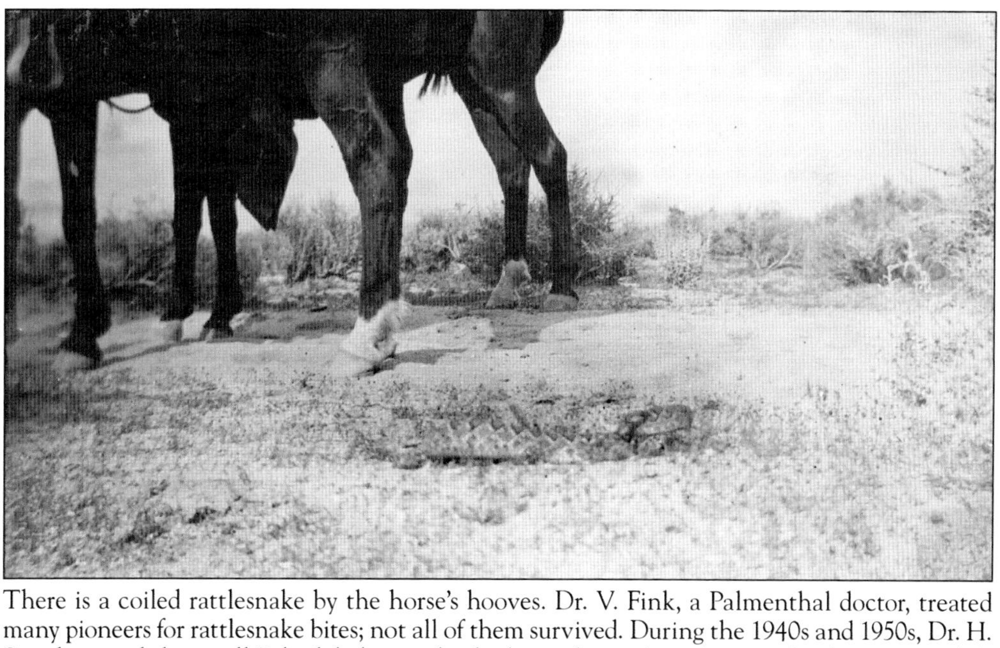

There is a coiled rattlesnake by the horse's hooves. Dr. V. Fink, a Palmenthal doctor, treated many pioneers for rattlesnake bites; not all of them survived. During the 1940s and 1950s, Dr. H. Snook owned the small Palmdale hospital, which was located on Avenue Q-9 between Eighth and Ninth Streets East, in the vicinity of the present-day Poncitlán Square. Some other doctors included F. Brockett, Emerson Savage, and H. Senseman.

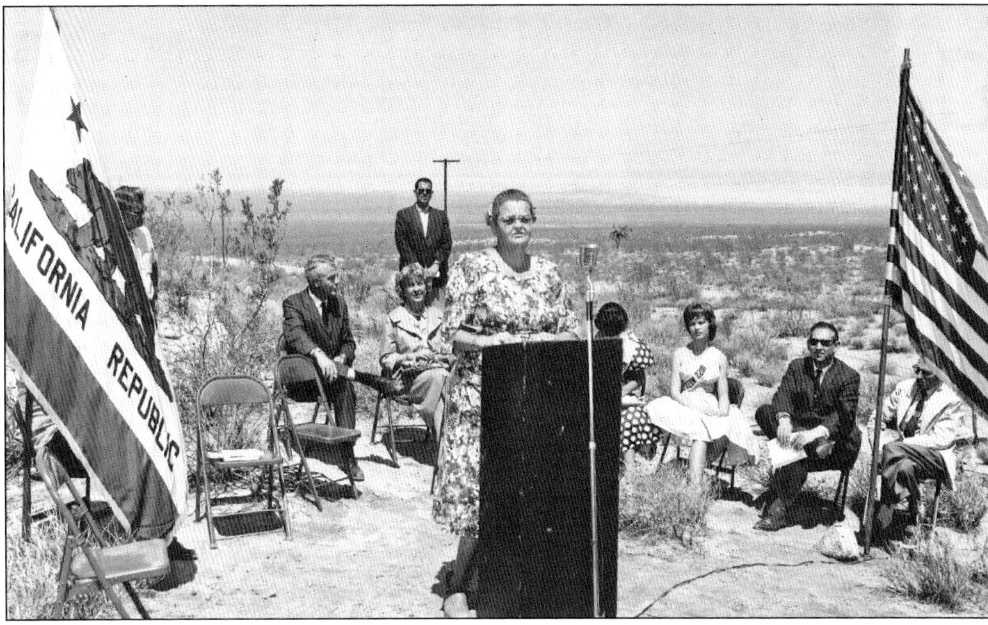

Mary Swan, shown right of the podium (1961), was the daughter of Dr. Alfred Swan of Pearblossom, who is generally credited with having been the first to propose a regional hospital. Swan reputedly saved Chiang Kai-shek's life in 1928 when he almost died from a tooth extraction. Swan came here in 1948. The old Swan Memorial Hospital in Palmdale was named after him. Swan's wife, Mary Ferris, was a renowned artist.

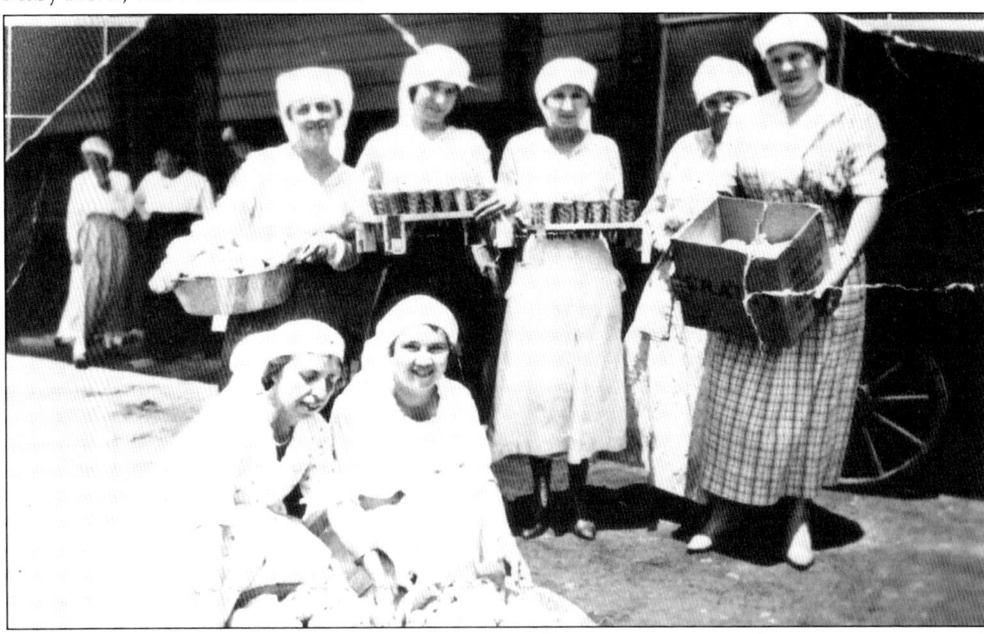

In November 1917, an auxiliary of the American Red Cross was organized at Moore's Mercantile in Palmdale with more than 50 members. Dances and baseball games were held as fund-raisers so the members could purchase sewing machines. The members made shirts, sweaters, socks, scarves, slippers, and hankies. These Red Cross members are at the old Mojave railroad ready to give sandwiches to soldiers as they passed by.

Albert Ritter was a soldier in 1917 (Camp Mills, New York). Glen Settle recalled that as a child, it was exciting living next to the railroad during World War I, as troop trains were passing through day and night. When the armistice was signed, Palmdale celebrated most of the night. Residents beat big wash tubs to make loud noises, and those with cars honked their horns as long as possible.

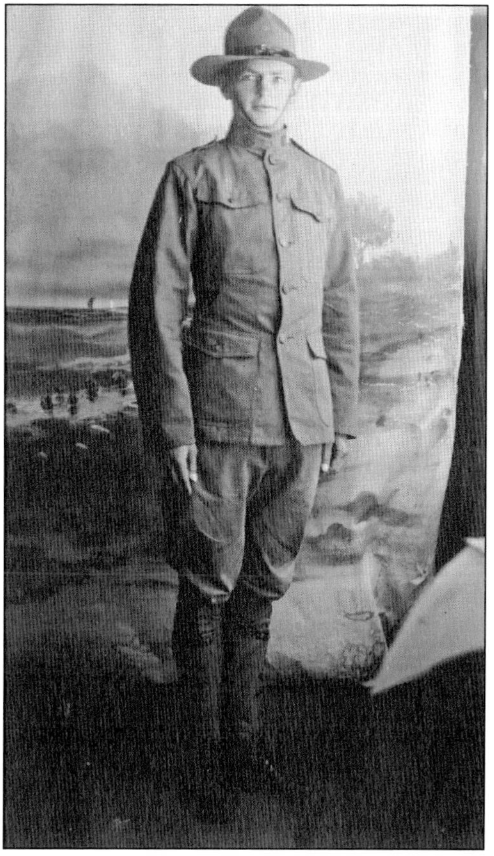

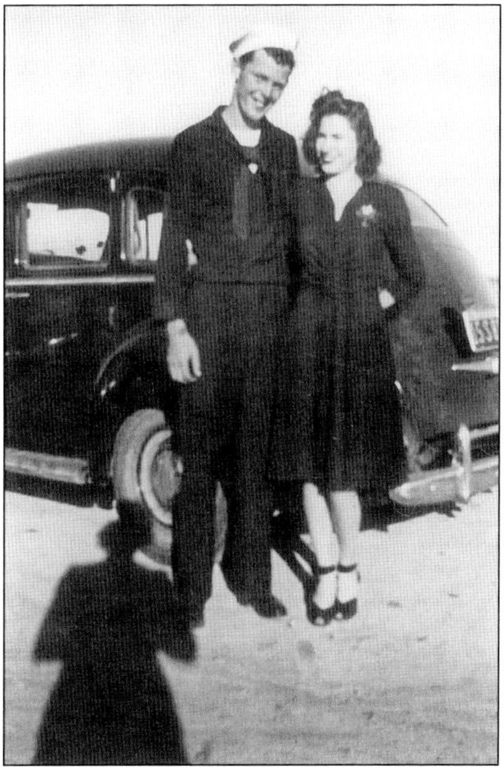

George Bones Jr. was born in Littlerock in 1925. He attended grade school in Littlerock and then Antelope Valley High School. In 1943, Bones started sailing with the U.S. Merchant Marine Service. After training, he was assigned to the Pacific Rim and later departed to the Philippines. At the war's conclusion, he returned to Littlerock to his wife, Dorothy Zink. (Courtesy of Denece Bones Parsons.)

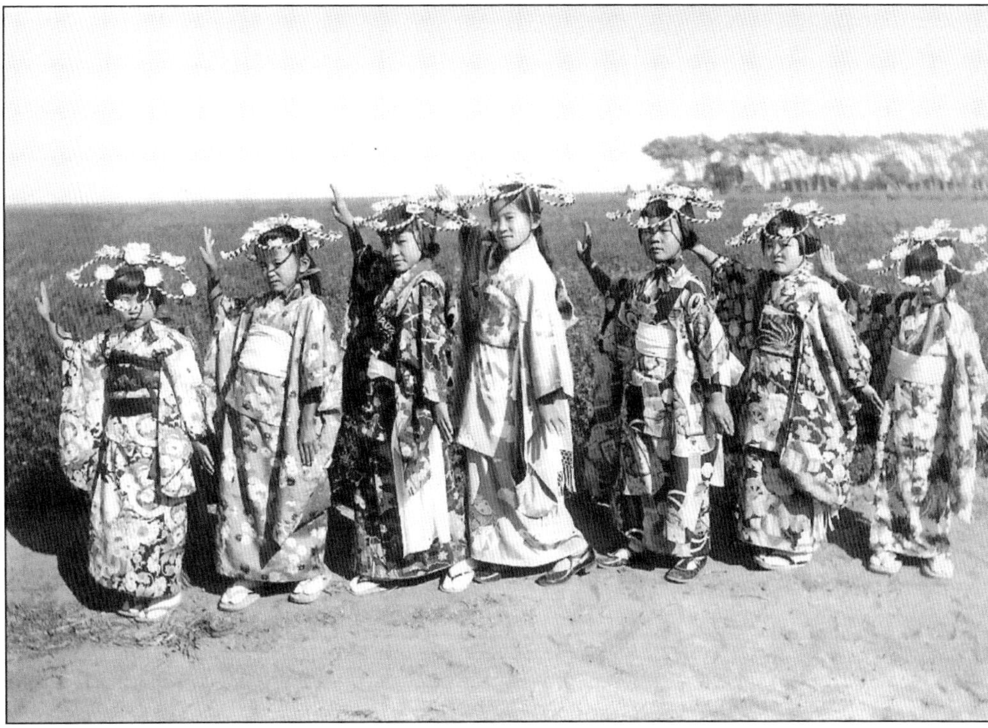

In 1920, Masakichi Hamada was an orchardist who lived in Palmdale with his family and two hired Japanese coworkers. Japanese farmers began settling in the Antelope Valley after 1910 and lived around Eightieth Street West and Avenue D in the Rogers area. The settlers formed a Japanese Farmer's Association in 1916 and built a community hall that was used as a church and a Japanese-language school. (Courtesy of Tom Shiokari.)

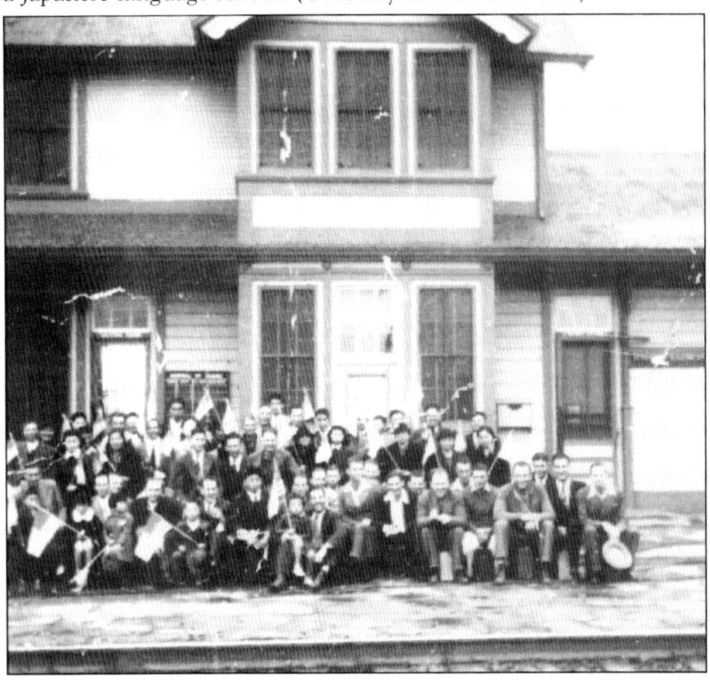

A group of local World War II army inductees and relatives are shown waiting for the train in Palmdale. This photograph was taken by Yoshio Ekimoto, a longtime valley resident, who died during the writing of this book. Yoshio and his family were among 85 Japanese immigrants and their American-born children loaded onto buses in May 1942 at the Palmdale depot and taken to Arizona. (Courtesy of Yoshio Ekimoto.)

Eight

Mining, Water Resources, Ranching, Disasters, and Protection

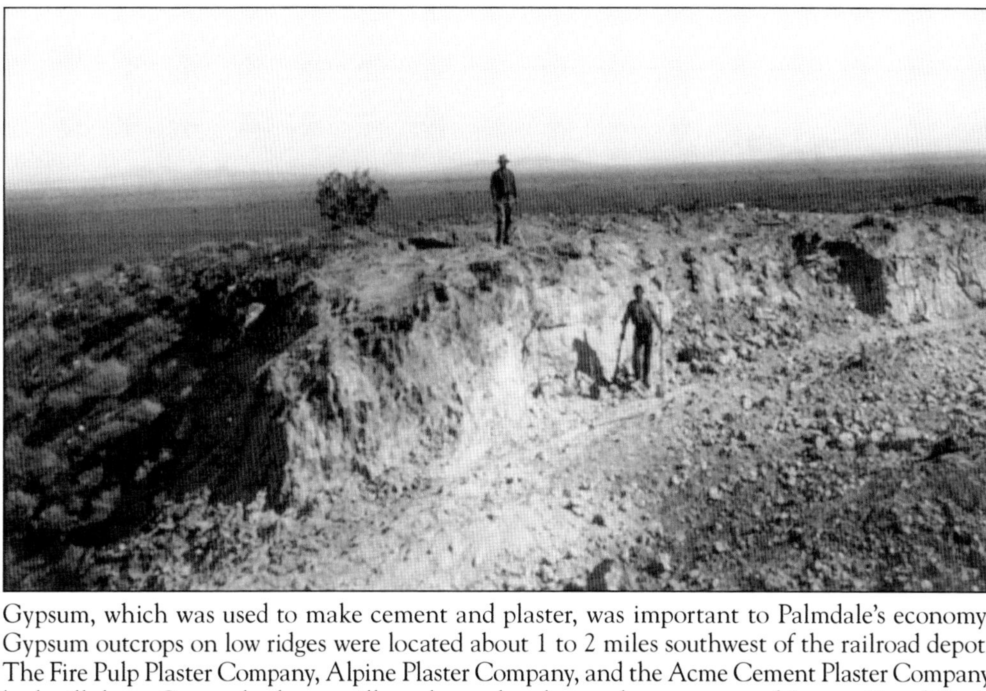

Gypsum, which was used to make cement and plaster, was important to Palmdale's economy. Gypsum outcrops on low ridges were located about 1 to 2 miles southwest of the railroad depot. The Fire Pulp Plaster Company, Alpine Plaster Company, and the Acme Cement Plaster Company had mills here. One early plaster mill was located at the northwest corner of Avenue R and Sixth Street East. (Courtesy of U.S. Geological Survey.)

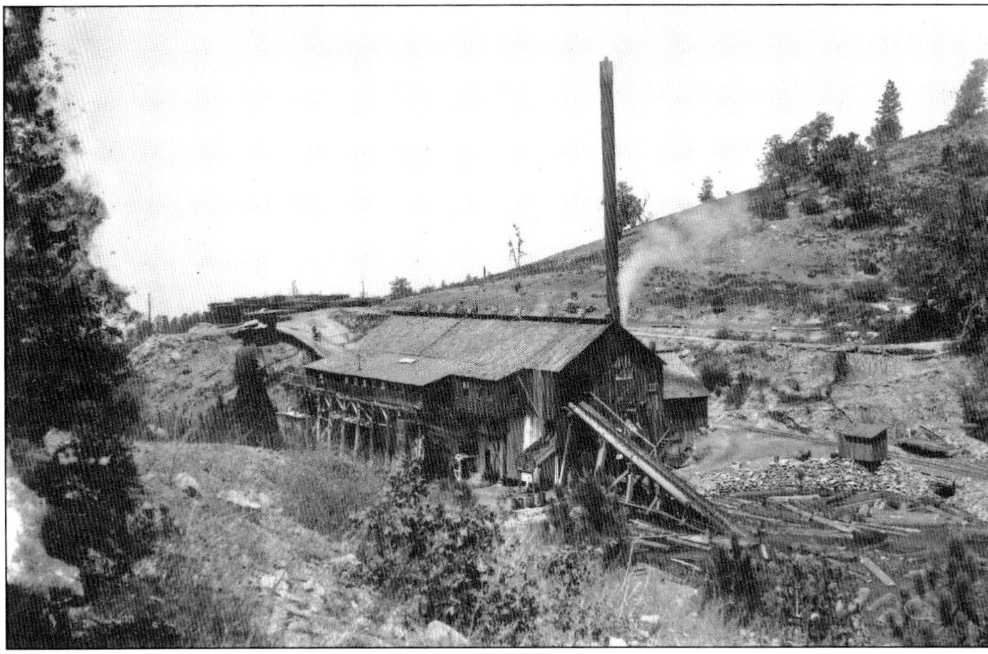

Located on the slopes of Mount Baden-Powell at almost 7,600 feet in the San Gabriel Mountains is the Big Horn Gold Mine. Its peak period of operation was from 1903 to 1906, when it employed more than 50 men. Supplies for the small community were brought in from Palmdale and hauled as far up the mountain as the road went and then taken to the mine by a pack team.

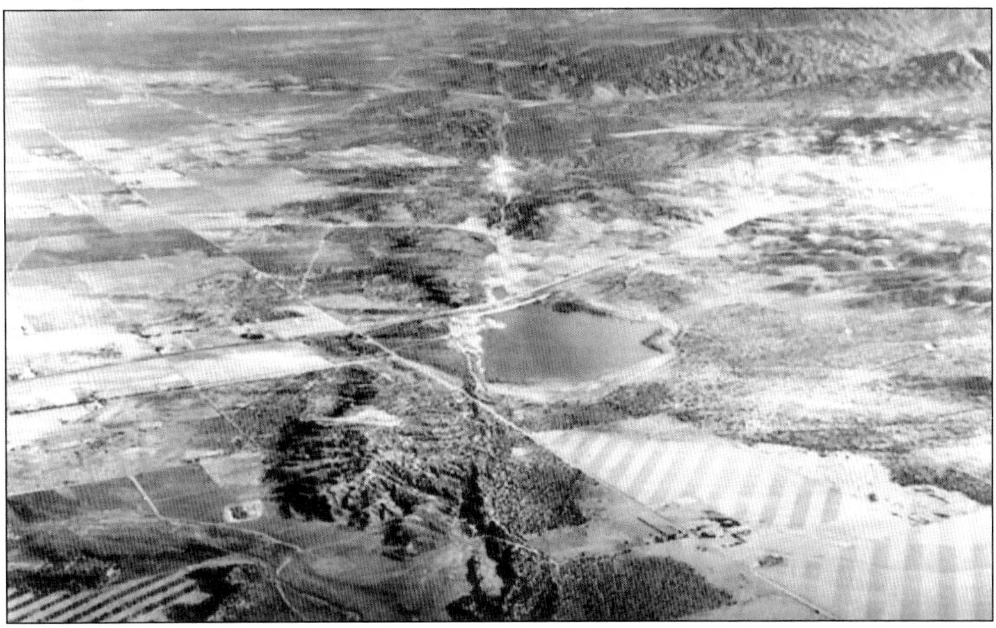

The highly active San Andreas Fault forms a straight, trench-like fault, running through the mountains and hills along the southwest margin of the western Mojave Desert. One of the best places to view the fault is on the Antelope Valley 14 Freeway, just north of Avenue S. On June 29, 1925, the Santa Barbara Earthquake struck, causing the large depot clock in Palmdale to stop exactly at 6:44 a.m.

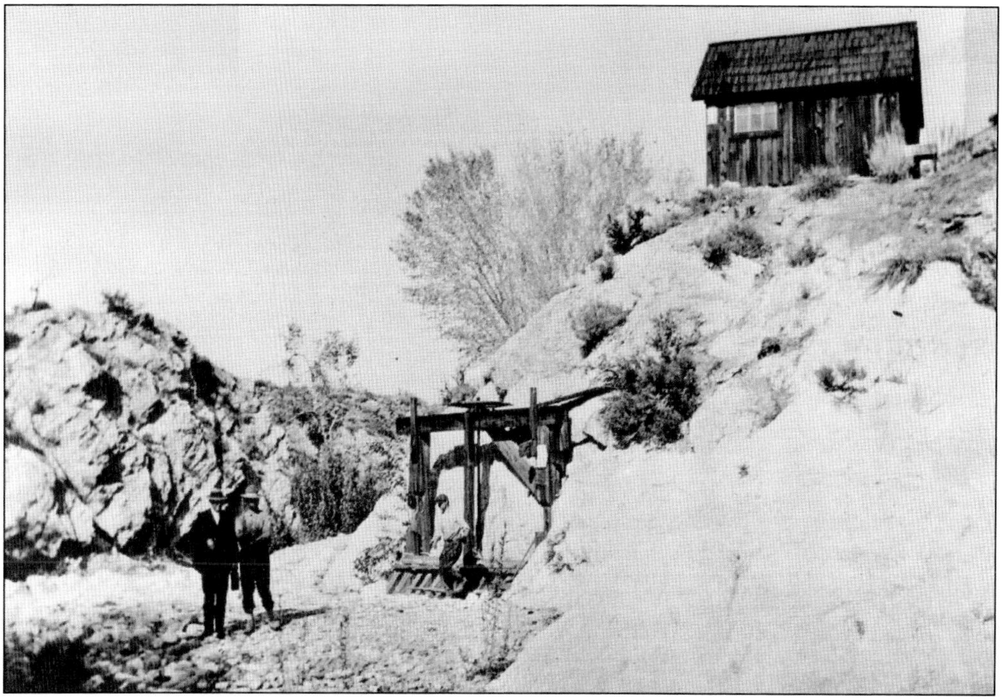

Paul Schoeller (right), a surveyor, and another man are examining the headgates for Palmdale's water supply (1896). He was a prominent resident and a strong community supporter. Schoeller's life took a dramatic turn when he was convicted of falsifying some Palmdale Irrigation District records. Palmdale was divided over his conviction, as some thought he had been railroaded. He died in prison in 1951. (Courtesy of *Antelope Valley Press*.)

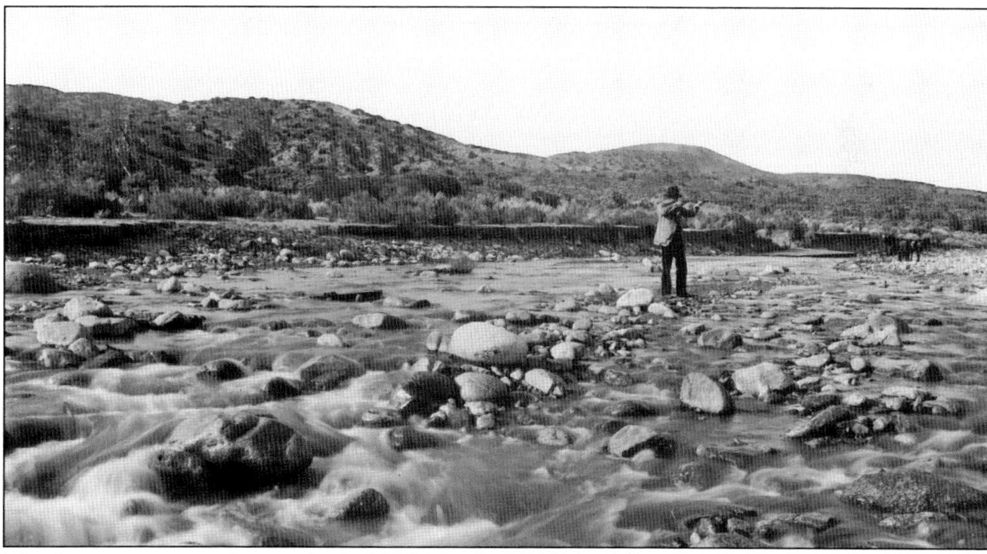

This brave man is wading in Little Rock Wash, which could be quite treacherous at times. The Antelope Valley floor can experience flood hazards during periods of heavy rain or melting snowpack from surrounding mountains. The major watercourses flowing through Palmdale are Amargosa Creek and Little Rock Wash. (Courtesy of University of Southern California, on behalf of the USC Special Collections.)

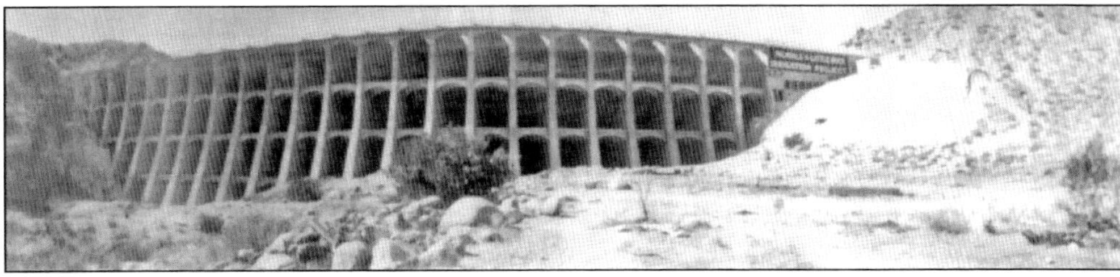

In addition to being of great historical significance to the development of south Antelope Valley, the Littlerock Dam is also significant in the history of structural engineering. Designed by John S. Eastwood, the Littlerock Dam was built for the Littlerock and Palmdale Irrigation Districts between late 1922 and early 1924. At the time of its construction, it was the tallest reinforced concrete, multiple-arched dam in the world.

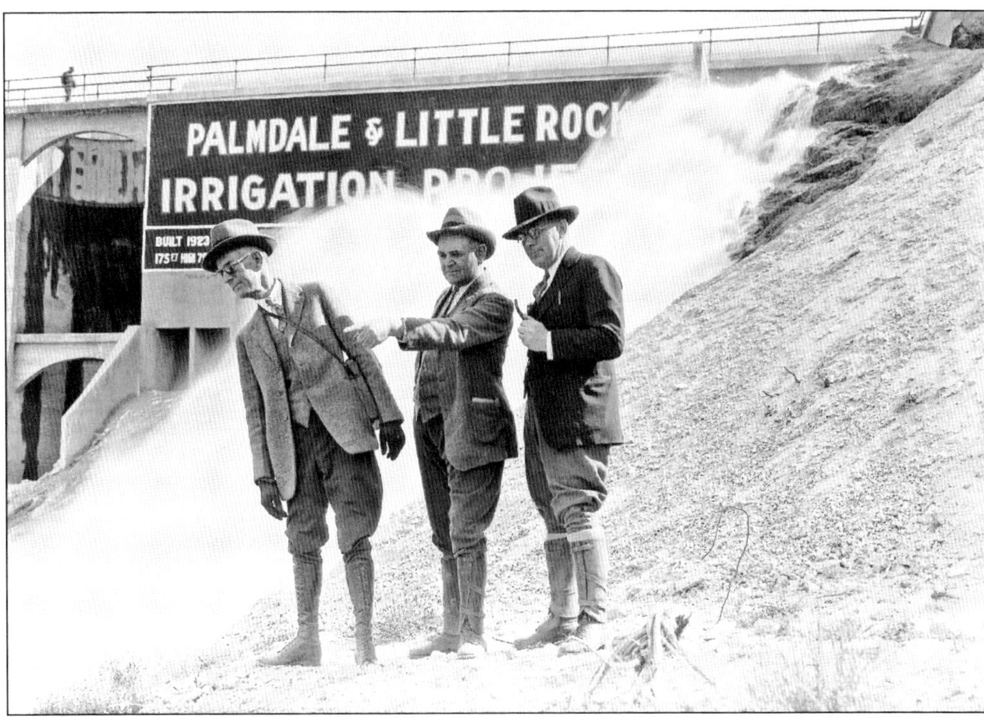

In 1923, in Harold, there was a large sign that read "This way to the Littlerock Dam, the highest multiple-arched dam in the world, being built by the Bent brothers." The three men at the Littlerock Dam in April 1926 are, from left to right, Arthur Bent, W. C. Petchner, and George Clements. (Courtesy of University of Southern California, on behalf of the USC Special Collections.)

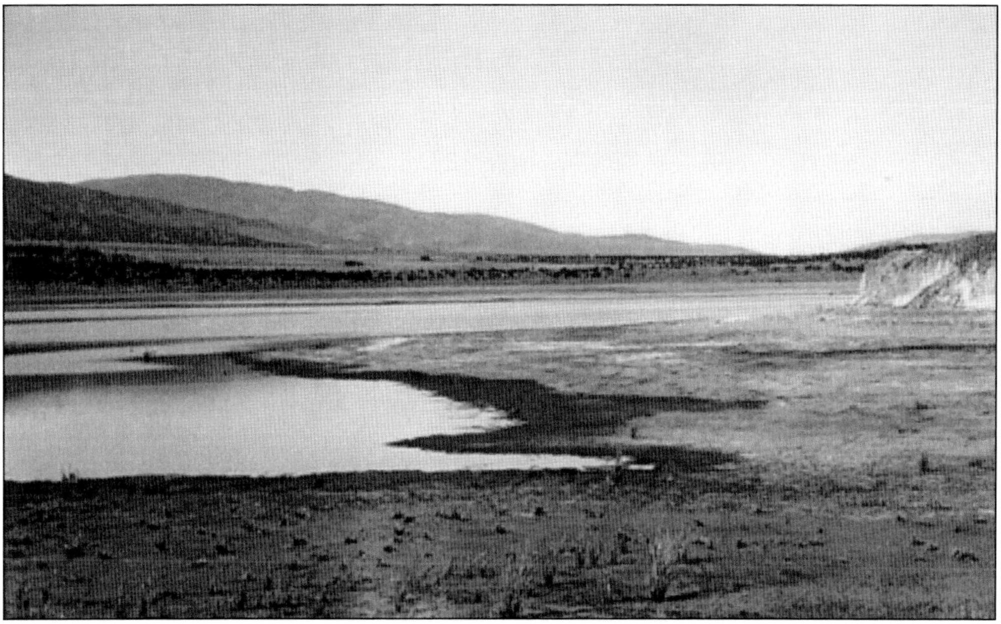

Like most desert towns, Palmdale would not have been able to exist if not for water. Before the Littlerock Dam was constructed, there was the Palmdale Reservoir, which was completed in 1897. It was originally called Lake Yuna or the Harold or Alpine Reservoir. Workers with mule teams were paid 50¢ per day to scrape out the reservoir. This scene dates to January 1920. (Courtesy of U.S. Geological Survey.)

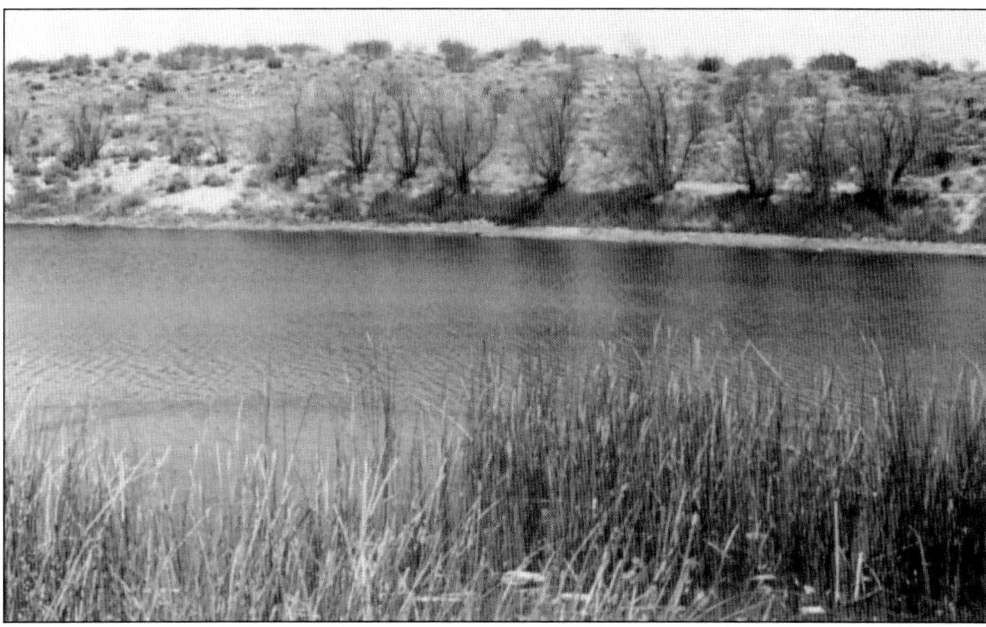

Lake Una got its name from the nearby Palmdale Reservoir. The reservoir was originally named Lake Yuna, in honor of a sister of the Cole brothers. That name was later transferred to the nearby small lake and changed to Lake Una. It is possible that the depression in the ground that created the supposedly "bottomless" Lake Una was caused by the awesome Tejon Earthquake of January 1857.

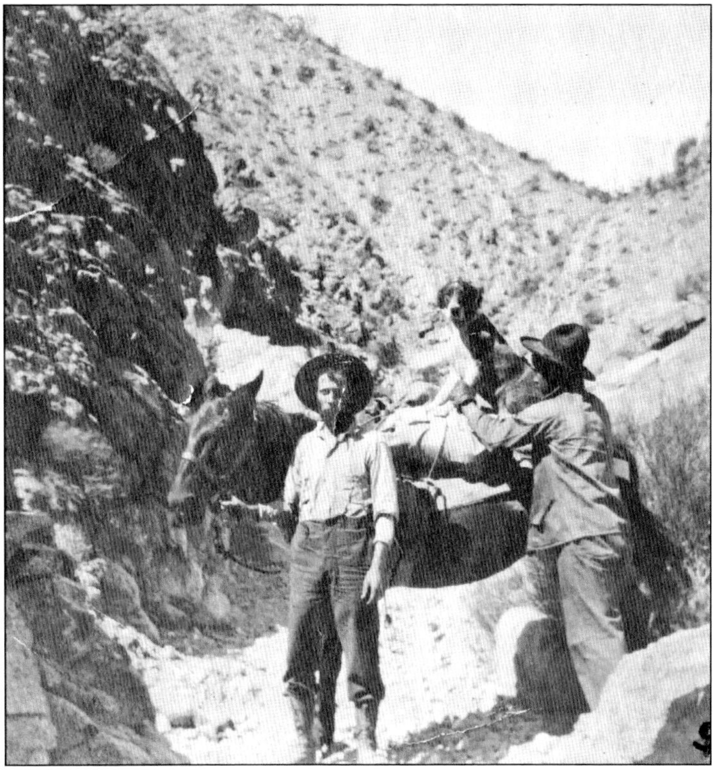

From 1908 through 1913, approximately 6,000 men helped to construct the Los Angeles Aqueduct, which drew water from more than 200 miles away in the Owens Valley. Antelopian Winfield McNamee (left), with a coworker, like many others, toiled over rugged mountains and across sterile deserts, digging through hills, laying cement, driving tractors, hauling sections of pipes, and working with picks and shovels. The aqueduct's construction was also important for Palmdale's economy.

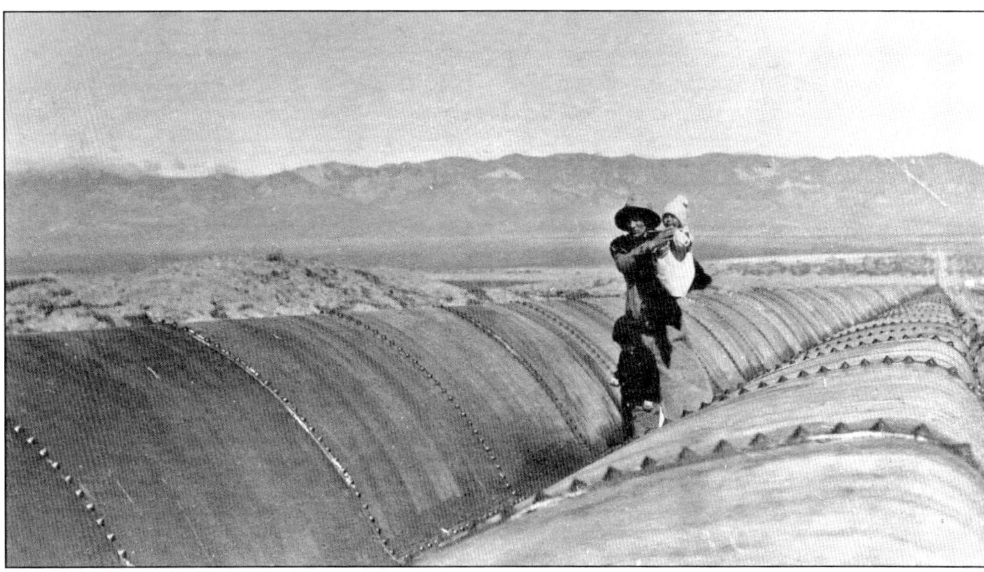

Even after the Los Angeles Aqueduct was finished, workers from the Antelope Valley had to maintain its pipes. Mrs. Nelson and her two children, John and Joe, are treading across a collapsed pipeline section in the Antelope Valley. One of the aqueduct's major engineers—besides chief engineer William Mulholland—was Joseph Lippincott. He stayed at the Palmdale Inn several times after the aqueduct's completion on trips for inspection purposes.

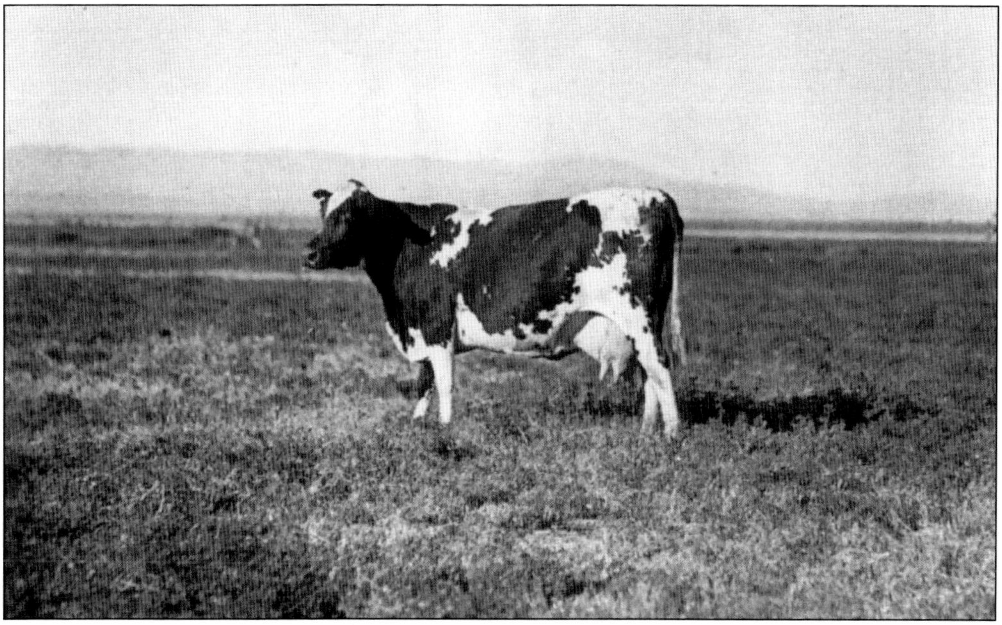

Although most Palmdale farms had their own small milk houses and did their own milking, several large dairies developed. The Carl Johnson family's Lake View Dairy was located in the Ana Verde area. Lake View Dairy supplied lunch milk for the Palmdale Grammar School on Tenth Street East. Some other dairies included the Palmdale Dairy and the Key Dairy. This is a prize-winning cow at Llano del Rio around 1915.

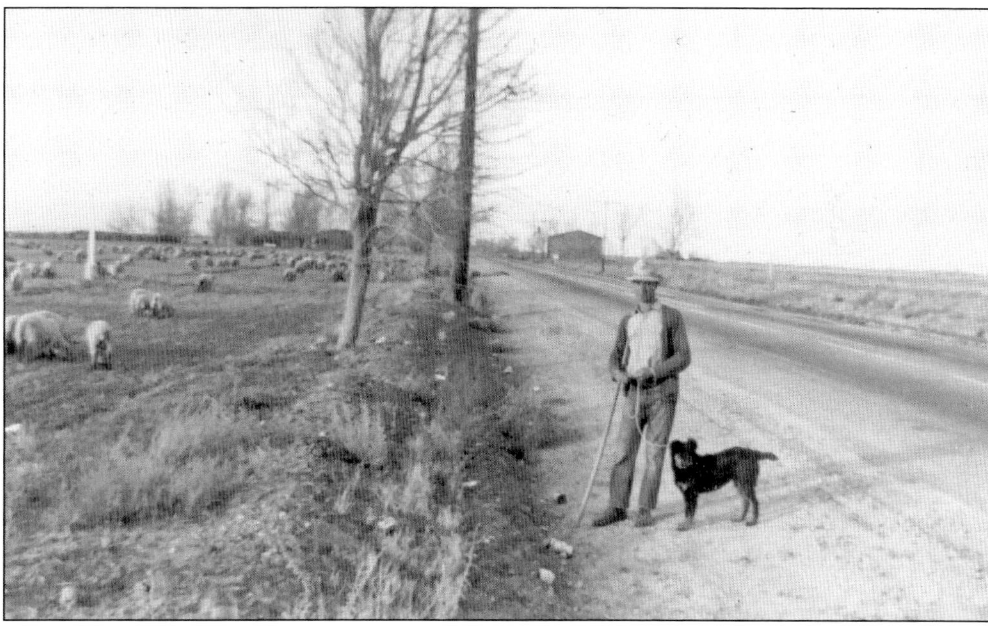

Cattlemen during the pioneer days did not look upon the seasonal migrations of sheep herds across the valley with great joy. Thousands of sheep close-cropped the available forage and could, in a short time, make an area temporarily useless for cattle pastures. In 1906, cattlemen said there would be "bloody" battles if the Basque sheepherders did not leave. This view dates to the late 1950s. (Courtesy of Charles Snodgrass family.)

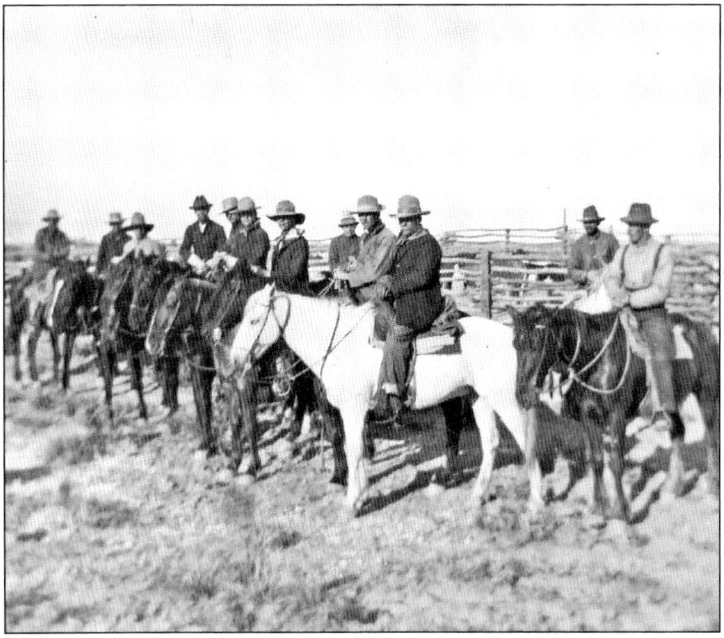

The cattle industry was important in the valley from 1886 to 1910. Some important cattle ranchers were Bob Pallet, Irving and Emery Kidd, and George Jane. Emery Kidd recalls driving cattle herds from Big Rock to Elizabeth Lake and even beyond Lake Hughes, which was about a three-day trip. The Palmdale railroad depot had cattle pens for several years. This photograph shows Harry Butterworth's corral north of Lancaster.

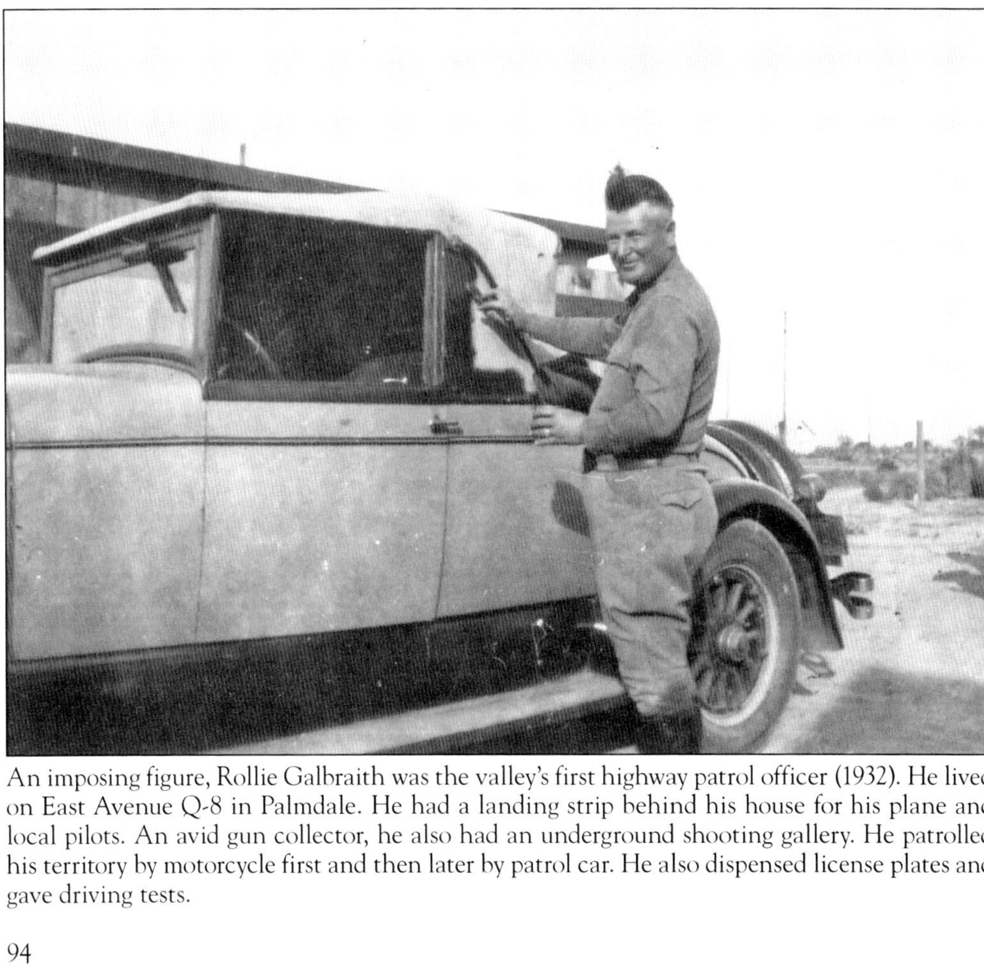

An imposing figure, Rollie Galbraith was the valley's first highway patrol officer (1932). He lived on East Avenue Q-8 in Palmdale. He had a landing strip behind his house for his plane and local pilots. An avid gun collector, he also had an underground shooting gallery. He patrolled his territory by motorcycle first and then later by patrol car. He also dispensed license plates and gave driving tests.

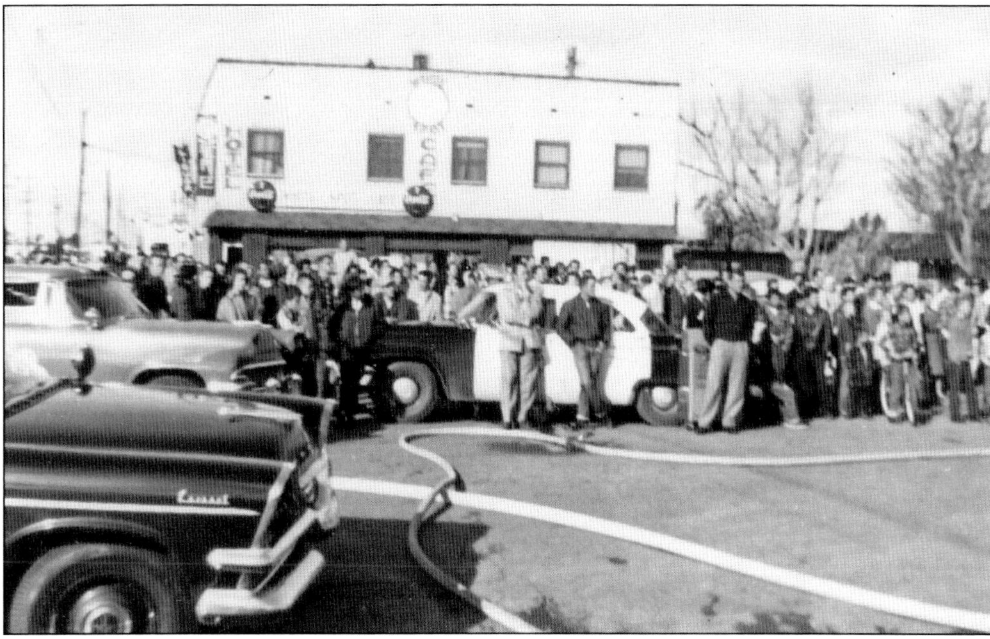

Local sheriffs are working hard to hold back a large, curious crowd in front of the popular White Spot Café during a fire on Sierra Highway in 1956. Palmdale and Harold's pioneer constables, such as Frank Dowler and Mr. Mitchell, were kept busy chasing burglars, horse thieves, cattle rustlers, hobos, and the occasional murderer. They often had second jobs as blacksmiths or hotel keepers. (Courtesy of Charles Snodgrass family.)

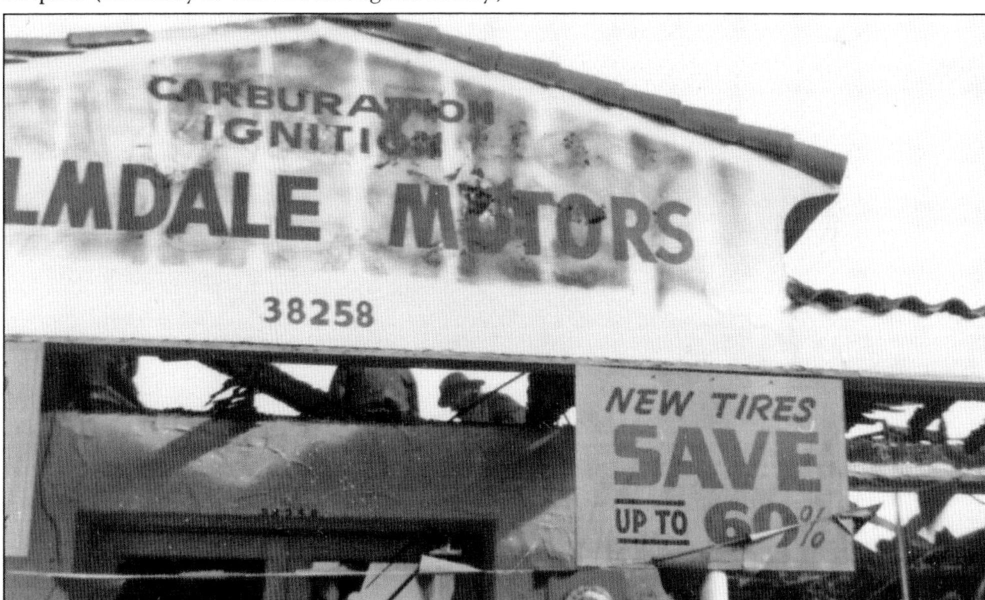

Fires were constant problems in the Palmdale area. The volunteer Palmdale Fire Protection Department was formed in December 1923. In November 1926, there was a fire in the Chinatown area of Palmdale; this is the only mention of a local Chinese section. The devastating fire shown here in 1956 occurred at the Palmdale Motors Garage on Sierra Highway near Avenue Q-10. Note the fireman at work. (Courtesy of Charles Snodgrass family.)

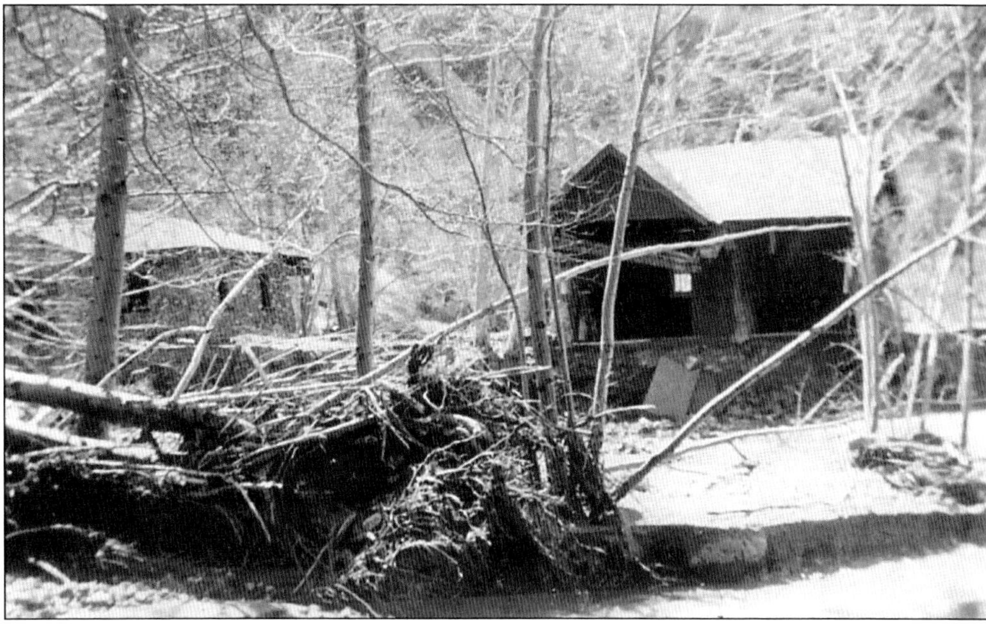

Heavy floods were recorded in 1891 and 1910 in the Littlerock area. Floods turned the streets into gushing rivers, tearing down wooden structures and holding townspeople captive until the water subsided. Due to freak weather conditions, some of the worst flooding occurred during several days in March 1938, which damaged the Littlerock Dam and cabins in the Valyermo and Big Rock Creek areas. (Courtesy of Cora Sweet McCrumb family.)

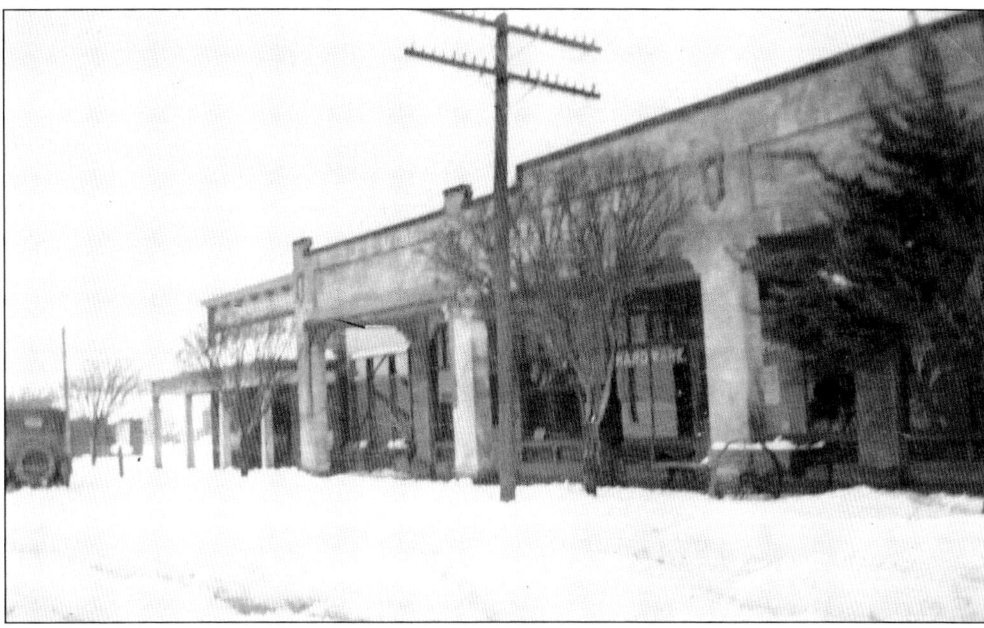

Snow days could be fun in the old days but not when they stranded people in homes and hotels. Without proper snow removal equipment, traveling became very dangerous. This snowstorm took place in downtown Palmdale on Sierra Highway in January 1922. Some pioneers stated that more recent snowfalls do not compare to the old days when 2 feet or more of snow were common occurrences.

Nine

Fun and Games

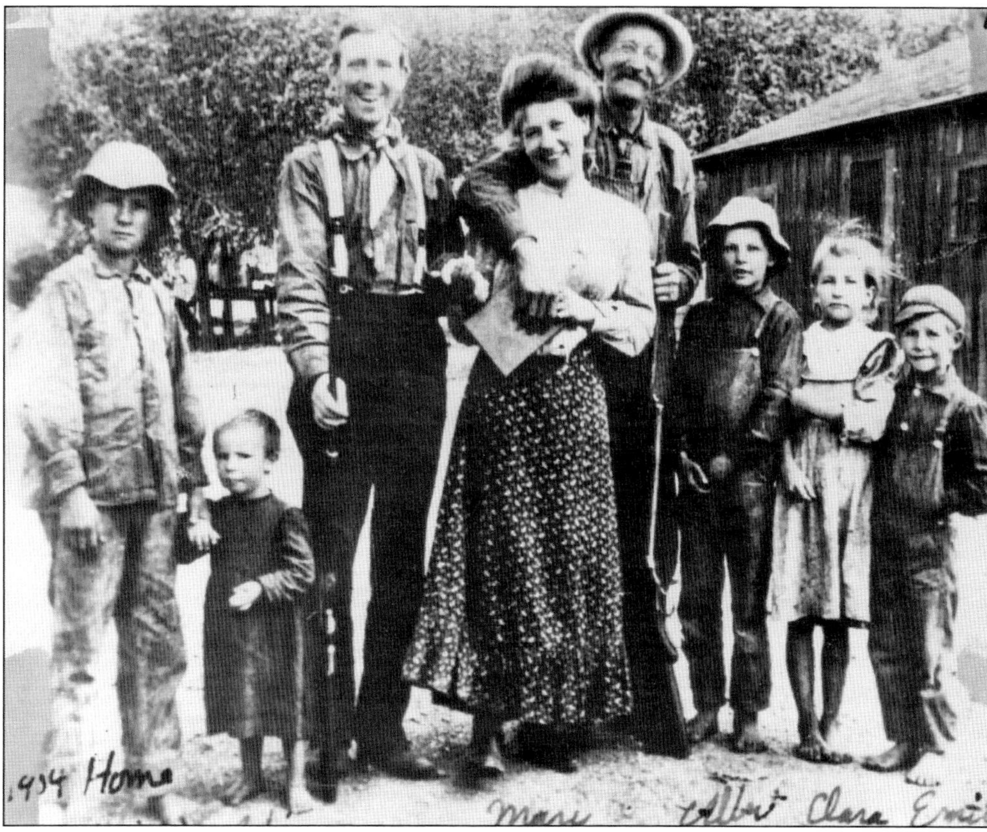

John G. Ritter and his wife, Anna Marie, moved to Palmenthal in 1886. They were forced to leave their home when water problems developed. The family later settled in Leona Valley. They planted grapevines on their homestead and erected a large winery of rock and brick hauled from Valyermo. Around 1904, the happy pioneers are, from left to right, Willie, Johnny, John Ritter Sr., Mary, unidentified, Albert, Clara, and Emil.

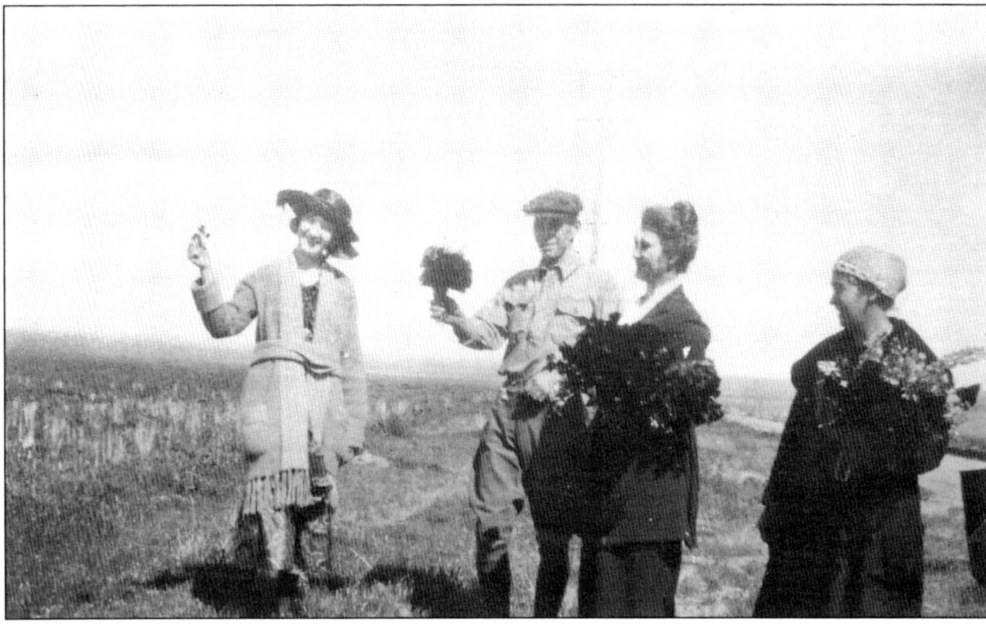

Mabel Jones and Maude Settle are enjoying some local poppy fields during the 1920s. Early explorer and trailblazer John C. Frémont noted the abundance of poppies in his journals written during his exploration of California in 1844. The California poppy (*Eschscholtzia californica*) was designated the state flower in 1903. In addition to the west end of the Antelope Valley, poppies also bloomed in Palmdale and surrounding areas.

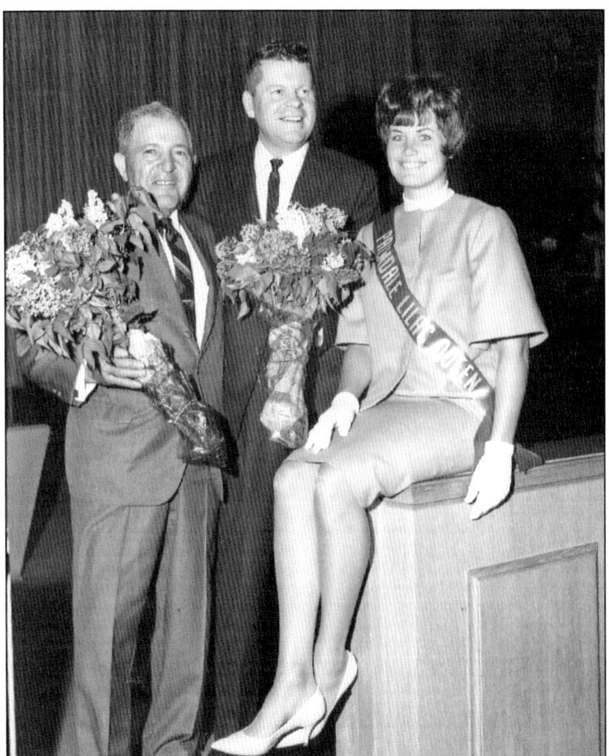

In 1947, the first Lilac Show was displayed in the store window of Gil Morse's Market at Sierra Highway and Avenue Q-7. It was organized by the Morses, Mr. Harris, and Mrs. Wilson of the Palmdale Woman's Club. The chamber of commerce later sponsored it. Pictured from left to right are councilman Domenic Massari, supervisor Warren Dorn, and the 1966 Lilac Queen, Heidi Harris. (Courtesy of Palmdale City Library.)

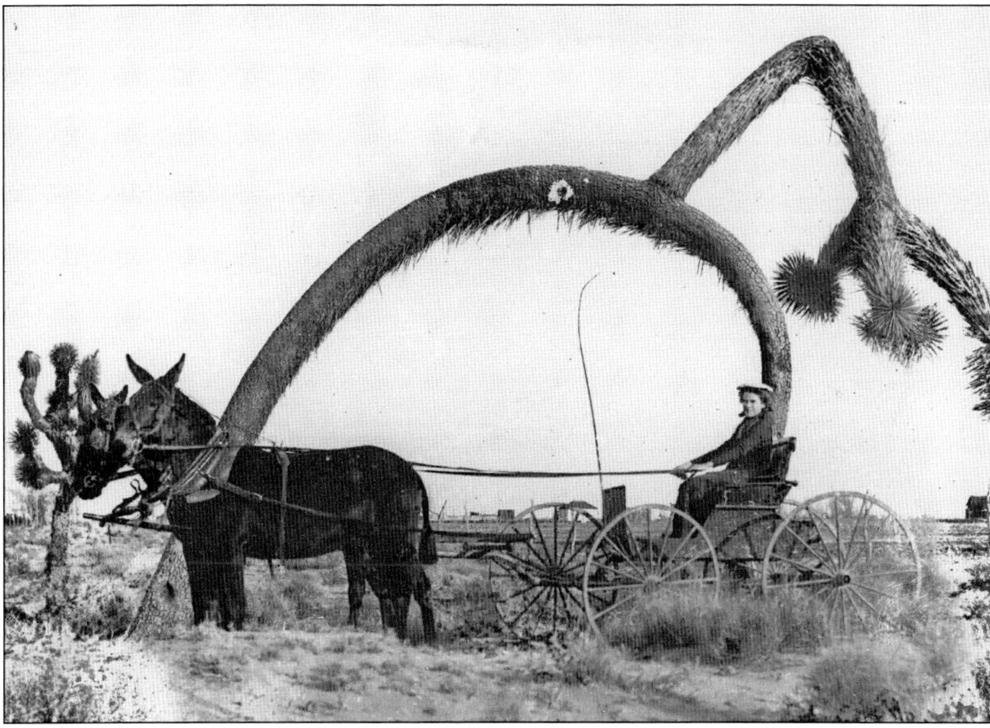

Sometimes Palmdale residents would take a buggy ride to Lancaster's famous arched Joshua tree (pictured here in 1903). Joshua tree wood was used for fuel, fence posts, and during World War I, for splints. Several Palmenthal pioneers, such as the Nagels, built large sheds completely from Joshua trees. One did not always need an ax to chop down a tree; sometimes dynamite was placed in the tree's center to blow it up.

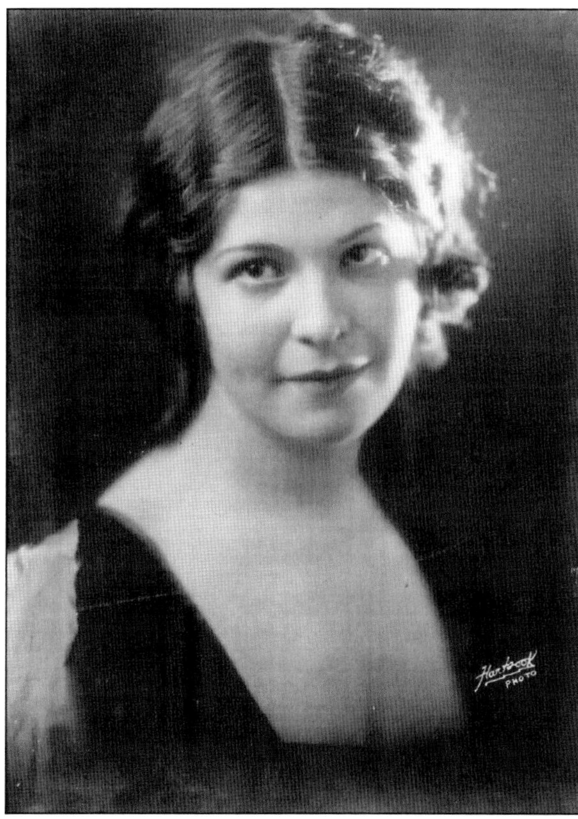

Cecile Kibre Bosworth was the second wife of Hobart Bosworth, the "Dean of Hollywood Cinema." She worked at early movie studios and founded Hollywood's first research department. In 1950, she moved to Littlerock and became a longtime community activist. Among her many local achievements, she was proudest of opening the Littlerock Library branch in 1957. (Courtesy of Littlerock Library, County of Los Angeles Public Library.)

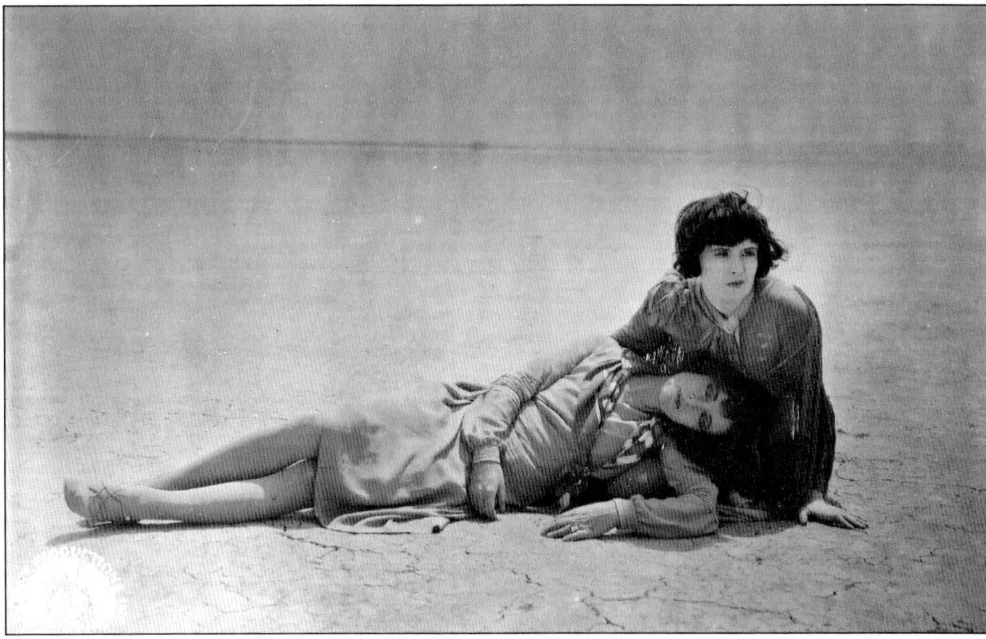

In June 1927, a troupe of 25 actors stopped in Palmdale for several days to film the movie *Lightning*, based on a Zane Gray novel. The cast and directors stayed at the Palmdale Inn. The film was shot in Palmdale, the dry lakes area, and Randsburg. An airplane also came to town to film the movie. Actresses Jobyna Ralson (left) and Margaret Livingston are shown at a local dry lake.

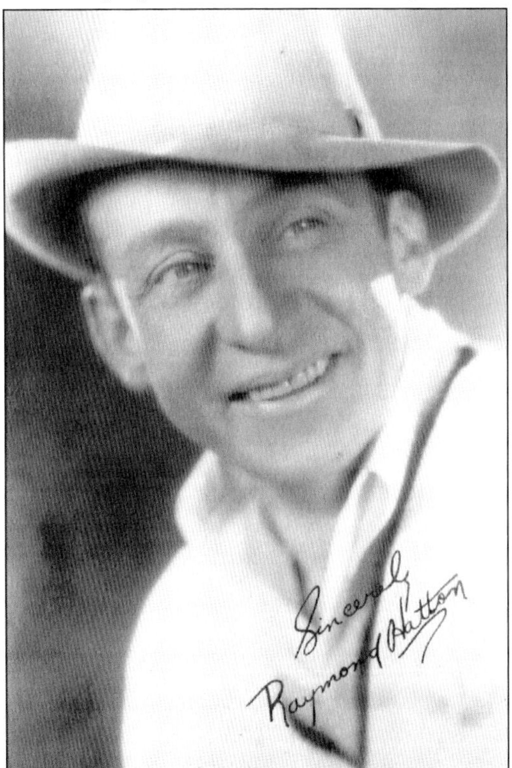

Raymond Hatton acted in hundreds of movies, especially Westerns. He appeared in *Hell's Heroes*, which was filmed near Palmdale in August 1929. One of his costars in this movie was Fritzi Ridgeway, who later lived in Lancaster. In 1963, he and his actress wife, Frances, moved to Palmdale. They lived on East Avenue Q-4. He has a star on the Hollywood Walk of Fame. The Hattons are buried in Lancaster.

It has been said that Gale Henry East, an early actress and comedienne, was the likely inspiration for the cartoon character, Olive Oyl, Popeye's girlfriend. Gale's husband, Henry, was a famous movie animal trainer who worked with Asta, an early canine star. The Easts lived in Ana Verde Hills and owned several attractive properties in the Littlerock and Pearblossom areas. Gale also wrote a column for the *Valley Press* newspaper.

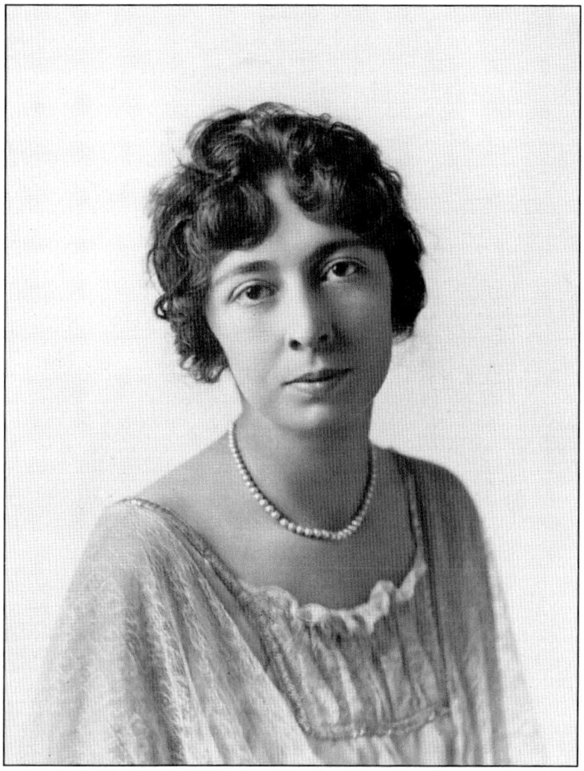

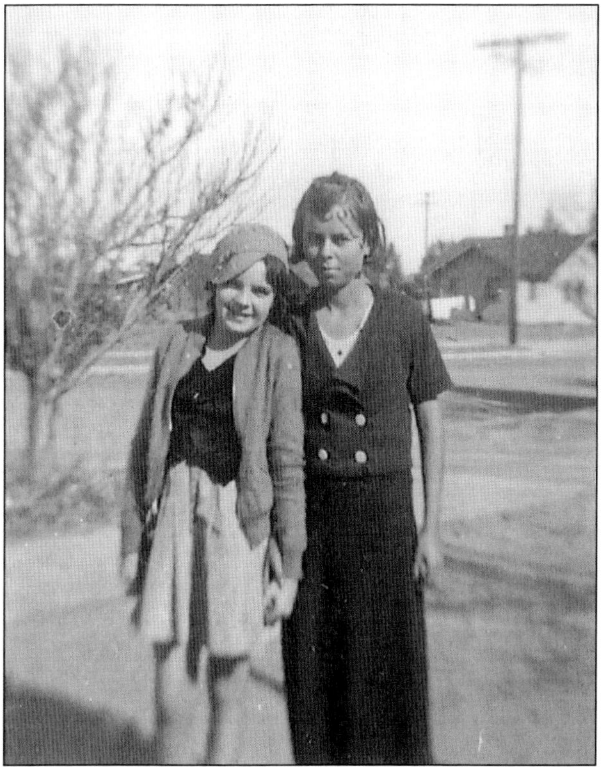

Actress Judy Garland (Frances "Baby" Gumm) was one of Lancaster's famous residents. The Gumm family lived there from 1926 to 1933. She and her family performed at many local functions, including a 1930s musical program at Keppel School. This photograph of Judy (left) and Esther Story on Newgrove Avenue in Lancaster was taken by Irma Story with a little box camera around 1932. (Courtesy of Irma "Babe" Story.)

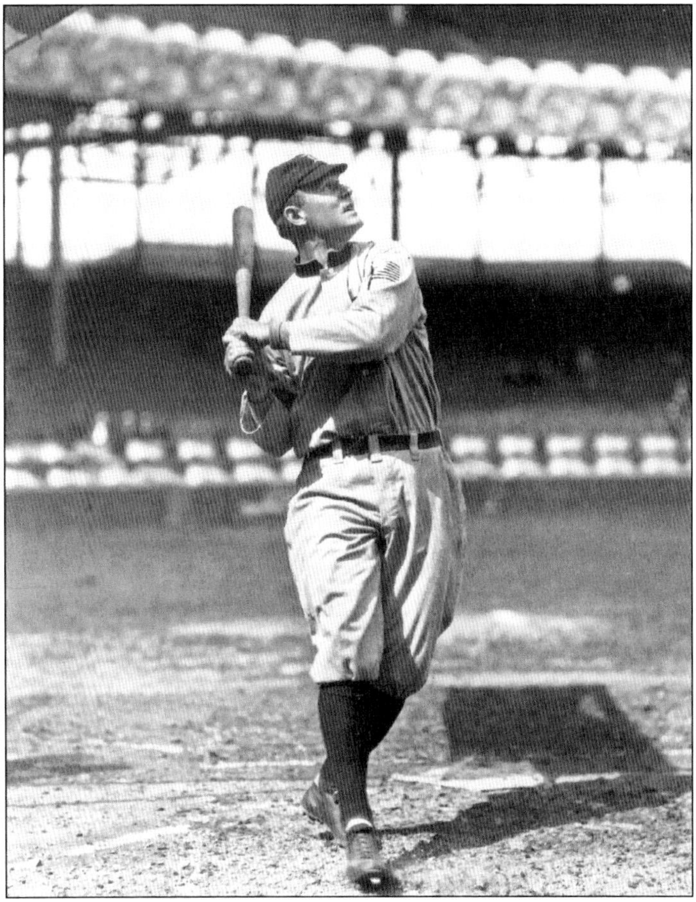

Samuel Earl Crawford was a Major League Baseball player who played outfield for the Cincinnati Reds and Detroit Tigers. In 1957, Crawford, whose nickname was "Wahoo Sam," was living in quiet retirement in Pearblossom when he was inducted into the Baseball Hall of Fame. Most of the community was unaware of Crawford's professional baseball background. (Courtesy of Ron and Maddi Kleit.)

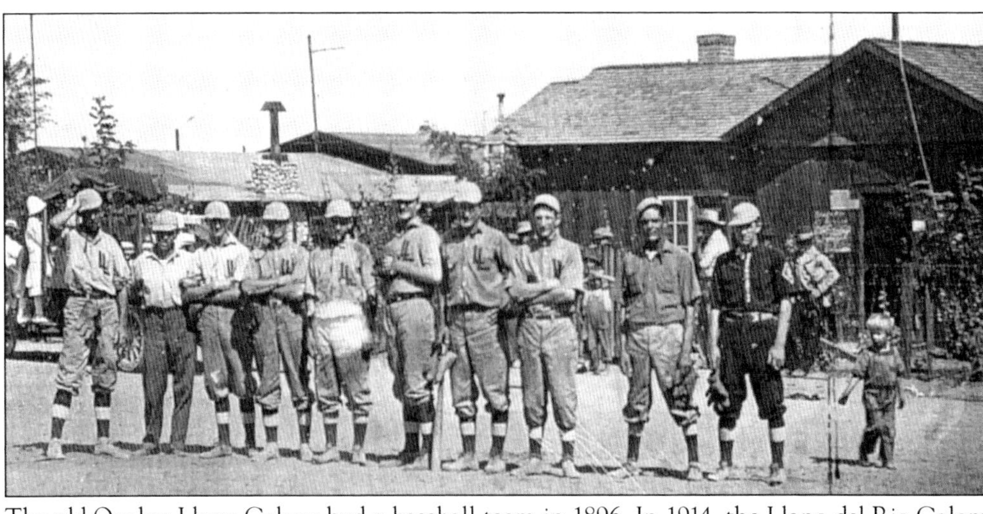

The old Quaker Llano Colony had a baseball team in 1896. In 1914, the Llano del Rio Colony developed an invincible red-suited baseball team that routinely beat nearby teams. In this photograph, the seventh player from the left is Charles Farrell, who became an actor. During the 1950s, he starred as Gale Storm's father in the popular television series *My Little Margie*. (Courtesy of Cora Sweet McCrumb family.)

Spencer "Shorty" Lindsey, holding B. Jones in 1915, was the manager of the Palmdale baseball team. Glen Settle was a batboy for the team. In 1908, Lindsey and his wife, Anna, came to Palmdale by wagon. They built a two-story house at Twenty-fifth Street East and Avenue S where they later planted a 10-acre pear orchard. Lindsey was also a drummer who performed at local musical programs.

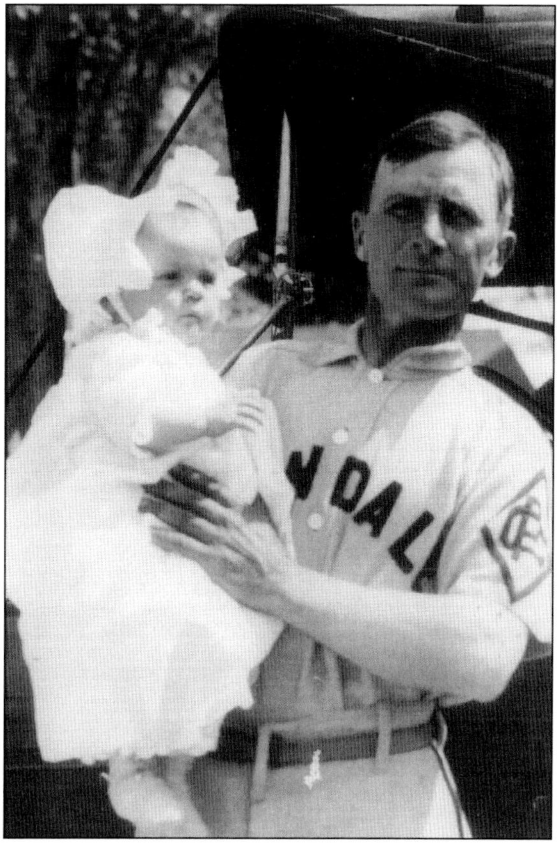

In May 1964, groundbreaking ceremonies took place for the new Jackie Robinson Park in Littlerock. Breaking the color barrier, in 1947 Jackie Robinson became the first black person to play in baseball's major leagues. Robinson is shown here with Dorothy Sweet, a community leader, and his wife, Rachel. The Los Angeles County Board of Supervisors proclaimed June 16, 1965, as "Jackie Robinson Day." (Courtesy of Cora Sweet McCrumb.)

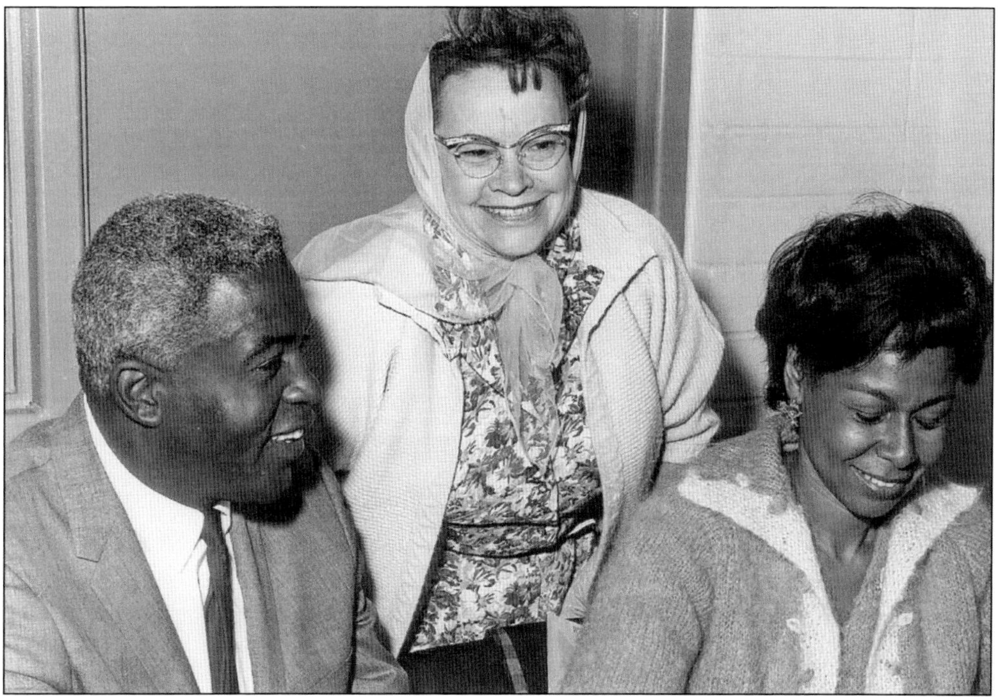

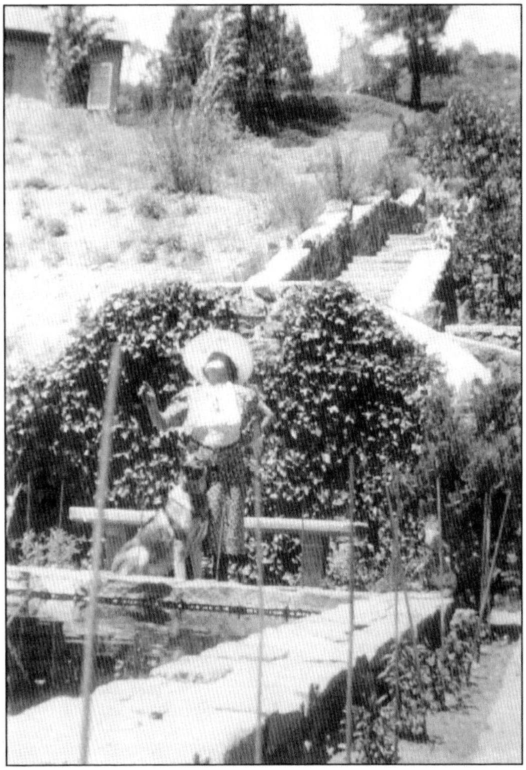

Flamboyant countess Jeannie La Marr was at one time the world's champion female boxer. While living in Hollywood, she established several health and fitness clubs. She later lived below Jackson Lake on a mountain ridge overlooking the entire Antelope Valley. She fought at the Valyermo California Conservation Corps Camp where boxing matches were staged. Petite La Marr fought mostly against men. In one fight, she knocked out two male contenders.

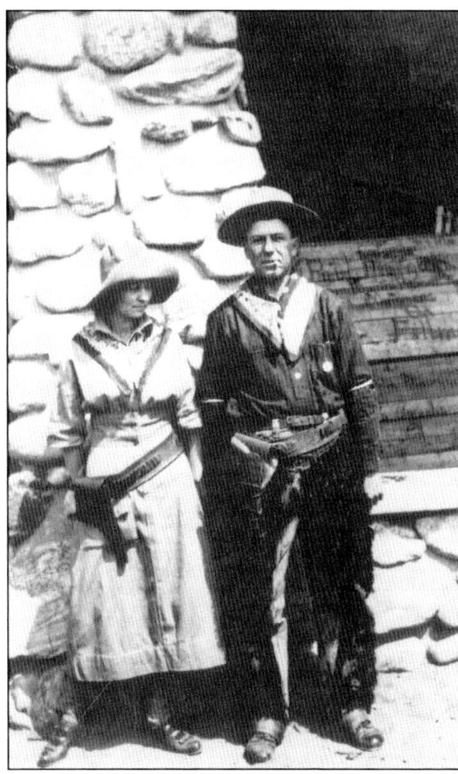

According to the 1920 Federal Census, the first Antelope Valley resident to have his or her occupation listed as an "actor" was Irish-born Joseph Allen (age 69), who was probably a stage actor. In 1917, electricity provided by generators was used for stage productions and the occasional silent movie at Llano del Rio. These are two cowboy actors at the colony. (Courtesy of WAVHS.)

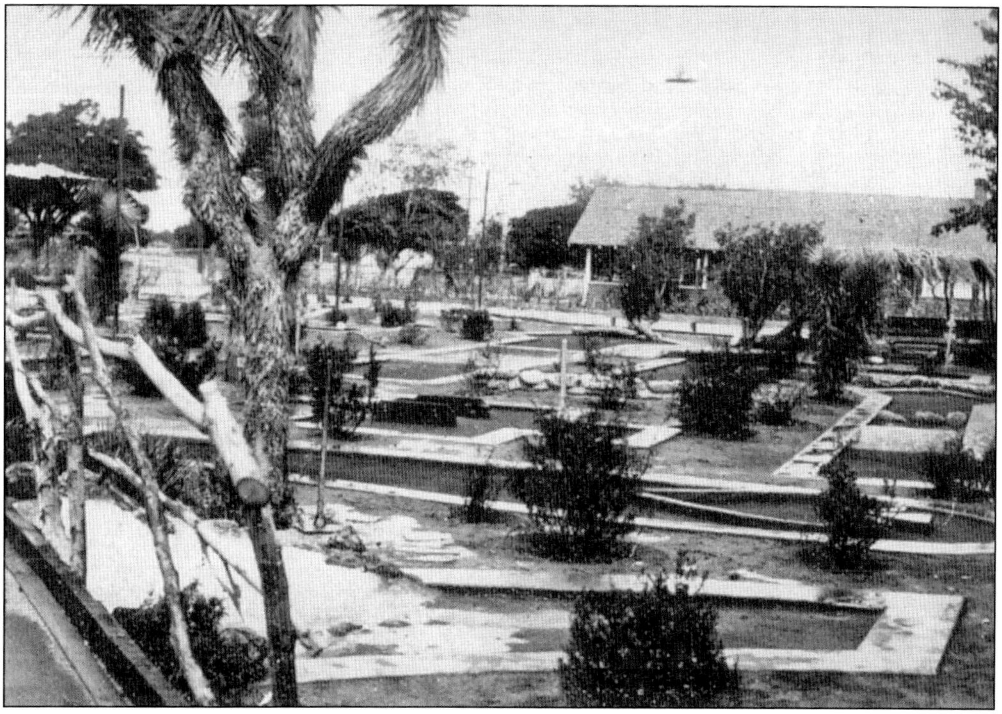

In 1930, Palmdale residents built the valley's first miniature putt-putt golf course. It was located on Sierra Highway. During the late 1920s, the Settle brothers, Buddy Redman, Don Hartfield, and others decided to build Rattlesnake Gulch, a nine-hole golf course with tomato cans serving for holes. They selected an area about 1 mile west of the present-day Antelope Valley Country Club in Palmdale.

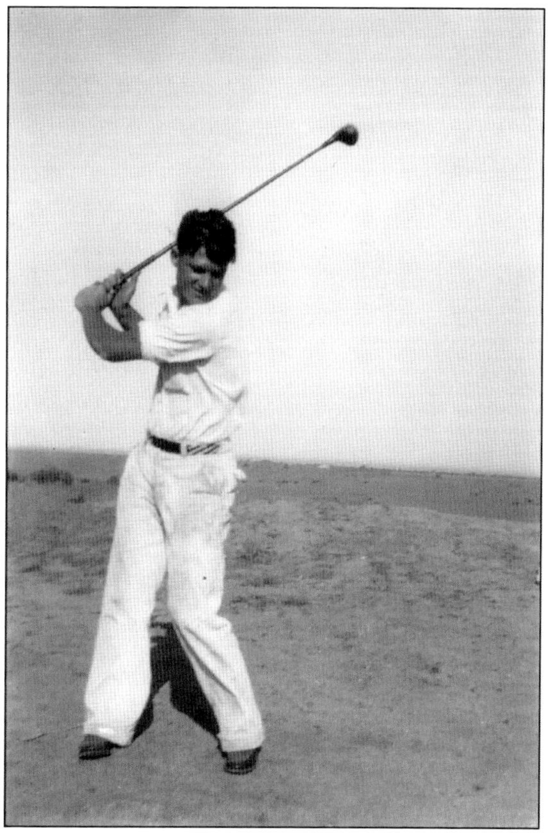

In 1935, the great Buster Keaton filmed a short baseball comedy, *One Run Elmer*, near Rattlesnake Gulch. Jim Thorpe, who was voted the greatest athlete of the first half of the 20th century, also appeared in this movie. Thorpe returned to the Antelope Valley in May 1939 for a high school program. Glen Settle, who is playing at the Rattlesnake Gulch golf course, was an extra in this movie.

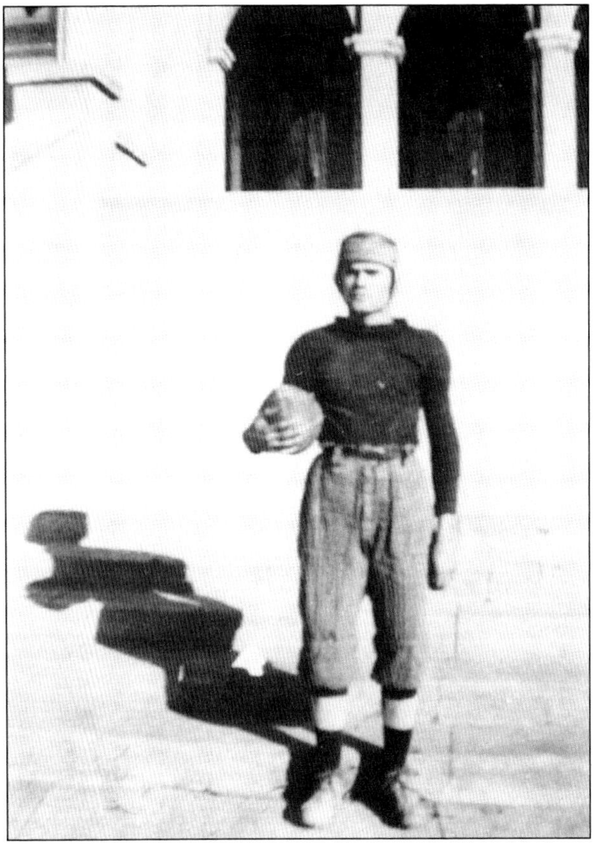

Ken Sadler was a popular football player at the old high school. Another Palmdale resident, Vernon Valdez Jr., who graduated from Antelope Valley High School and Community College in the mid-1950s, later became a defensive back for the Los Angeles Rams. He then played for the Buffalo Bills (1961) and the Oakland Raiders (1962).

In the late 1930s, a group of local men arranged with the Palmdale Irrigation District to use the Palmdale Lake for recreational purposes and organized the Palmdale Fin and Feather Club. The preserve and 310-acre lake provided readily available fishing and hunting activities for members throughout Southern California. Fred Snodgrass—now 99—displays a day's catch at the club during the 1950s. (Courtesy of Charles Snodgrass family.)

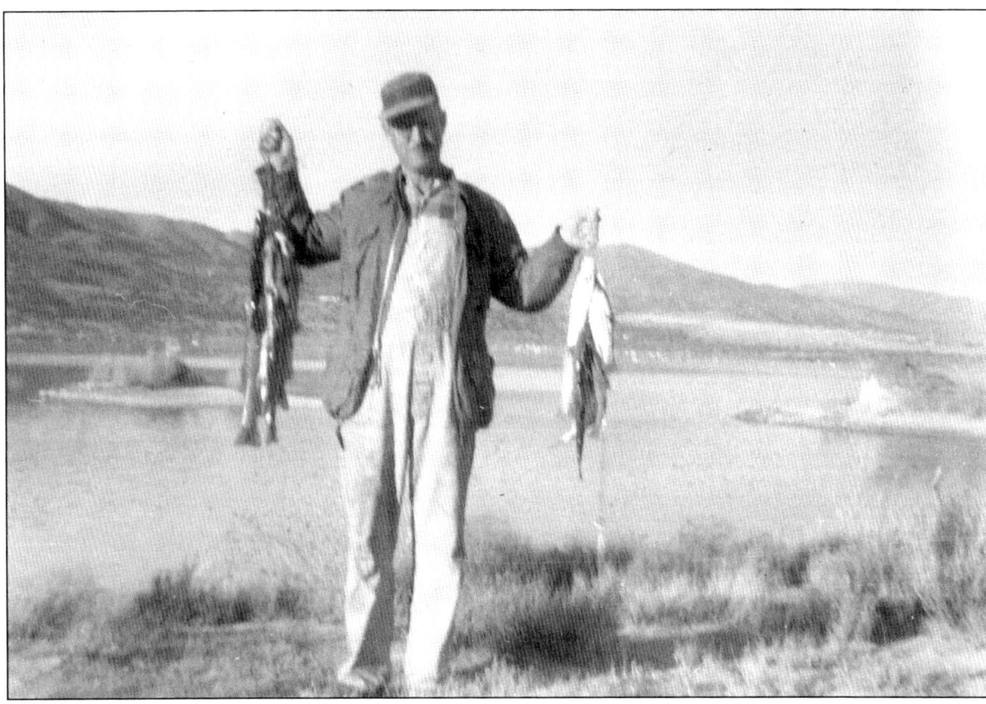

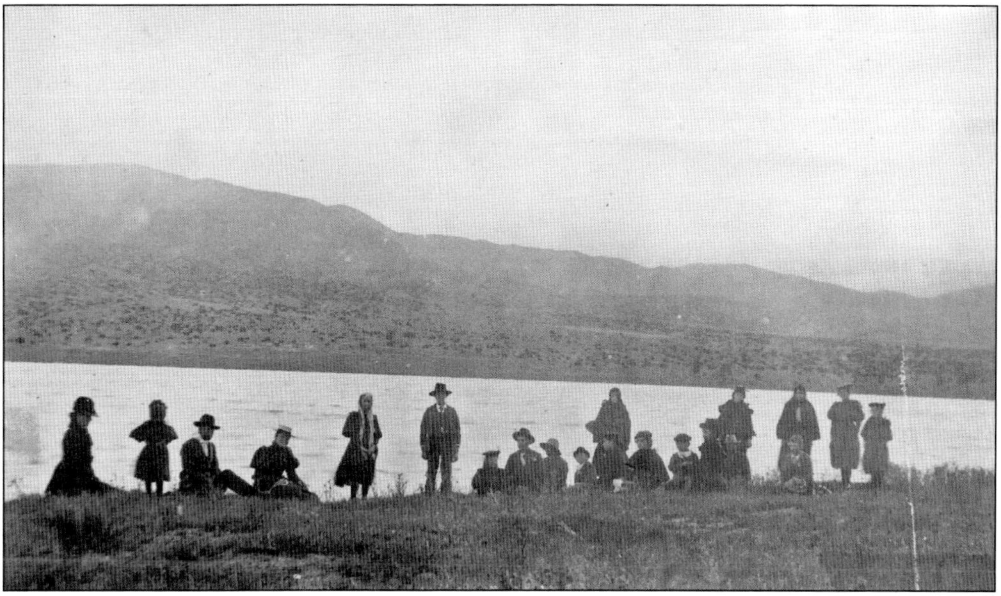

The Palmdale Reservoir was a popular recreation area for pioneers. Mrs. Nagel, fifth from the left, is enjoying herself during an 1896 picnic. It was a great spot for swimming and going fishing. Pioneers Nellie and Jacob Lansing, who lived in the Ana Verde Hills during the 1890s, thought that their views looking over the lake and wildflowers were the best in the valley.

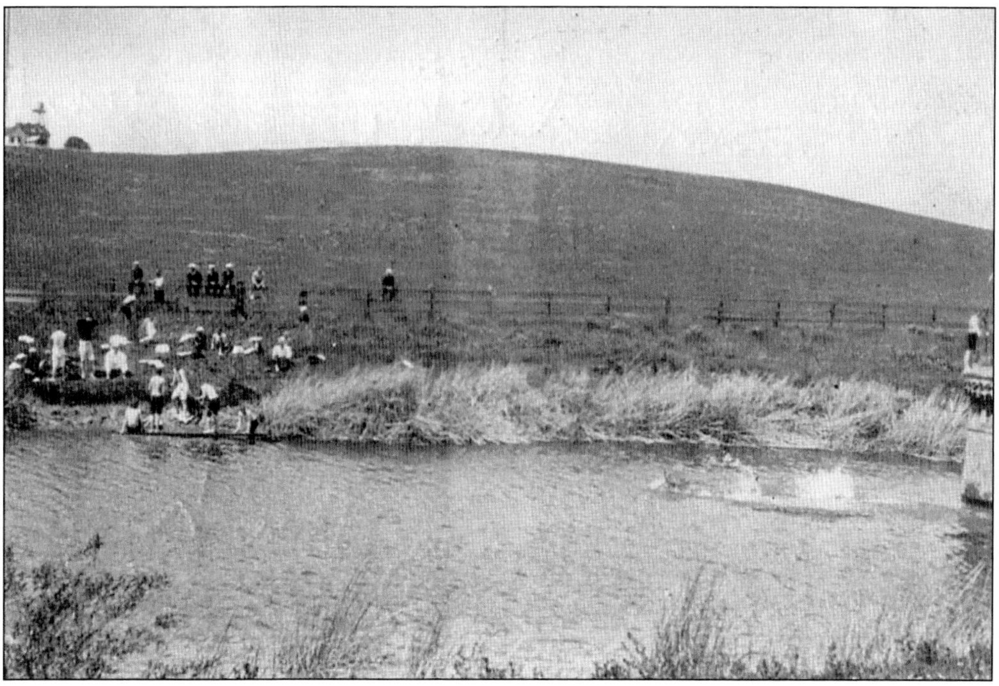

Besides Palmdale Reservoir, pioneers also enjoyed going on fun trips to Elizabeth Lake. Members of the Palmdale Community Church are playing and wading in the lake's shallow water in 1919. Fishing was always a popular sport. Favorite fishing spots included Tweedy Lake, Quail Lake, Munz Lake (Lake Hughes), Pallet Creek, Little Rock Creek, and Jackson Lake. Fish such as bass, trout, pike, catfish, and perch could be found in different areas.

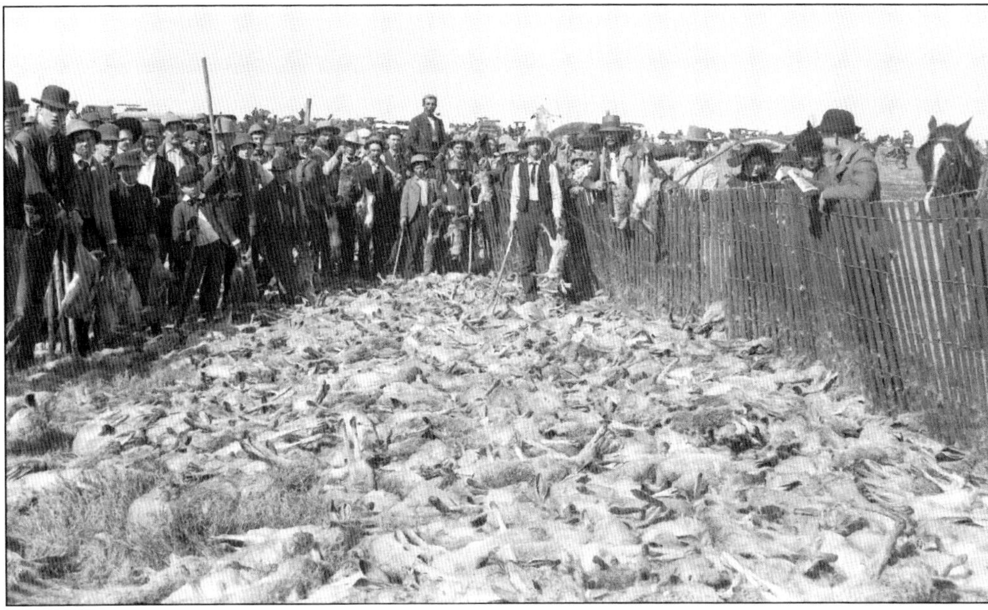

Early settlers saw themselves threatened by large hordes of jackrabbits, which were destroying their crops. Rabbit drives were one of many control measures needed to keep the population down. Participants flushed rabbits into corrals and then clubbed them to death. But not all "clubbers" enjoyed this sport. One participant said the horrible noises made by the jackrabbits sounded like wailing babies and he could never kill a living animal again.

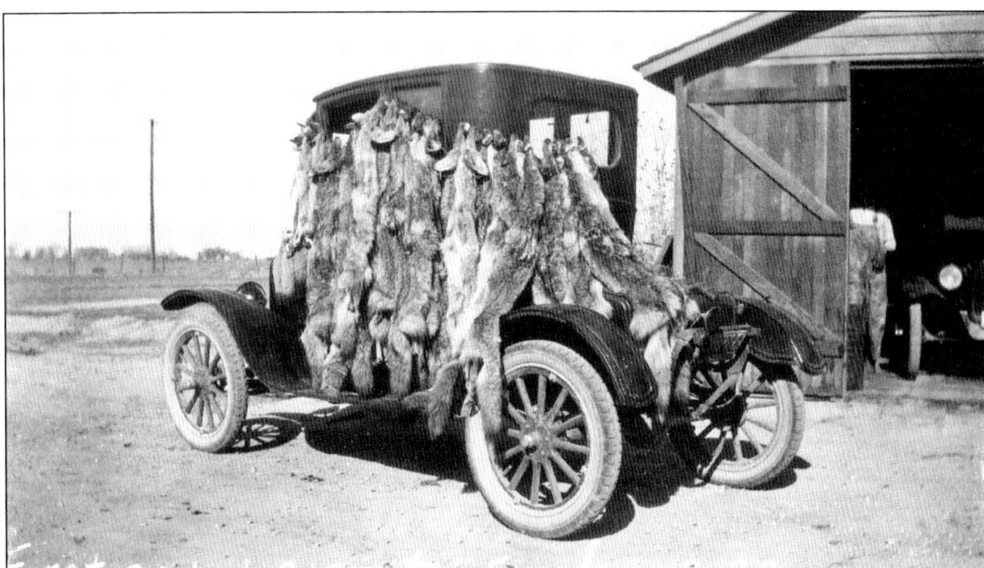

Coyotes are cunning, mobile, and highly adaptable. Early Antelope Valley settlers did not like coyotes since they attacked their poultry, stock, and small pets. Pioneers also hunted coyotes for their fur, which was sometimes used for clothing. In the 1890s, one could receive $2 for a coyote skin. All of these coyote fur pelts dangling from the automobile belonged to trapper Harold True.

Hunting was a necessity and a favorite sport during the pioneer days. Hunters, or "nimrods," as they were called by the newspapers, hunted bears, deer, antelope, coyotes, rabbits, ducks, and other animals in the valley, foothills, and neighboring forests. Hunting was not necessarily a safe sport as many hunters accidentally shot themselves or others. This hunter and his faithful companion are resting after a successful day. (Courtesy of Josephine Williams.)

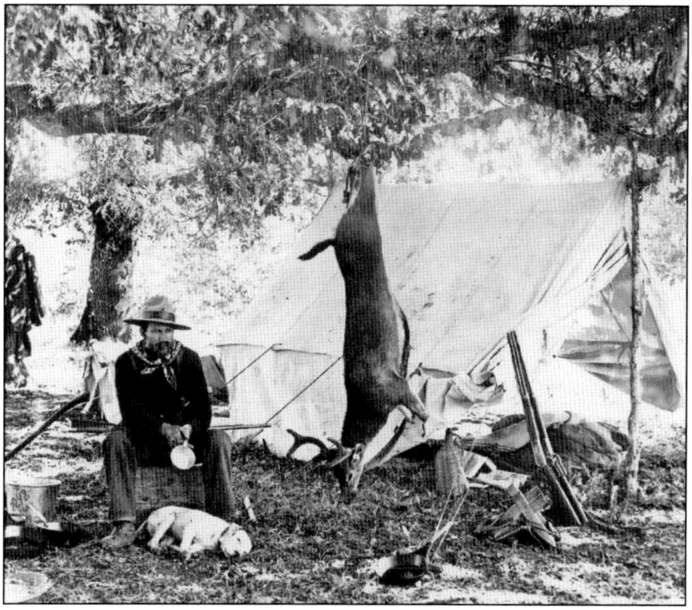

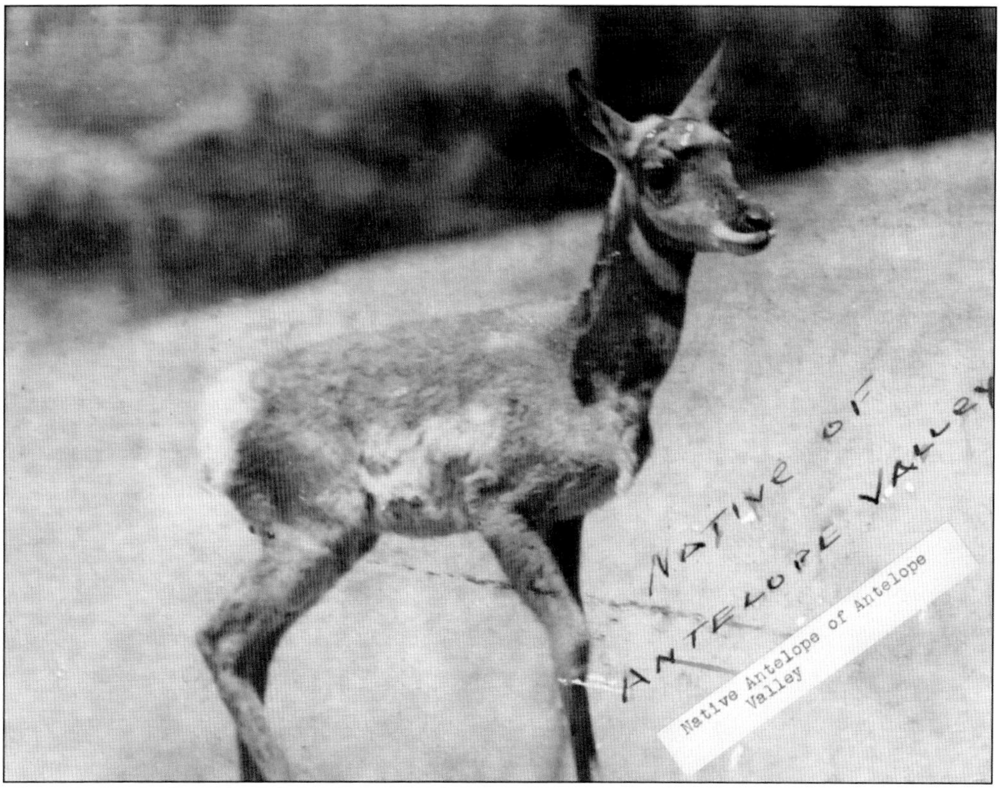

The existence of antelope (pronghorn) in the Antelope Valley has been debated for decades. Few photographs exist showing them. Most early antelope sightings occurred in the west end of the valley around Fairmont. They were also seen in the foothill regions of Palmdale, Littlerock, and Valyermo where there were juniper trees. They did not roam in areas covered extensively with creosote bushes such as Lake Los Angeles.

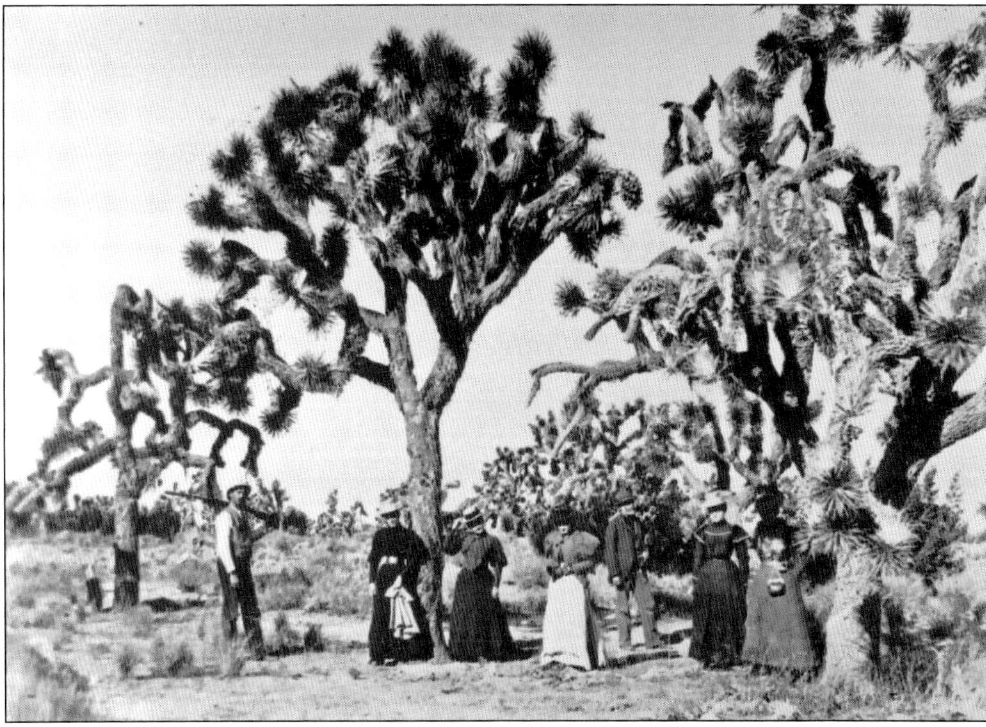

Women also enjoyed hunting as a sport. They were members of the Palmdale Gun Club (1927), which held events at the Palmdale Reservoir for hunting, shooting, and recreational purposes. There were several newspaper reports of women shooting mountain lions in self defense. Shooting domestic turkeys for Christmas was another popular pastime. These pioneers are trekking near Palmdale in 1905. (Courtesy of Fred Strasburg.)

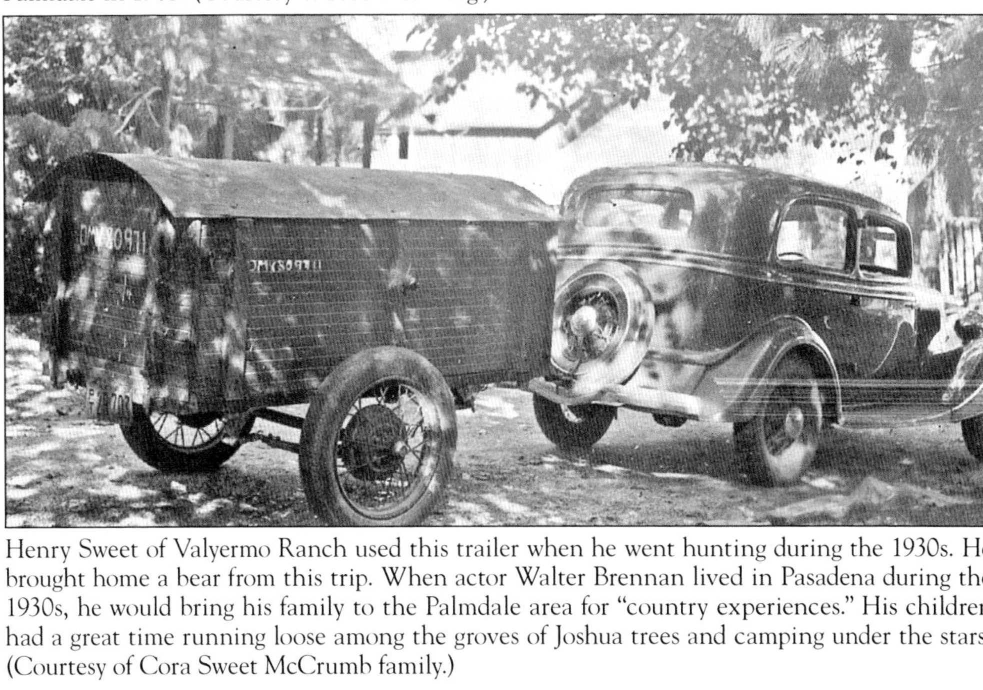

Henry Sweet of Valyermo Ranch used this trailer when he went hunting during the 1930s. He brought home a bear from this trip. When actor Walter Brennan lived in Pasadena during the 1930s, he would bring his family to the Palmdale area for "country experiences." His children had a great time running loose among the groves of Joshua trees and camping under the stars. (Courtesy of Cora Sweet McCrumb family.)

The Antelope Valley Fair has always presented beautiful artwork displays (1949). Palmdale was home to artist George Van Saake, who was well known for his portraits of early movie stars. Another Palmdale (and later Lancaster) artist, Charles LaMonk, was noted for his paintings of Indians and for his contributions toward the preservation of Native American pictographs and petroglyphs. Otto Farsky, an early-20th-century artist, frequently painted near Palmdale.

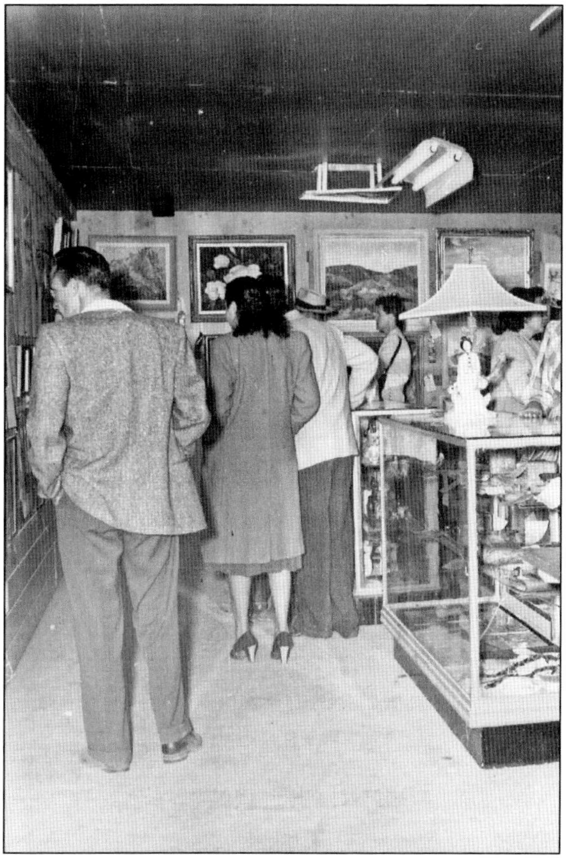

Fourth of July celebrations held in Palmdale and at Big Rock and Little Rock Creeks presented fun activities for the entire family. There were barbecues, dances, rodeos, three-legged races, sack races, greased pigs, greased pole-climbing, horse and foot races, boxing, and wrestling matches. Although fireworks were allowed in Palmdale during the early days, they were prohibited by 1925. Maude Settle riding on a tricycle makes an interesting Uncle Sam.

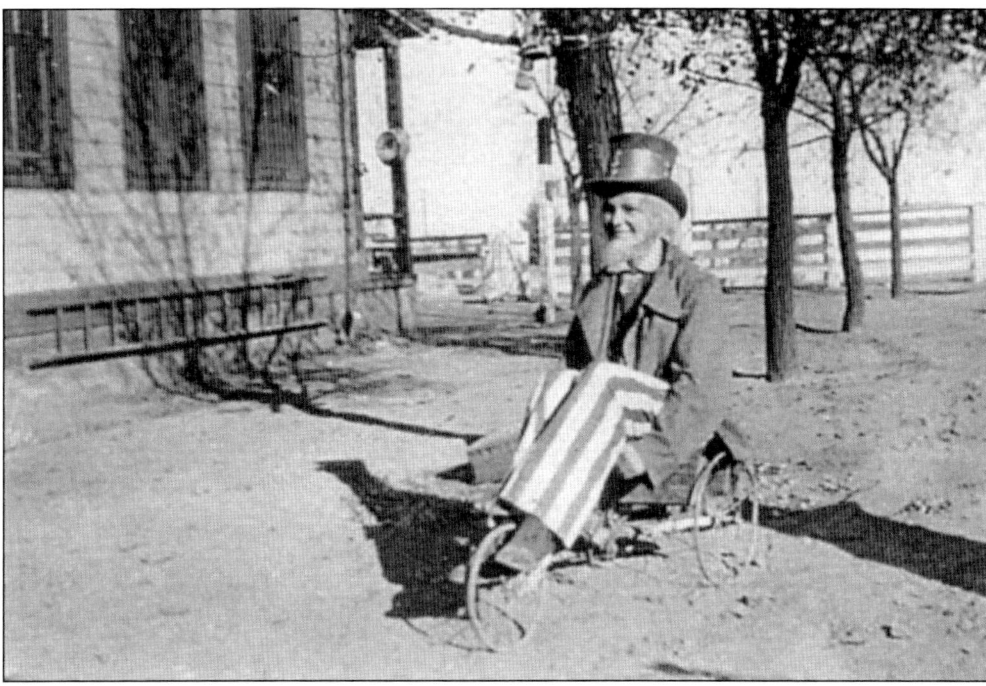

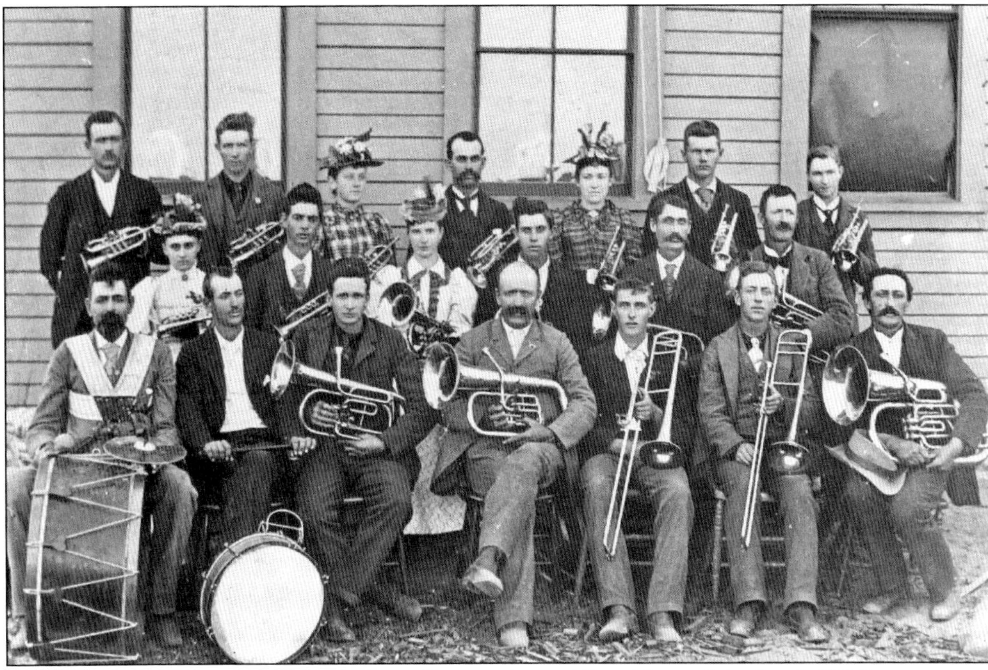

Music has always been important for valley residents. The Almondale Band (1896) was one of the valley's first bands; it was made up of 26 pieces. Later there were orchestras of different sizes, mandolin players, and barbershop quartets. During the 1950s, J. Russel Robinson, a famous ragtime and Dixieland jazz pianist and a composer of jazz, blues, and popular tunes, lived in Palmdale. He died in Palmdale in 1963.

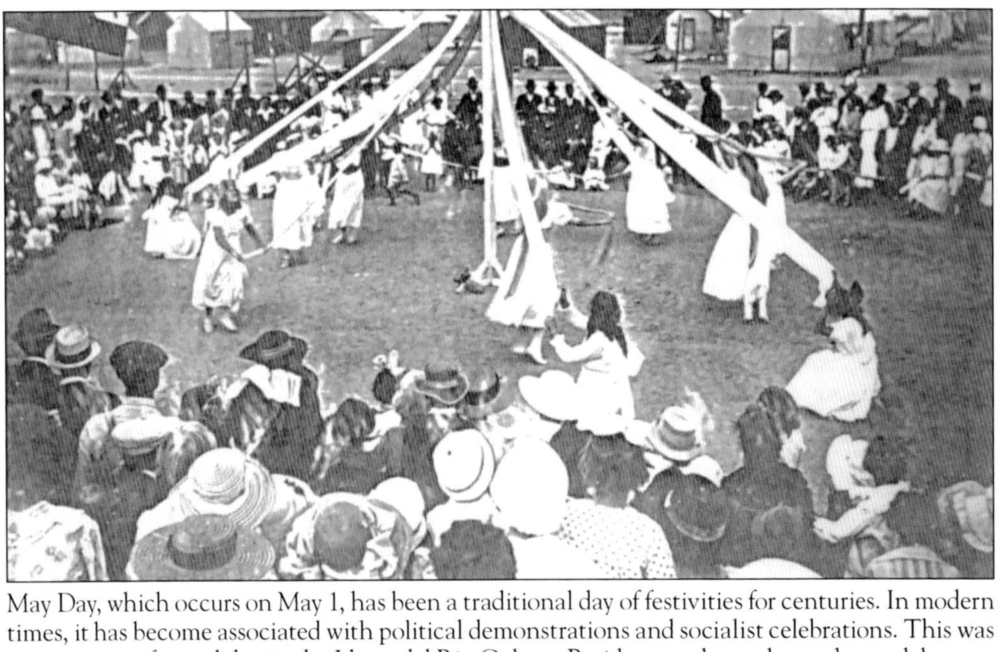

May Day, which occurs on May 1, has been a traditional day of festivities for centuries. In modern times, it has become associated with political demonstrations and socialist celebrations. This was an important festival day in the Llano del Rio Colony. Besides parades and speeches, celebratory activities always included young female dancers circling a Maypole with long ribbons (1917). (Courtesy of Cora Sweet McCrumb family.)

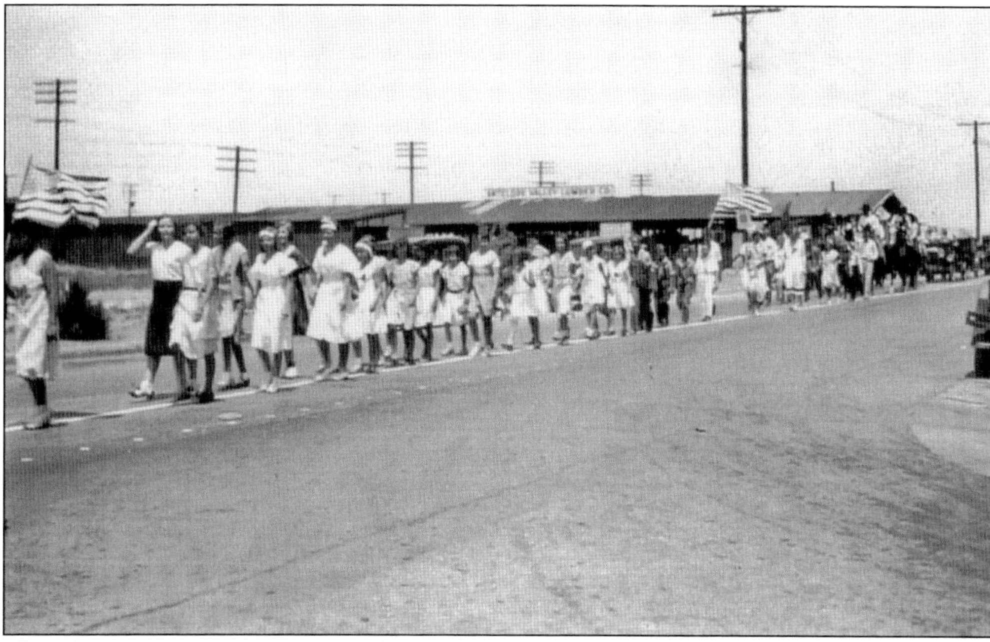

These happy participants are marching in a 1931 Palmdale parade on Sierra Highway near Palmdale Boulevard. Behind the celebrants is the Antelope Valley Lumberyard. Farther south, near Avenue R, was another lumber business, the Palmdale Lumber Company. Parades like this were truly a community event when stores would close down, and everyone participated or watched the parade. (Courtesy of WAVHS.)

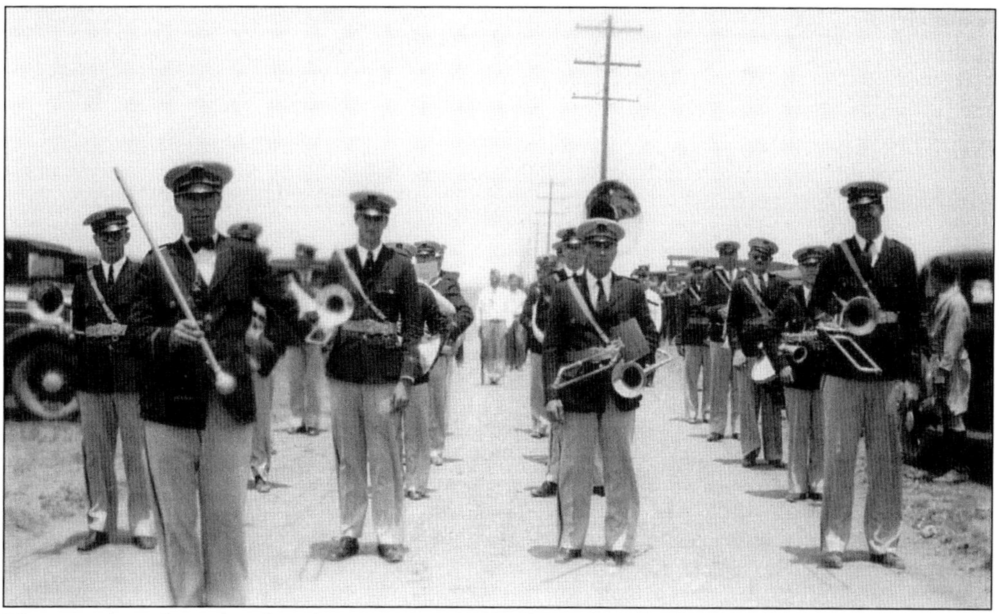

This marching brass band is also participating in the 1931 Palmdale parade. Considerable pride was taken in the various musical presentations. Local and out-of-town bands were constantly in demand to play for parades, dances, and other events. Three of the most popular dances were the special Fourth of July celebrations, harvest dances, and hard-time themed parties. (Courtesy of WAVHS.)

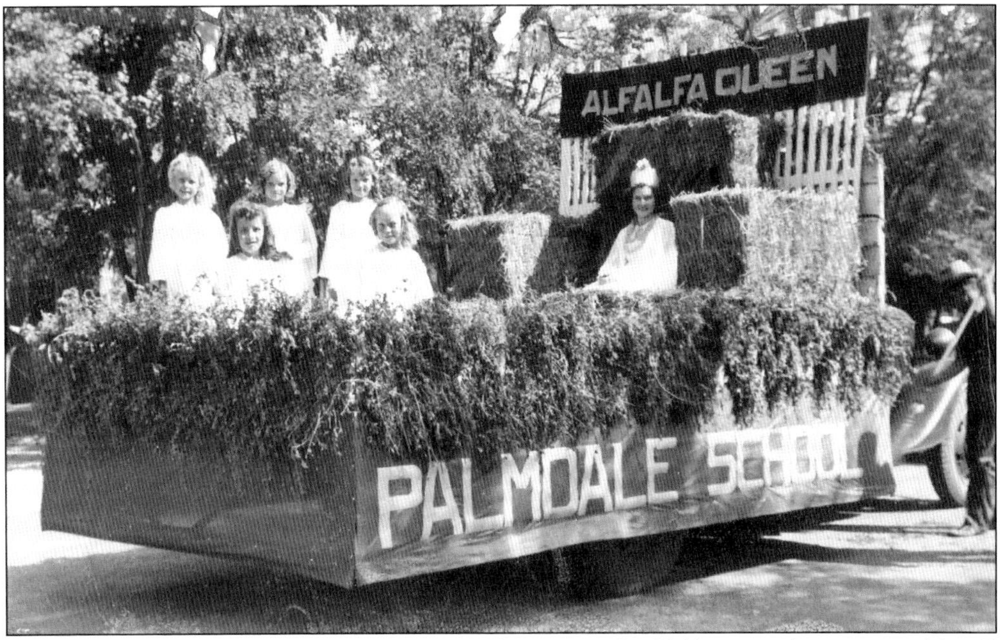

Although held in Lancaster, the Antelope Valley Fair and Alfalfa Festival was enjoyed by all valley residents. Presented at the end of summer, residents would come together to celebrate the valley's agricultural heritage. Floats such as this one carrying Palmdale Grammar School students and the Alfalfa Queen were built for the fair's parade. (Courtesy of WAVHS.)

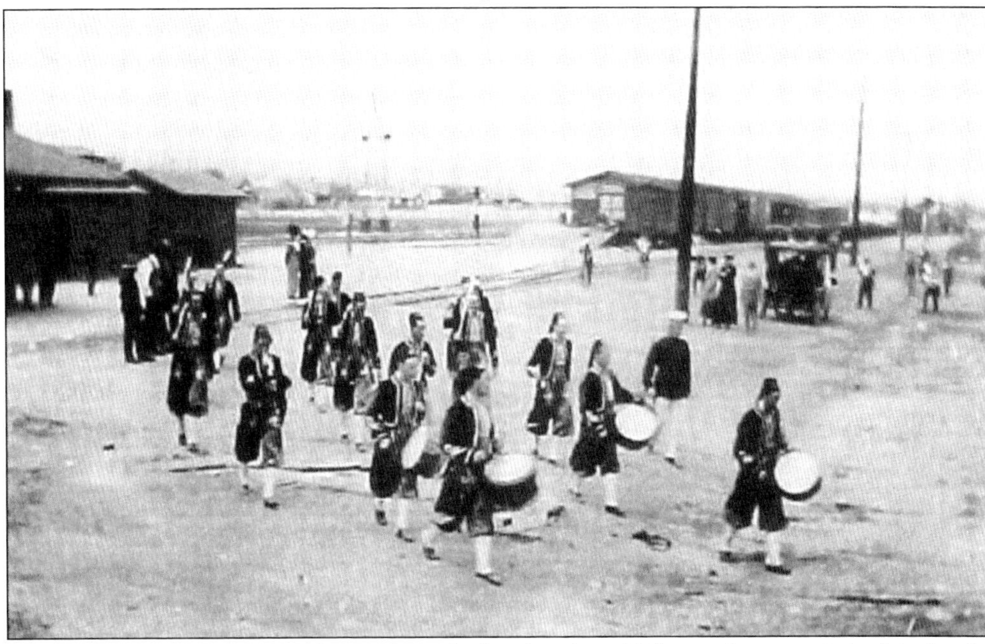

Sometimes circus trains would pass through the Antelope Valley and stop at Palmdale for the engines to take on water. There was always a mad scramble by the excited children to see all the exotic animals and colorful circus cars. On several occasions, circus performances were staged near Sixth Street East and Avenue Q-12. This photograph shows the Sells Floto Circus band arriving in neighboring Mojave in April 1913.

Ten

Moving Along

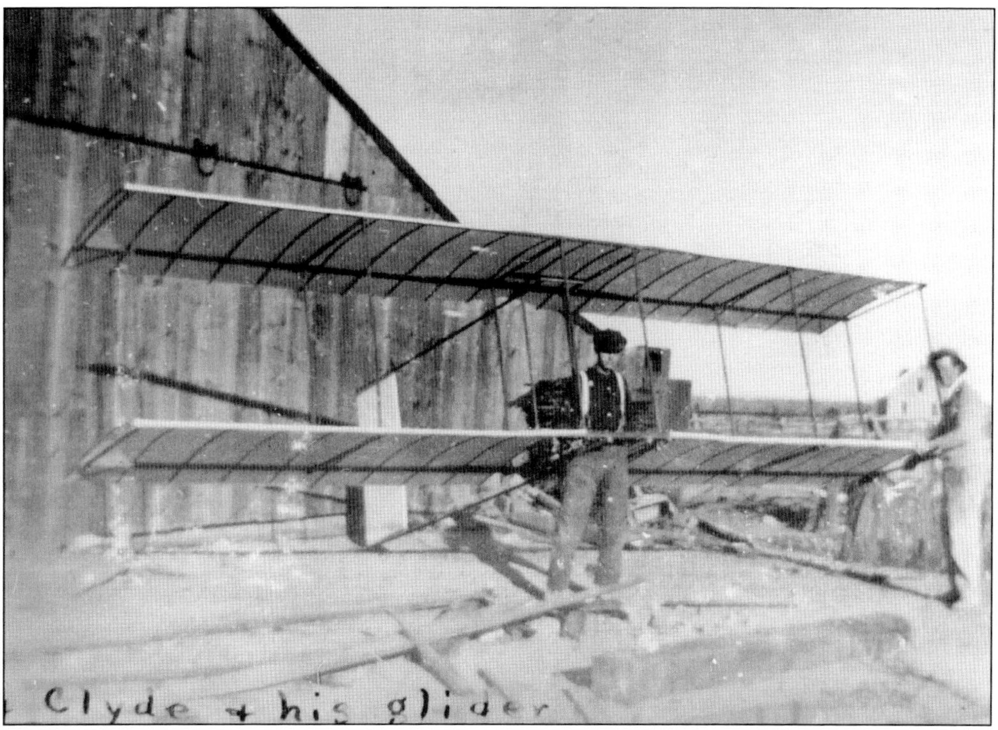

Walt Primmer's father, Clyde, was possibly the first flyer in the Antelope Valley. He built a Chanute hang glider from plans in a *Popular Mechanics* magazine. Lew Bones helped his future brother-in-law, Clyde, clear a hillside just west of Little Rock Creek in 1912 so he could fly his homebuilt glider. Clyde loved aviation and owned a plane until the 1970s. (Courtesy of Walt and Mickey Primmer.)

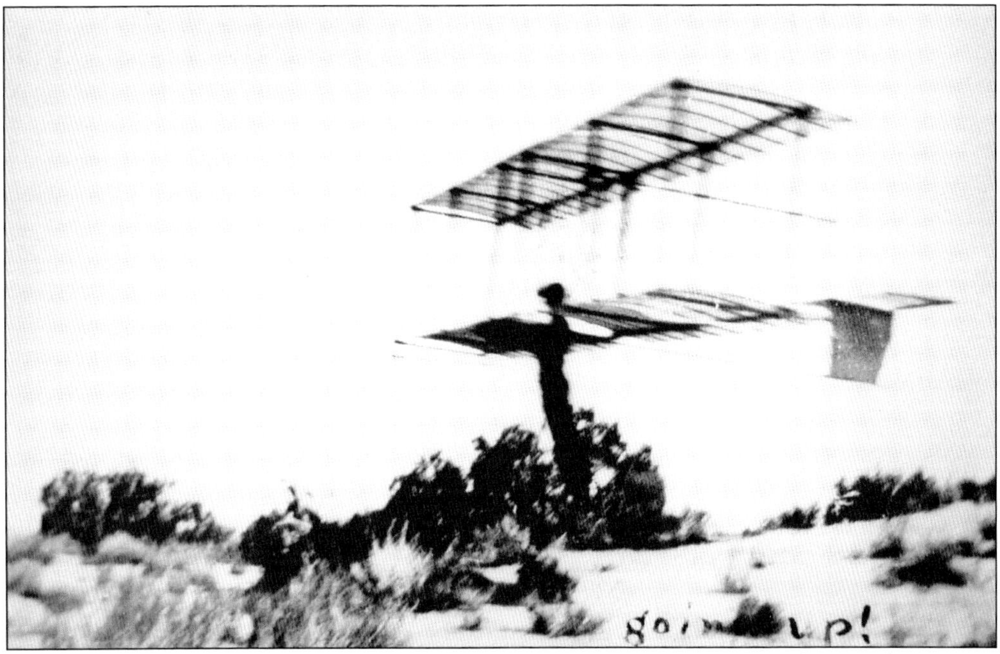

Clyde Primmer is up in the air near Little Rock Creek in 1912. It is not known how many glider flights he made. Alfred Meek, a Harold resident during the 1920s, became known as the "human kite" in Los Angeles (1905), when, wearing a gigantic kite on his back, he climbed a 137-foot-high pole at Redondo Beach and cast himself into the ocean. (Courtesy of Walt and Mickey Primmer.)

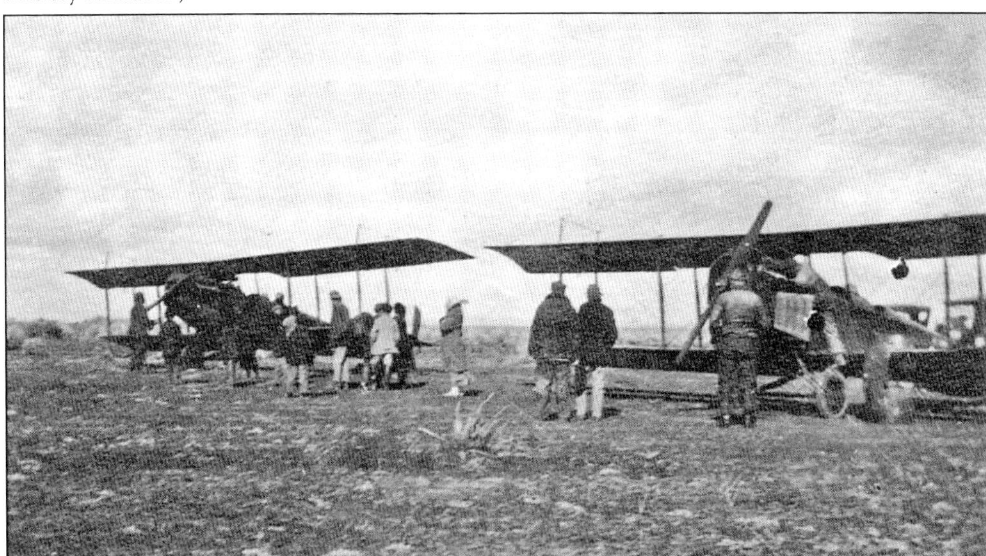

The progress of regional aviation has a fascinating history. Palmdale helped to make the Antelope Valley become America's "Aerospace Valley." The first airplane landings in Palmdale (shown here), and perhaps in the Antelope Valley, took place in late 1917 or early 1918. They were two World War I "Jennies" that needed to refuel. The planes landed near the community's baseball field. This area became the town's first airfield.

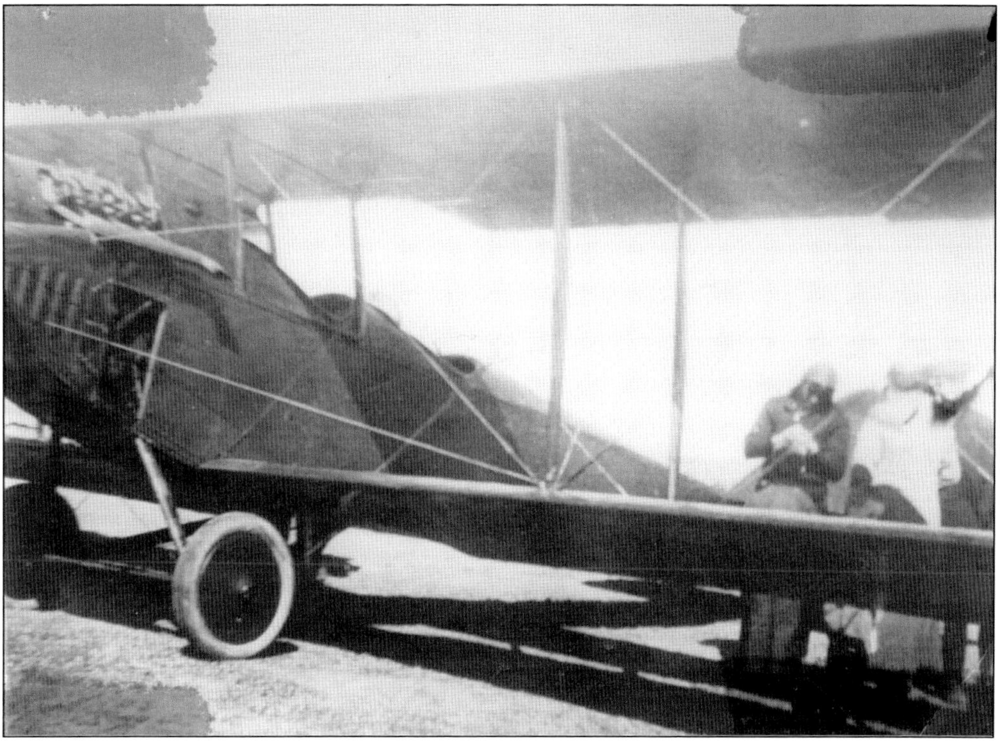

One of the first pilots to land in Palmdale is signing autographs. Planes began to stop here for gas or to stay overnight while filming movies. Movie stunt pilot extraordinaire Arthur Goebel, who landed here three times, later became the first flyer to span the Pacific from California to Hawaii in the 1927 Dole Race. *Flying Mail* (1925), *The Man from Lone Mountain* (1925), and *The Air Hawk* were filmed locally.

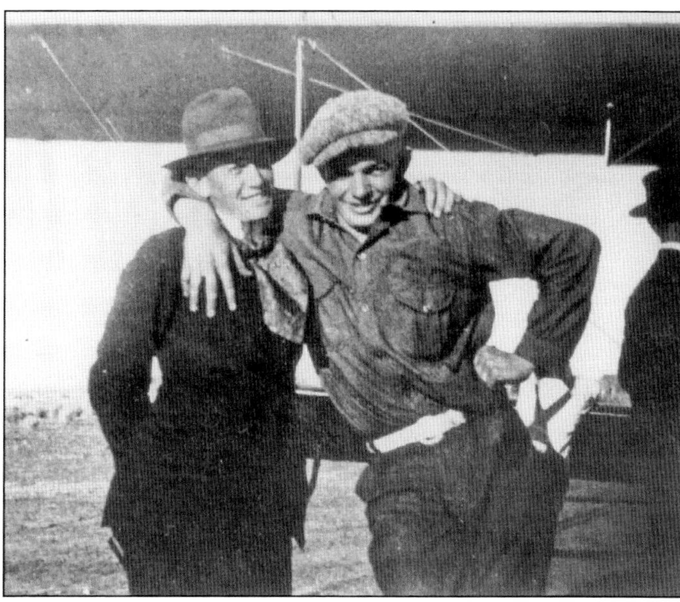

An early pilot (right) greets a fan at the Palmdale airfield. Before Edwards AFB and USAF Plant 42, there was another government facility, the Hugh Denny Aviation Field. In 1925, a small government airport was built south of Palmdale at Alpine Springs (Harold) to provide a convenient landing place for government fliers. Several hundred people attended its dedication to Lieutenant Denny on July 11, 1925.

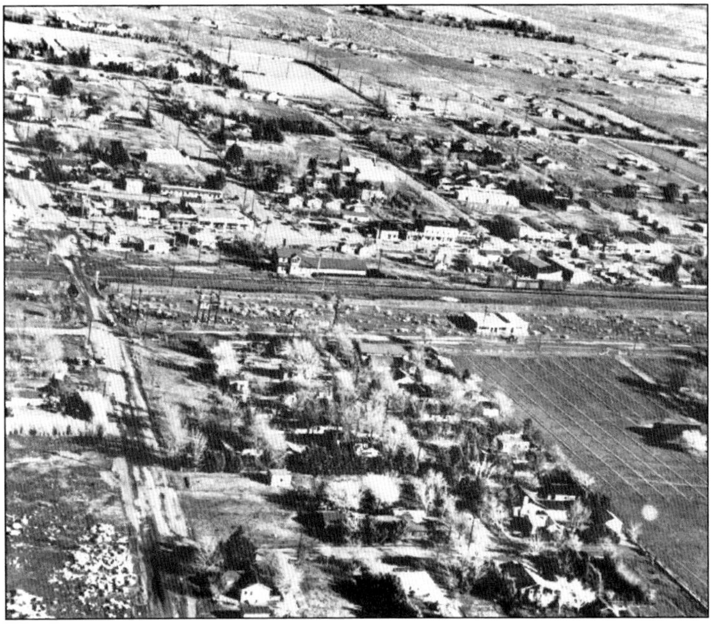

The first airfield was located near present-day Avenue Q-12 and Sixth Street East, in the lower right-hand corner of this photograph. Many residents were interested in becoming pilots during the 1920s. In 1929, Fred Alley, who had 10 years flying experience, was offering flying lessons in Palmdale. This airfield slowly lost its importance and was abandoned as pilots began to keep their planes at Rollie Galbraith's airfield. (Courtesy of WAVHS.)

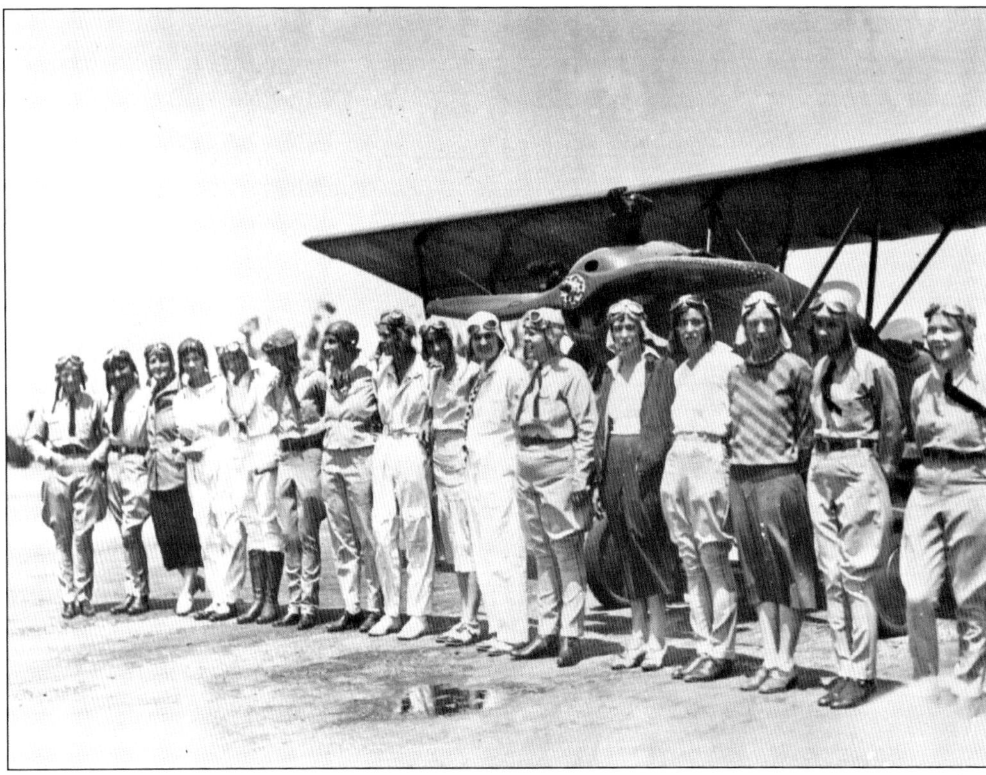

Pioneer aviatrix Clema Baxter Granger (1893–1983) took up flying in 1929, earning a pilot's license signed by Orville Wright. From their hangar at Santa Monica Clover Field, she and her husband, James, gave flying lessons. Clema competed in air races with Amelia Earhart, Pancho Barnes, and many other aviation notables. She later resided in Palmdale with her son, Harry Granger; Clema, ninth from the left, died in Palmdale.

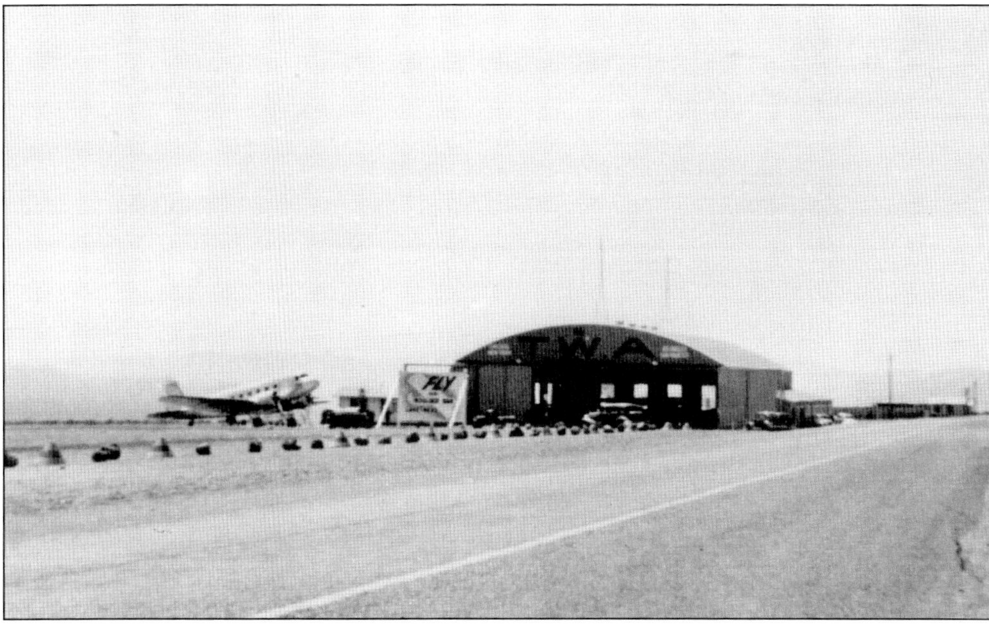

Rollie Galbraith's airstrip became known as the Palmdale Airport. There was also another dirt airfield, which belonged to the Palmdale Irrigation District, located near the site of the present-day Palmdale Regional Airport. This strip was used as early as 1930–1931 by local aviators. By 1933, the U.S. government wanted to use it, and minor improvements were made. Airlines also used it when Los Angeles area airports were fogged in.

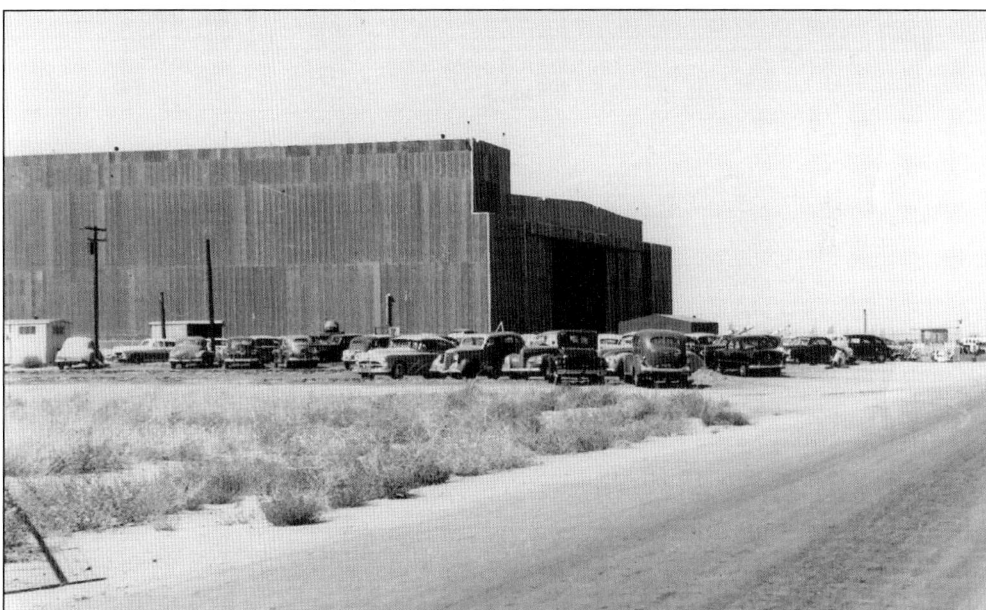

In 1940, the federal government built concrete runways at the airfield. They were used by Army Air Corps fliers for emergency landings and for training purposes. After the war ended, the airport was returned to Palmdale Irrigation District and Los Angeles County civilian control but later was reacquired by the USAF. In 1949, Lockheed became the first defense contractor here and constructed a large hangar. (Courtesy of Palmdale City Library.)

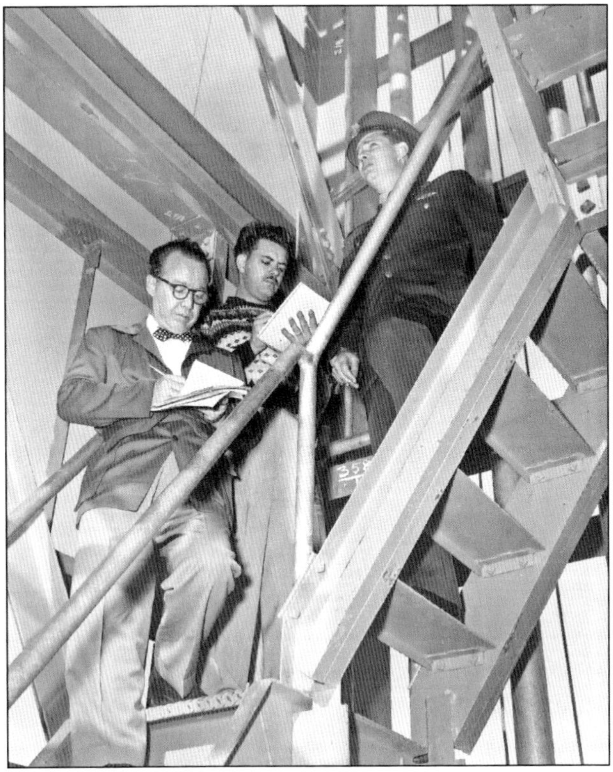

Valley Press reporters Leonard Murnane (left) and Vern Lawson listen intently to Lt. Col. M. P. Elvin. The air force became interested in the airport as a base to assure the continued delivery of jet aircraft and began negotiations with Los Angeles County to purchase the field. Plant 42 made available all the airport's facilities to airframe manufacturers for use on a common basis. (Courtesy of *Antelope Valley Press*.)

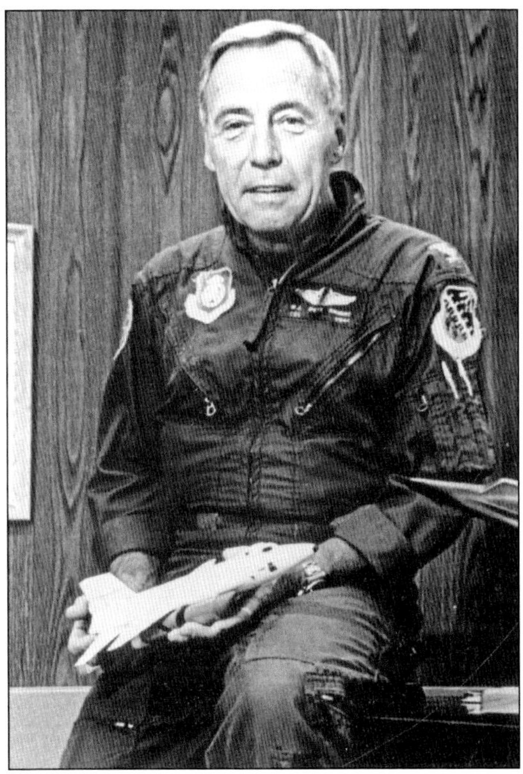

William J. "Pete" Knight was a combat pilot, test pilot, astronaut, and politician. In 1984, he was elected to the Palmdale City Council and four years later became the city's first elected mayor. In 1992, he was elected to serve in the California State Assembly, representing the 36th District, and later as a state senator representing California's 17th Senate District from 1996 until his death in 2004.

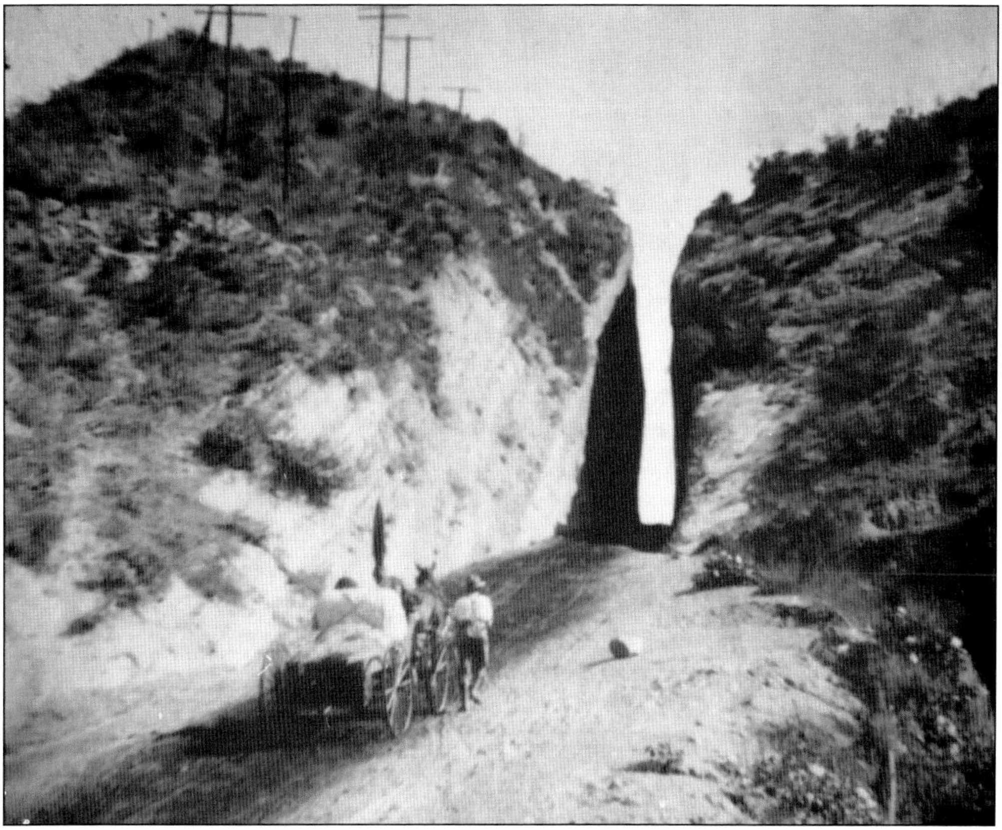

Early travelers and miners entered the Santa Clarita Valley gateway to the Antelope Valley through Beale's Cut. Beale's Cut is a long, narrow slit through the mountains between San Fernando and Newhall. The cut followed an old Indian and Spanish route. By 1860, it was already called the "Old Road." It was also called Frémont's Pass after John C. Frémont. Winfield McNamee is leading his wagon through the cut.

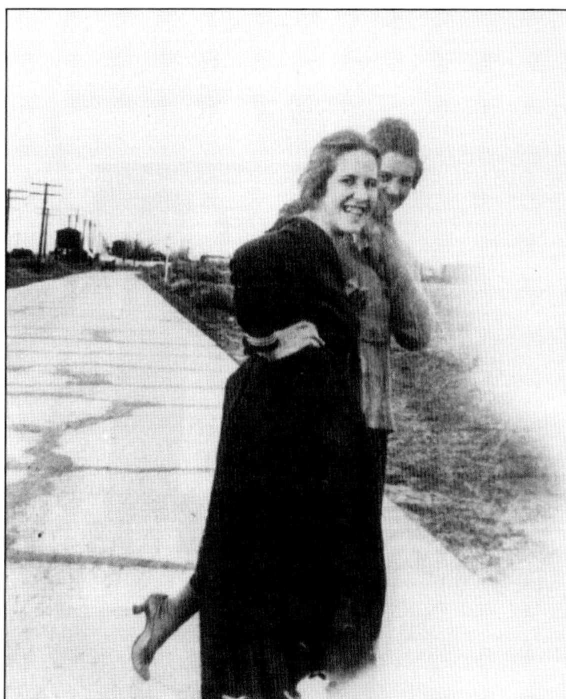

Sierra Highway was a rough dirt and sand road large enough for only one vehicle until 1916, when the first oiled road was started from Saugus and finished at the south end of the Antelope Valley in 1918. By April 1921, concrete had been laid on the road to Palmdale. There was a huge celebration at its completion. Mabel Jones (left) and Marie Hicks are standing on the new highway.

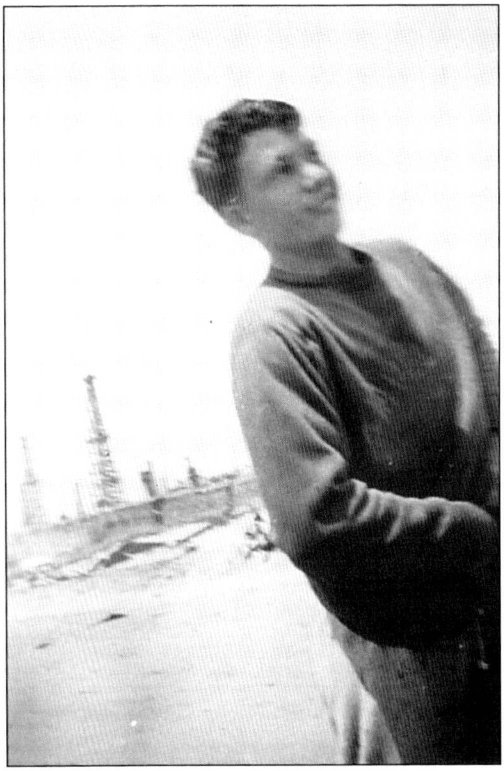

These oil wells are behind Glen Settle at the high school in Lancaster in 1929. There were also some unsuccessful oil wells in Southeast Antelope Valley. The Palmdale Oil Company drilled for oil between Palmdale and Littlerock in July 1921. In June 1926, an oil well was established midway between Palmdale and Lancaster. There also were a few derricks off Avenue R/ Rayburn and Division Street in the 1920s.

This Standard Oil Service Station was located at the southeast corner of Palmdale Boulevard and Sierra Highway. Several other gas stations served Palmdale in the 1920s: Clarence Gustave's City Square Service Station, Hughie's Service Station, and the Pagenkopf Service Station. There was a gas war in December 1924 when one station sold gas for 18¢ a gallon as compared to 19¢ charged by other dealers. (Courtesy of WAVHS.)

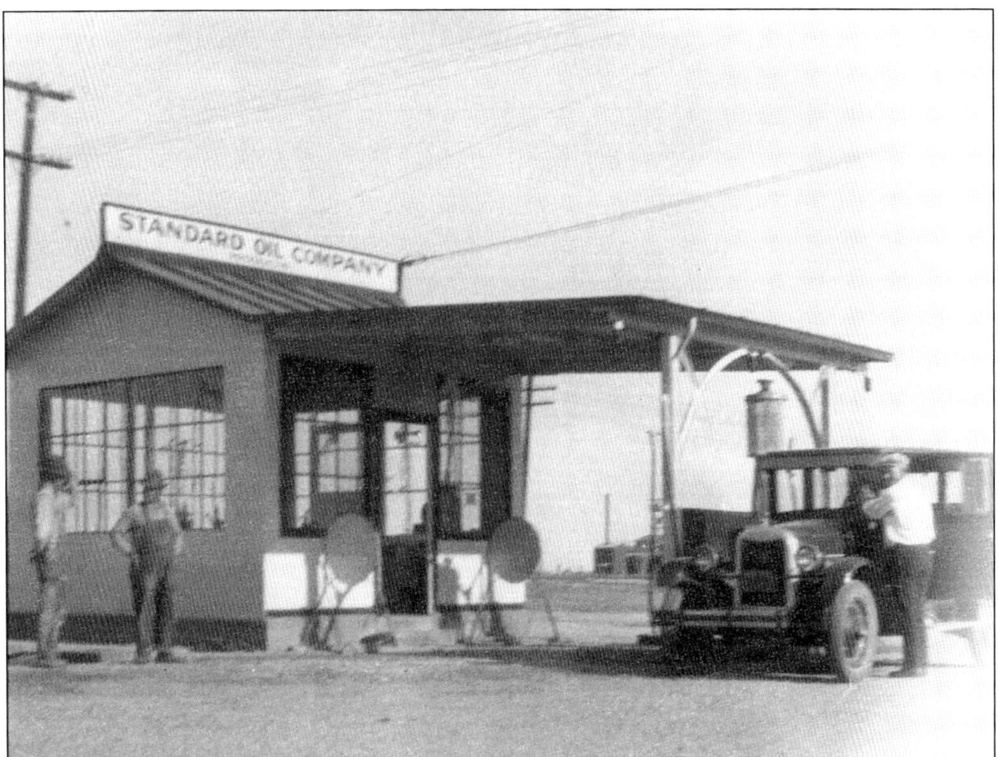

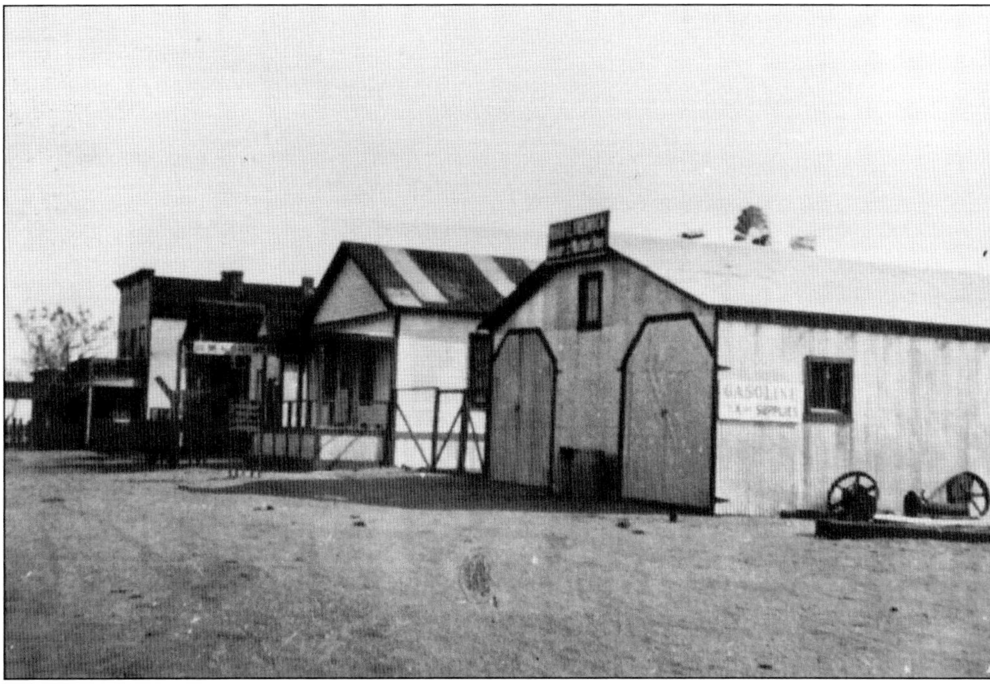

In February 1909, Lewis Tilghman bought an Auburn Touring Car, perhaps the first automobile in Southeast Antelope Valley. Fortunately there were soon several dealers and garages to service cars: Fred A. Alley of the Mission Garage, Moore's Garage, and the Palmdale Garage. In Littlerock, there was Hart's Garage and further east, the Pearblossom Service Company. The 1913 business district of Palmdale shows a garage at the right, along with hotels.

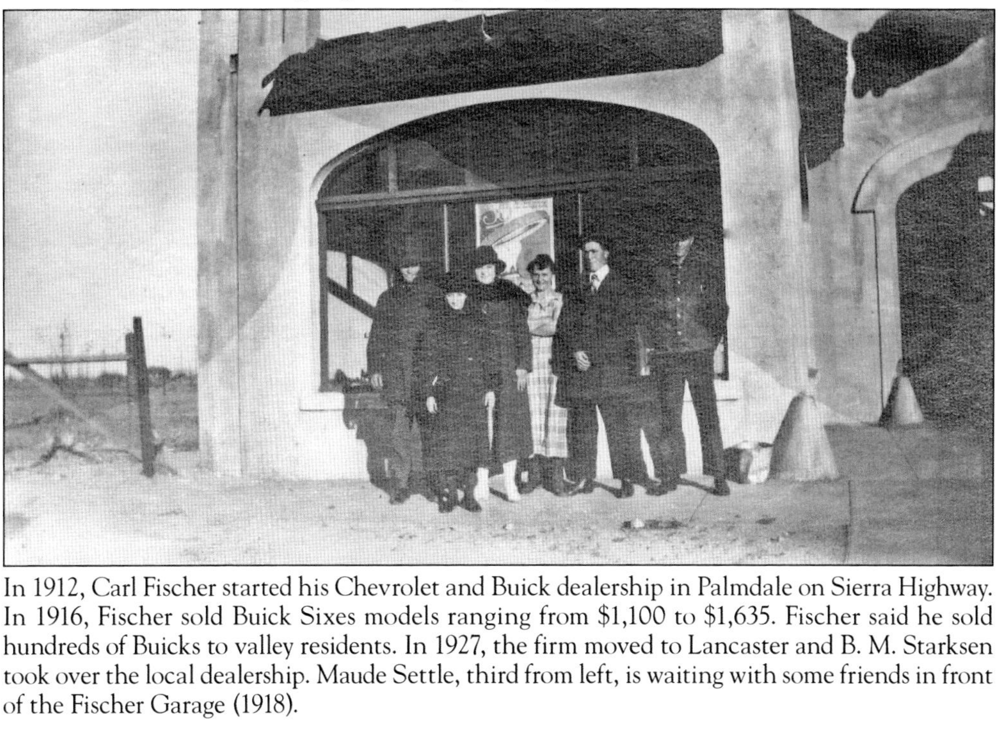

In 1912, Carl Fischer started his Chevrolet and Buick dealership in Palmdale on Sierra Highway. In 1916, Fischer sold Buick Sixes models ranging from $1,100 to $1,635. Fischer said he sold hundreds of Buicks to valley residents. In 1927, the firm moved to Lancaster and B. M. Starksen took over the local dealership. Maude Settle, third from left, is waiting with some friends in front of the Fischer Garage (1918).

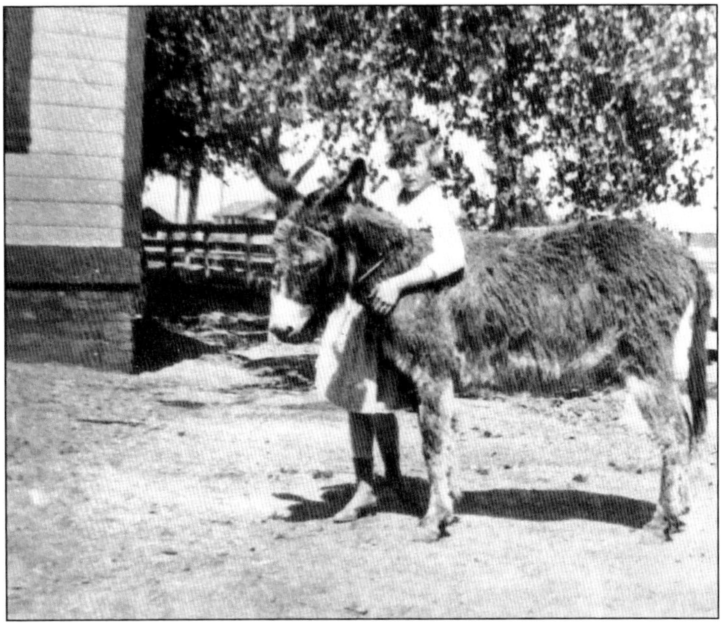

If one's automobile broke down, he or she could always depend on some other form of reliable transportation. Horses and buggies were still commonly used through the 1920s. Mamie Atmore and her friend are in the Palmdale railroad section yard. In 1905, there was a famous racehorse named Palmdale that won many notable horse races. During the 1920s, Mrs. Jason Parker of Palmdale entered her horses in numerous races.

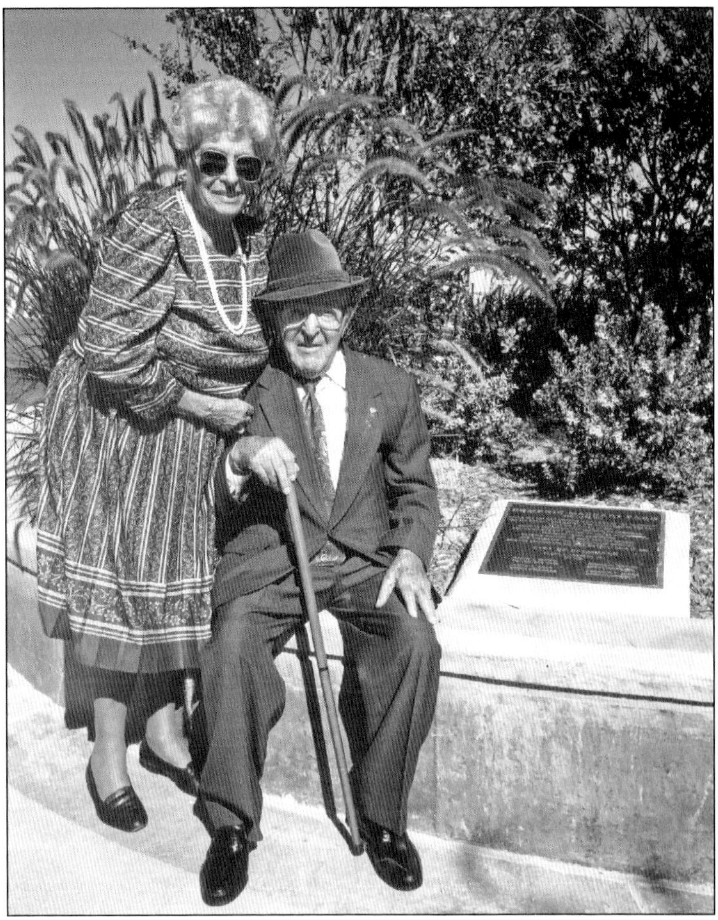

Domenic Massari and his family owned an early Palmdale gas station. He also became the Wilshire Oil Company distributor from Saugus to Mojave. Massari spent 10 years on the Palmdale City Council. In 1993, Palms Park at Fifty-fifth Street East and Avenue R was renamed in his honor. Massari ("Mr. Palmdale"), shown here with his wife, Teresa, died in 1996 at 102. (Courtesy of *Antelope Valley Press.*)

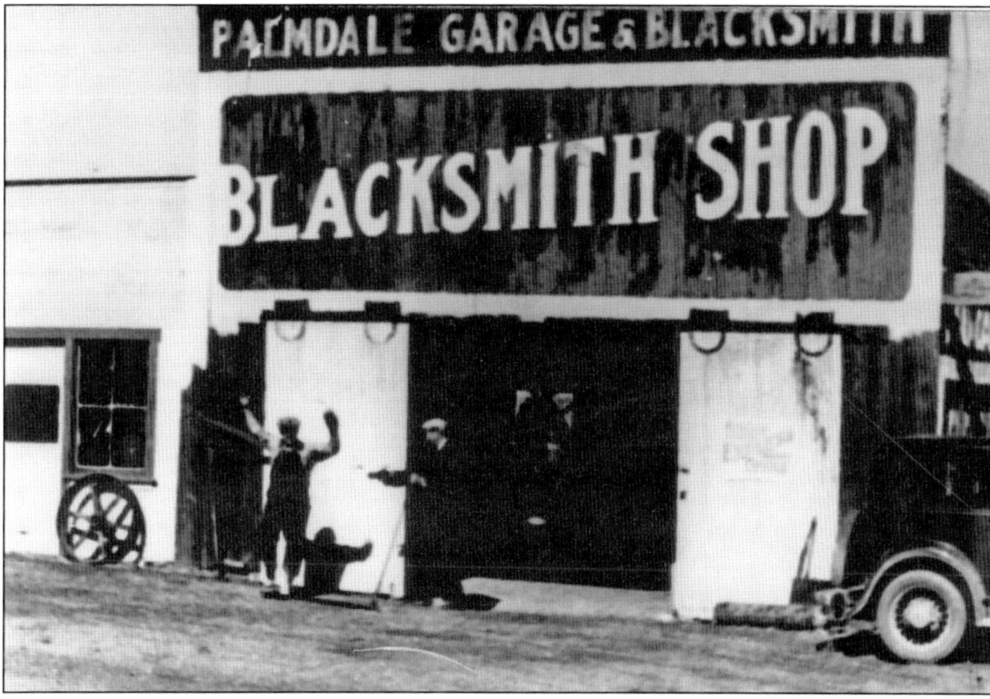

Frank Dowler was a Palmdale constable and blacksmith during the 1890s. During the 1910s and 1920s, Manuel Mariscal was the town's popular blacksmith. This old blacksmith shop was located on Avenue Q-7 and Eighth Street East. It was frequently used in early movies. In Littlerock, Amasa Martin, who is often called the "father of the local pear industry," also had a blacksmith shop in the 1890s. (Courtesy of WAVHS.)

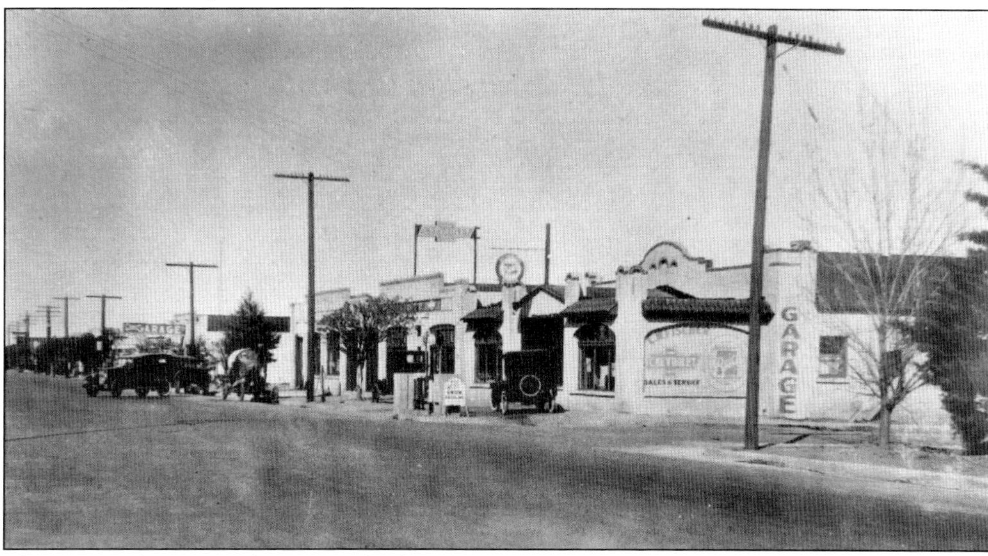

This scene of Sierra Highway in Palmdale shows two garages. The road is in good condition due to proper road maintenance. Evan Evans came to the Antelope Valley in 1889. In 1906, he was hired by Los Angeles County Road Maintenance and became a supervisor in 1909. In 1936, there was a county road maintenance yard in Palmdale with 49 employees. It was the town's largest employer. (Courtesy of WAVHS.)

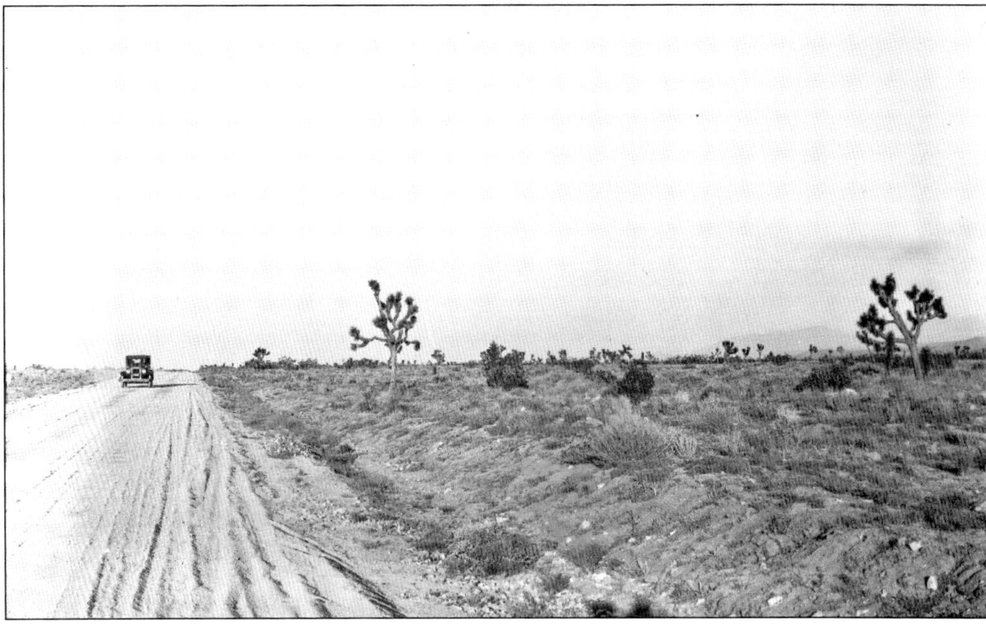

In 1921, the dirt road leading to the Llano area was simply known as the Llano Road. Paved in 1925, it was officially named Pearblossom Highway in April 1926, by the Los Angeles County Board of Supervisors. Now also known as Highway 138, during the 1980s, Pearblossom Highway was made famous by David Hockney's photographic collage. (Courtesy of University of Southern California, on behalf of the USC Special Collections.)

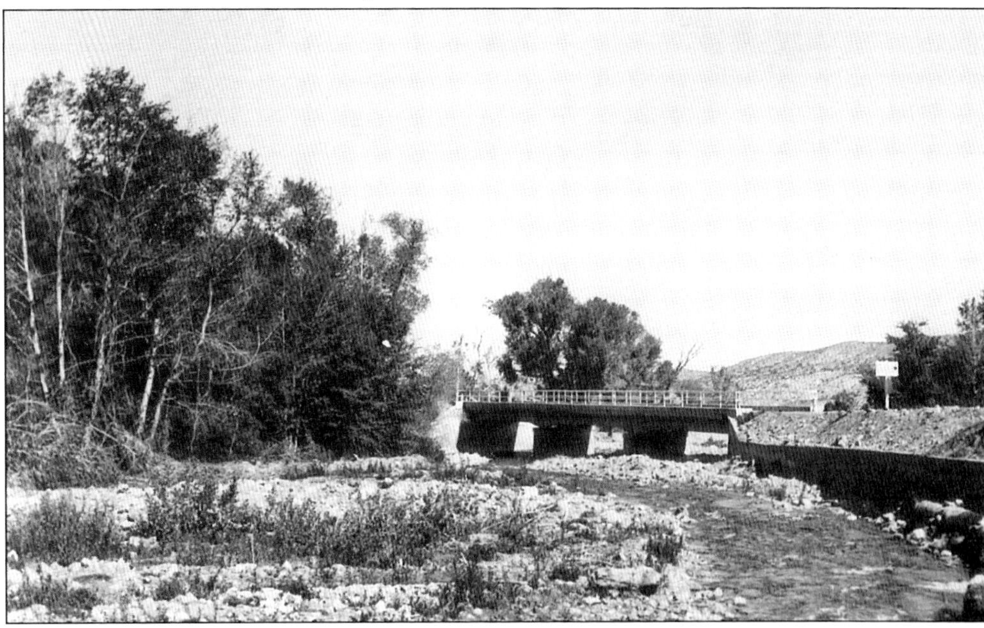

As modern motorists drive on valley bridges, they tend to forget their historical importance. With the numerous creeks traversing the Southeast Antelope Valley, good bridges are a necessity. The Big Rock Creek concrete bridge, shown here, was built in 1927. At Twenty-fifth Street West and Elizabeth Lake Road in Palmdale, the first little wooden bridge crossing Amargosa Creek was erected in 1929. (Courtesy of Cora Sweet McCrumb.)

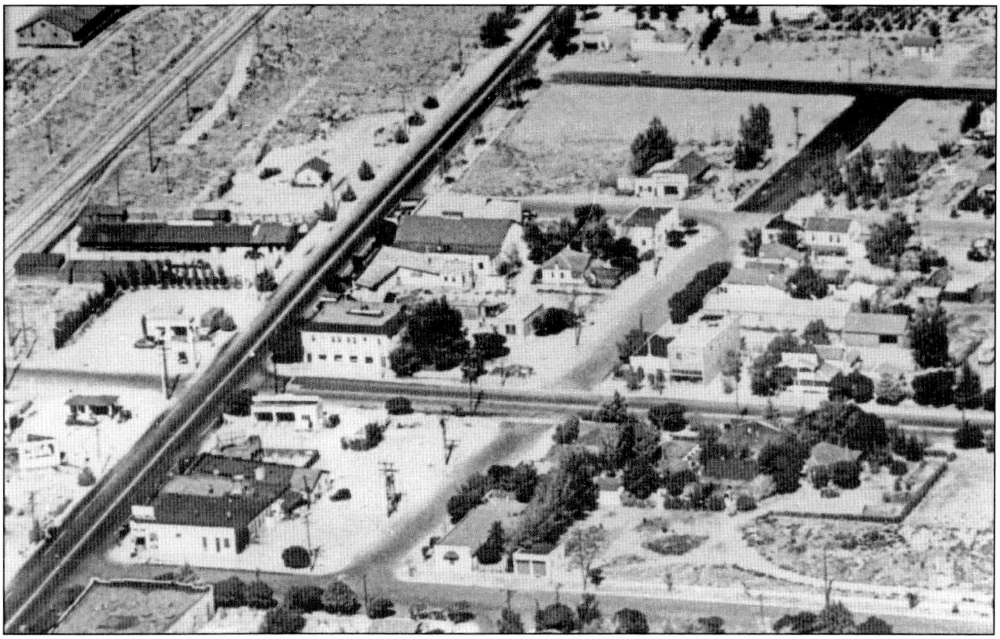

Palmdale, like many communities, suffered growing pains following the Depression. This 1930s photograph shows a Palmdale that was not much different from 1915. During the 1950s, however, Palmdale experienced a tremendous population boom spurred by aerospace industry hiring. New schools, housing, roads, and stores were built to meet the area's new demands. Palmdale was incorporated on August 24, 1962. (Courtesy of WAVHS.)

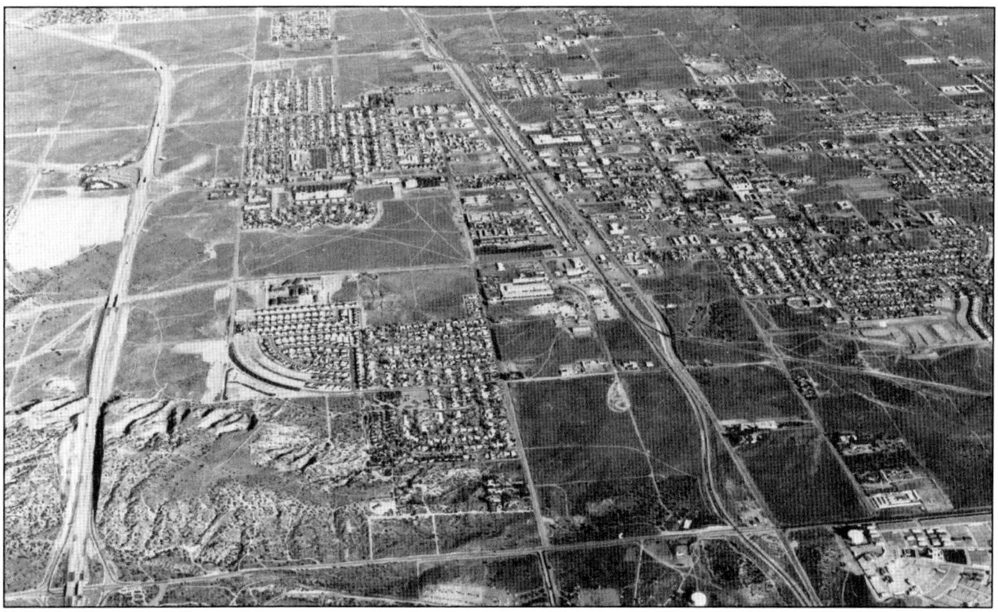

In 1914, Palmdale had 125 residents. In 1950, it had 3,000. Today Palmdale's population surpasses 152,000, and the city measures over 104 square miles. Neighboring communities are also growing. This 1986 view of Palmdale shows the Antelope Valley 14 Freeway snaking through the region. When the first freeway section opened in the summer of 1963, a caravan of nearly 1,000 automobiles cruised along its lanes. (Courtesy of WAVHS.)